Better Crime Prevention

Better Crime Prevention provides a critical guide to theory, research, ethics, and politics in relation to crime prevention policy and practice. It concludes with an agenda for continuous improvement. The book also demonstrates what is involved in doing theoretically informed and realistically applied social science orientated to reducing harms.

The focus throughout this book is on ethical and effective ways to reduce crime-related harms. There are chapters on how to target crime prevention efforts, crime prevention theories and frameworks, ethical issues in crime prevention, the practical conduct of crime prevention, evidence-based crime prevention, the politics of crime prevention, and the need for continuous adaptation in crime prevention.

Student readers will obtain an overview of, and capacity critically to engage with, crime prevention theory and practice. Policymakers and practitioner readers will be able to make better-informed decisions about what to do and how to allocate crime prevention resources. Social scientists interested in contributing realistically to harm reduction will better understand how they can go about doing so.

Nick Tilley has taught or conducted research at Coventry University, Nottingham Trent University, the University of Minnesota, Griffith University, the Home Office, and, most recently, University College London. He is an elected Fellow of the Academy of the Social Sciences (FAcSS) and has been awarded an OBE for services to policing and crime reduction. The Tilley Award for police problem-solving is named in his honour. He is Honorary Professor at UCL, Emeritus Professor at Nottingham Trent University, and Visiting Professor at Huddersfield University. He is the author or editor of 15 books and more than 200 chapters and journal articles, mostly to do with evaluation methodology, policing, and crime prevention.

Better Crime Prevention

2nd Edition

Nick Tilley

Routledge
Taylor & Francis Group

LONDON AND NEW YORK

Designed cover image: Yusuf Sabqi, 'a red and orange sunset', Unsplash

Second edition published 2024
by Routledge
4 Park Square, Milton Park, Abingdon, Oxon, OX14 4RN

and by Routledge
605 Third Avenue, New York, NY 10158

Routledge is an imprint of the Taylor & Francis Group, an informa business

First edition published by Willan 2009

British Library Cataloguing-in-Publication Data
A catalogue record for this book is available from the British Library

Library of Congress Cataloging-in-Publication Data
Names: Tilley, Nick, author.
Title: Better crime prevention / Nick Tilley.
Other titles: Crime prevention.
Description: Second Edition. | New York, NY : Routledge, 2024. | Revised edition of the author's Crime prevention, c2009.
Identifiers: LCCN 2023050417 | ISBN 9780367404390 (hardback) | ISBN 9780367404369 (paperback) | ISBN 9780429356155 (ebook)
Subjects: LCSH: Crime prevention. | Crime prevention—Philosophy.
Classification: LCC HV7431 .T548 2024 | DDC 364.4—dc23/eng/20231030
LC record available at https://lccn.loc.gov/2023050417

ISBN: 978-0-367-40439-0 (hbk)
ISBN: 978-0-367-40436-9 (pbk)
ISBN: 978-0-429-35615-5 (ebk)

DOI: 10.4324/9780429356155

Typeset in Sabon
by Apex CoVantage, LLC

To Jenny, as always

Contents

Figures

Tables

Boxes

Preface

This book has three aims.

First, it updates my 2007 book *Crime Prevention*, although less than ten pages of the original have survived. *Crime Prevention* was written as a textbook and was badly in need of updating. Routledge asked a bunch of people about the possibility of a second edition. They all said they thought it was a good idea, and all made suggestions. I've tried to deal as best I can with what they proposed. Only they can judge how well I've done. You will find a brief exercise towards the end of each chapter where I ask readers to build on the material covered in it. I'm hoping that students, teachers, and researchers will find the material in this book interesting, useful, and digestible.

Second, the book embodies a manifesto for the future of crime prevention. It packs a particular argument in favour of a non-stop orientation to improvement and a manifesto for what this involves. The focus on improvement is inspired in part a) by Herman Goldstein, whose problem-oriented policing was improvement focused; b) by the U.S. Institute for Healthcare Improvement and the work of Donald Berwick who headed it for many years, as well as Paul Batalden who has spearheaded much effort to improve healthcare and make it safer; c) by Karl Popper, the Anglo-Austrian philosopher of science, who stressed that ever-ending improvement is built into scientific method and who promoted its application in piecemeal harm reduction; and d) by Mel Mark, Gary Henry, and the late George Julnes whose position on evaluation complements Ray Pawson's and my own and who stress social betterment as its major aim. I hope that politicians, officials, organisational managers, and frontline practitioners will all have something to take from what I say.

Third, the book demonstrates what is needed to conduct theoretically informed applied social science focused on reducing harms. For these purposes, crime prevention serves as a case study to exemplify what can be done and what needs to be done for applied social science to help to identify ethical and effective harm-reducing interventions. This type of endeavour lost favour in sociology in the late 1970s and never fully recovered. I speak in this respect specifically to readers who are not concerned with crime prevention but with social science more generally. Here, my main target is tyro social scientists who will decide the direction of social science over the coming years. The only chapters that largely speak only to crime prevention are Chapters 1, 2, and 4.

I have tried to write this book as an argument where later chapters are built on earlier ones. However, because not everyone will read it this way I have tried to make each chapter as self-contained as possible. This means that there is a little repetition. Apologies if this irritates you.

I owe major debts to some fellow travellers. Gloria Laycock provided an intellectual and practical lifeline to the Home Office which enabled me for around a decade to conduct theoretically informed empirical applied social science. Gloria went on the establish the Jill Dando Institute of Crime Science at UCL, which initially had just a skeleton staff including a bit of me, but has since grown to be a large and thriving interdisciplinary applied science department conducting exemplary applied research. My relationship with Ray Pawson goes back to the times when we both worked at the then Lanchester Polytechnic (now Coventry University). We talked about methodology as we wended our way from Earlsdon, where we then both lived, to work in the centre of Coventry. A common interest in evaluation methods arose in the 1990s. We shared incredulity at shortcomings in the methods being used, and this eventually led us to write *Realistic Evaluation*. Ray followed that book up with further work on realistic review and realist research methods more generally, and I followed it up by applying our ideas in the field of crime prevention. The thinking behind *Realistic Evaluation* washes through most of this book.

I have been fortunate to have collaborated with many fine scholars and practitioners. In addition to Gloria and Ray, Troy Allard, Kate Bowers, Steve Brookes, Rick Brown, Karen Bullock, Jyoti Belur, John Burrows, Ron Clarke, John Eck, Paul Ekblom, Graham Farrell, Mick Gregson, Sarah Hodgkinson, Matt Hopkins, Mike Hough, Shane Johnson, Johannes Knutsson, Matt Manning, Ken Pease, Susan Rayment-McHugh, Tim Read, Amanda Robinson, Aiden Sidebottom, Steven Smallwood, Anna Stewart, Steve Taylor, Mike Townsley, Machi Tseloni, Barry Webb, Janice Webb, Gill Westhorp, and Richard Wortley have all at some point been collaborators and have exerted memorable influences. A large cast of others have been involved in collaborative applied social science projects, where their contributions have been important, often more so than my own.

I have sent drafts of various chapters of this book to Rick Brown, Karen Bullock, Matt Hopkins, Gloria Laycock, Matt Manning, Ray Pawson, Aiden Sidebottom, Jenny Tilley, and Richard Wortley. The book is better for their comments and suggestions. I'm enormously grateful to all of them. Nicole

Mantl did a fine job in helping me finalise the text and also meet Routledge's sundry requirements. She deserves great credit for her patience, hard work, cheerfulness, and intelligence in helping to improve the final product.

Jenny has had to put up with absent-mindedness, moodiness, crises in confidence in what I've been trying to do, and failures to be around when needed. All I can say is 'Sorry' and 'Thanks.' As with the errors you spot in this book, they are all my fault! Dear readers, I urge you to try to do better.

1 Introduction

Crime prevention knowing and doing

Think about health promotion. There's a massive knowledge base. Different people who have a role to play in health improvement need to grasp different parts of that knowledge base. Each group of specialists, be they pharmacists, cardiologists, radiographers, physiotherapists, health visitors, paediatricians, public health officers, geriatric nurses, vascular surgeons, midwives, or orthodontists, has its own distinctive body of knowledge to draw on in what they do. All have a part to play in promoting health, as do government ministers, officials, and ordinary citizens. Yet, what they know and how they make use of what they know vary widely.

This book is about knowing and doing in crime prevention. As with health promotion, crime prevention falls to a host of different specialists, as well as citizens and their governments. While it might be helpful if they all knew everything relevant to what can be done to prevent crime, this is not practicable. This book tries to lay out a common knowledge base, while recognising that there will be additional specialist knowledge for those with different preventive roles. Is common sense enough for us to prevent crime? Sadly, no. Some crime prevention measures fail against widespread expectations that they will succeed. Some crime prevention measures succeed against expectations that they will fail. Worse, some common-sense measures can backfire, producing more harm than good.

We are often faced with emerging crime problems with no well-tested common-sense responses to draw on. This book is premised on the assumption that we can do better by being better informed. Just as healthcare has improved and unintended harms reduced as interventions become better informed, so too for crime prevention. Again, just as research efforts drawing on what is already known can expedite the development of effective responses to emerging health problems, as has been the case with COVID-19 (see Gilbert & Green, 2021), so too for responses to emerging crime threats.

This chapter begins by discussing what crime prevention is for, and who has an interest in it. It shows that concerns about, capacities for, understanding

DOI: 10.4324/9780429356155-1

of, and responsibilities to deliver crime prevention are spread very widely. It also shows that the conceptions of crime prevention are far from being uniform and have changed over time. The chapter then argues that human crime prevention has continuities with predation prevention in nature, before providing brief summaries of the chapters that follow.

The focus of crime prevention

A man rapes his wife. Why do we care? It might be because he breaks the law in doing so and can therefore be arrested, charged, brought before the courts, and given a penalty. It might also be because we think that the harms caused by him are so serious that we believe it to be important to try to prevent the same behaviour. For a long time, marital rape was not unlawful, but that didn't mean it wasn't harmful to its victims, likewise slavery and genital mutilation. Crime prevention can focus on rule infraction, in which case concerns with marital rape begin only when the behaviour is formally made unlawful. Alternatively, it can focus on intentional behaviours that cause so much harm that we want to prevent them. Of course, making behaviours such as marital rape, slavery, and genital mutilation unlawful is one way of signalling that the behaviour is unacceptable and subject to penalty, which may be sufficient to prevent many from engaging in it.

If we concentrate on lawbreaking, then laws of course produce crimes in the sense that without a law proscribing or prescribing behaviours, there can be no infractions and therefore no crimes. Hence, the more behaviours that are covered by laws the more possible crimes. If we concentrate on harms, we will welcome the formulation of laws that create both crimes and licence efforts to regulate the harmful behaviour involved. We will also welcome the decriminalisation of behaviours where that criminalisation tends to produce harms, such as consensual sexual intercourse between same sex adults or abortion, the criminalisation of which has produced a range of notoriously damaging consequences.

What is considered deviant varies by place and period (Curra, 2000). Unsurprisingly, therefore, laws also change over time and vary by jurisdiction. Think, for example, about suicide, drug-taking, gambling, prostitution, slavery, and violence against children. Hence, the focus on crimes as lawbreaking will cover behaviours that vary by place and change over time. The particular laws that prevail will reflect the processes that create them and often reflect the interests of those well placed to enact laws or influence those who can. That said, interests shared across space and time lead to the widespread regulation of some behaviours, such as killing others or taking their possessions without permission. I use the term 'regulation' here advisedly to acknowledge that these behaviours are seldom unconditionally unlawful.

Some killing in some circumstances by some people, such as that by members of the police and army doing their duty, is not made unlawful. Also, there have been many circumstances in which the confiscation of others' goods against their will has been lawful, as when children are deprived by their parents of their toys.

Many laws create crimes that are unrelated to behaviours producing direct harms to third parties. Defacing currency, blasphemy, public nudity, and burning the national flag have all been crimes in some places at some times but are unrelated directly to harm production. Many status offences by youths in the United States cause no direct harms to others. What causes affront may not cause any intrinsic harm but may still be legislated against. Likewise, some behaviours by some population subgroups may be proscribed for paternalistic reasons, such as non-attendance at school.

The law surrounding Khat (or 'Khatt') furnishes one example. Khat is a flowering plant native to parts of Africa. It is a mild stimulant. To elicit its effects, users of Khat chew it at length – the effects are produced gradually and are said to amount roughly to the consumption of strong coffee. Khat chewing has a long history in some countries, for example Somalia. Somalians like to chew Khat as a social activity. The almost universal religion in Somalia is Islam. Alcohol is not consumed. Khat seems to serve an analogous function – something chewed in company with mild effects that are conducive to social intercourse. Somalians have evidently been chewing Khat for centuries. It is also widely consumed in Yemen in the Arabian Peninsula and in much of Africa: Armstrong (2008, p. 63) reports estimated the rates of usage as 98% (men) in Djibouti, 50% in Ethiopia, 75% in Somalia, 32% in Uganda, and 82% (men) and 43% (women) in Yemen. Unsurprisingly, the Somali diaspora in particular has taken the Khat chewing habit with them. In 2019, the production and sale of Khat were controlled or illegal activities in many countries, including for example China, Australia, the United States, Canada, Sweden, Norway, France, Germany, and the United Kingdom, while they were legal in Yemen, Thailand, and in much of Africa including Somalia, Ethiopia, and Djibouti. The direct harms to self and others from Khat chewing are far from being clear (Armstrong, 2008), although it can be seen as a nuisance for those who observe it and the unsightly, discarded remains of the chewed plant.

Figure 1.1 shows the relationship between criminal and harmful behaviours as potential targets of preventive attention. In practice, most crime prevention has focused on the area where the two intersect. This reflects a pragmatic, utilitarian orientation, whereby efforts are made to improve net well-being (the greatest happiness of the greatest numbers), while respecting human rights. Chapter 5 will focus on the ethics of crime prevention, where we return to these issues.

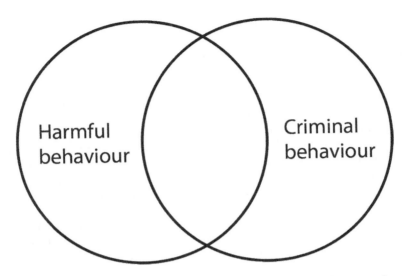

Figure 1.1 Harmful behaviour and criminal behaviour as potential targets of preventive attention.

The ubiquity of crime prevention

Crime and crime prevention in human societies

Sociologists have always been interested in the 'problem of order' faced by human societies. It is not necessary to adopt the Hobbesian view that in a state of nature, life would be 'solitary, poor, nasty, brutish and short' in the absence of some sovereign power to which we must subordinate ourselves (Hobbes, 1651). It is enough to see that rules governing many behaviours, no matter whose interests may be being served by those rules, underpin social order. Children learn rules. The powerful try to legitimate them. Authorities enforce them. Efforts are thereby made to reduce infractions of them.

The social responses to rule violations comprise one means of reinforcing those rules, reducing the risk of future violations. Hangings, floggings, denunciations, humiliations, degradation ceremonies, public trials, and restorative justice meetings comprise differing ways in which occasions of rule breaches are drawn on to reinforce and reproduce rules, enhance their legitimacy, and increase fear of the consequences of breaching them.

Pretty much everyone has an interest in crime prevention as harm reduction. We all want to enjoy some level of physical security. We don't want our possessions to be stolen. We don't want to be defrauded. We also share an interest in reducing bullying, even if it is not a crime. We all adopt some crime prevention measures in that we try to keep ourselves, our close kin, and our possessions reasonably safe, even if we vary in the level of precautions taken. As individuals and as members of groups and organisations, we have roles to play in the prevention of crime against others. For example as community members, most of us raise our children in ways orientated in part to reducing their criminal and antisocial proclivities. We also keep an eye on others with a view to reducing their risks of victimisation. Most teachers have some concern to reduce the risk that pupils harm one another in school and adhere to some rules over conduct both within the school and outside it. Most bureaucrats have some role in regulating behaviours of one sort or another. Public health workers are concerned with reducing violence. Planners' decisions affect the risks of criminal behaviour as do designers of products such as cars or phones and managers of retail premises – consideration of unintended crime consequences can avoid or reduce harms from them. And so on. Moreover, some have formal responsibilities that relate to criminal behaviour and its prevention. These include all those working within the criminal justice system, be they police officers, probation officers, prison officers, magistrates, or judges.

Because we all have some interest in crime prevention and play some role in it, we could all benefit from being as well-informed as we can be in deciding what to do.

'Crime' and 'crime' prevention in other species

Crimes as rule infractions are social constructs. If people enact laws and laws define crimes, then it follows that crimes are social creations. Although other members of the animal kingdom may behave in law-like ways, they do not formally construct the laws governing their behaviour. They simply act in accordance with laws. Thus, crime prevention as the prevention of lawbreaking does not apply in non-human parts of the animal kingdom.

However, crime prevention as harm reduction or as a form of security improvement is widely observed in nature. It is not surprising. Evolutionary processes involve both predation and protection. Those that survive are those where predation and protection are sufficient to allow for reproduction at the level of the gene, animal, or species. Hence, protection (read 'harm reduction'/'crime prevention'/'risk mitigation') is a biological imperative in which catastrophic failure results in extinction. Consider the flea. According to Ge et al. (2011), flea beetles (of which there are around 10,000 species) provide a good example of ways in which prey adapt to predators in nature. Ge et al. stress that similar protective strategies can emerge independently to help solve the problem of survival from a predator. Fleas basically quickly jump out of the way, when threatened. Genetic analysis finds that jumping evolved independently among the flea sub-species. It exemplified 'convergent evolution' rather than common ancestry. Jumping out of the way, however, is not the only technique used by fleas. As Ge et al. say, 'Chrysomelids (leaf beetles) display a wide range of avoidance behaviours, including flying, running, dropping, feigning death, mimetic concealing and, largely unique to this group, jumping' (Ge et al., 2011, p. 133). These again often follow from convergent evolution. The same goes for much human crime prevention.

There are many parallels between protective measures in nature and crime prevention measures in human society. Holly trees, brambles, hedgehogs, echidna, and spiny anteaters all use spikes to keep potential predators at bay. Humans use razor wire, barbed wire, and prickly plants to keep potentially harmful offenders at bay. Squirrels squirrel away their acorns to prevent their 'theft' by others with an interest in having them. Humans put precious assets in safes for the same reason. Seagulls squark and dive to deter predatory animals that jeopardise their offspring and to warn of impending risks. Humans likewise use personal alarms and car alarms for the same reasons. Deception is used in the animal and human kingdoms in the interests of crime prevention, as mentioned not only among leaf beetles but also for example in butterflies whose 'eyes' on wings make them appear threatening. Humans have in a similar way used pictures of eyes to reduce theft.

Non-human animals can, thus, be nifty at protecting themselves and their kin from predation. They can also be nifty predators. Indeed, the nifty predator and the nifty protector are often involved in long-running 'arms races' where the one adapts to the other and the other to the one. One example comprises 'crypsis.'

Crypsis describes predation prevention whereby the potential prey blends into the background and therefore becomes less visible to the potential predator (Davies, Krebs, & West, 2012, pp. 86–90). The forewings of underwing moths appear to be cryptic in this sense. The moths become hard to see when on bark. The moths also twist themselves best to fit with the bark patterns. Blue jays are potential predators of these moths. In some species of underwing moth, the cryptic patterns are fixed and in others variable (polymorphic). In an ingenious experiment, blue jays were presented with images of moths and were rewarded with a mealworm if they pecked a lever when they could discern one in an image on a slide but were 'punished' if they made a mistake, by increasing the delay in the arrival of the next image. The blue jays were better at discerning the cryptic moths when presented on a plain background on which they stood out. However, they began to worsen when the background was cryptic. That said, over successive slides, the blue jays improved their recognition of the fixed-image cryptic moth against the cryptic background, but they could not do so when the moth had polymorphic cryptic colouration, or when different patterns succeeded one another.

The term 'red queen evolution' has been used to describe long-term processes of mutual adaptation between predators and prey where each adapts to the other but where no overall change in levels of predation results (Davies et al., 2012, pp. 83–86)! The 'red queen' reference is to Lewis Carroll's *Through the Looking Glass*, where in response to Alice's remark that 'In our country you'd generally get to somewhere if you ran very fast for a long time,' the Red Queen retorted 'A slow sort of country! Here it takes all the running you can do to keep in the same place' (Carroll, 1871). In evolutionary terms, not to run could mean extermination. In crime prevention, similar processes of mutual adaptation occur as offenders learn to circumvent preventive measures, and preventers then adapt to make crime more difficult for offenders. The history of the safe is one of mutual adaptation.

The notion that security concerns and many of the associated crime prevention techniques that are used are entirely human and social is clearly a mistake. Human beings may decide to adopt or not to adopt specific measures or to regulate their use (which may sometimes be deemed not to be in the public interest on the grounds that some 'natural' measures cause more harm than good), but concerns about security and the routine measures taken are also part and parcel of our biological selves.

In our evolutionary past, crime prevention has been a necessary concern for all of us for our survival. Over time, the state has come to assume core responsibilities for it through the formalisation of laws and making provisions for their enforcement. We now also have specialist institutions and specialist occupations dedicated to crime prevention, albeit that, as this book will make clear, we all still have roles to play.

Chapter outlines

Chapter 2 provides a series of examples of crime prevention interventions and initiatives. These cover a range of different crime types including both acquisitive crimes and ones of violence; efforts to reduce specific offences such as car theft and vehicle theft as well as attempts to prevent the onset of criminality; and initiatives that have been unsuccessful as well as those that have succeeded. These examples show the range of focus for crime prevention, the uncertainty of outcome even with well-meaning measures, and the diverse personnel and agencies involved in crime prevention. The cases presented in Chapter 2 are picked up in discussions in later chapters.

Chapter 3 is concerned with the targeting of crime prevention efforts. Resources for crime prevention are always limited. They can be put to alternative uses. Those with a potential part to play in prevention must decide whether to allocate resources to it, what resources to allocate, and on what to target those resources. In this chapter, we discuss bases for those decisions. Harms caused by crimes, relative volumes of crimes, costs of crimes, demands for crime prevention measures, and the tractability of crimes for preventive interventions are all possibilities. These all raise tricky problems of principle and evidence.

The chapter goes on to highlight some of the evidence that can be drawn on when deciding where to allocate effort. It notes that across stolen goods, locations for crime, offenders, facilities, and systems, crimes are highly concentrated. The 80/20 rule applies: a relatively small proportion of targets, places, offenders, facilities of a given type, and systems of a given type account for a relatively large proportion of offences across the total population of targets, places, offenders, facilities, and systems. These findings can inform the targeting of preventive endeavours.

Chapter 4 focuses on frameworks and theories that can and have already usefully informed crime prevention. The range of theory that might be drawn on to inform crime prevention is vast. Anything that speaks about human behaviour could be relevant. That would include theories from sociology, psychology, human geography, economics, anthropology, and biology, as well as criminology and crime science which are themselves largely parasitic on these other areas of scholarship. It would clearly be impossible to do justice to all this in one book, let alone one chapter. Readers are invited to draw imaginatively and creatively on disciplines with which they are familiar to think through how ideas within them might be drawn on for crime prevention purposes. Read any issue of a popular science or social science magazine, and you should be able (especially when you have read this book to the end!) to mine it for ideas that can be drawn on in improving our understanding of and response to crime.

The chapter has had to be selective in the coverage of theory that might be germane to crime prevention. It covers theories and frameworks that relate specifically and explicitly to crime prevention. The chapter is in three main parts. The first notes the requirements for theories that will be most useful for crime prevention and outlines routine activities as a framework for understanding crime and differing preventive intervention point possibilities. The second discusses theories that speak about crime opportunities and their exploitation. The third moves on to the supply, availability, and capabilities of offenders. The chapter concludes by noting the examples of other theories that may be open to application in crime prevention.

Chapter 5 is concerned with the ethics of crime prevention. Crime prevention involves ethical choices, even if these are often not made explicit. Critics of crime prevention measures have highlighted the normative nature of crime prevention and have contested the moral assumptions that are built into measures. For example issues of distributive justice arise in the availability of crime prevention measures and in the effects they have on the distribution of crime as a harm; issues of rights arise in relation to the use of surveillance measures that may jeopardise civil liberties; and issues of aesthetics arise in the design of places and products to reduce the risks of crime. Decision-making about crime prevention measures inexorably involves moral as well as technical issues to do with efficacy and efficiency. The purpose of this chapter is to sensitise readers to those moral issues. This chapter takes the form of a dialogue between those involved in crime prevention challenging one another in relation to the ethical assumptions they make in decisions about what to do.

Chapter 6 is about the development and delivery of crime prevention strategies and interventions. It starts with private sector crime prevention undertaken in the interests of private sector organisations. It shows how this can be undertaken through problem-solving processes, using shop theft as an example. The chapter then moves on to public sector crime prevention. It discusses responsibilities and competences in crime prevention and outlines a series of ways in which those who are competent but reluctant to play a part in prevention can be persuaded to accept responsibility to help prevent crime. The chapter takes the reader through the SARA (scanning, analysis, response, assessment) processes of problem-solving which are widely used to work out what needs to be and can be done to reduce specific crime problems. The chapter also notes the substantial practical challenges in implementing effective preventive interventions.

Chapter 7 comprises a discussion of the production and use of evidence in crime prevention. Its focus is on decision-maker evidence needs and how they can be met. The latter part of the 20th century and the first decades of the 21st century have witnessed a rapid increase in 'evidence-based' policy and practice. The evidence-based movement began with medicine and has since spread to many other fields including crime prevention. This chapter discusses what counts as good evidence, and for what purposes, in crime prevention decision-making. It notes that many types can be useful, as is now recognised by the Medical Research Council regarding complex health-related interventions. The chapter considers the implications of changing assumptions about evidence hierarchies for those who produce and those who use evidence in crime prevention. There are different forms of evidence and research, and there are different ways in which evidence can be used by different types of decision-makers. Overall, this chapter aims to throw light on what kinds of evidence are most useful for practitioners and policymakers.

Chapter 8 turns to the politics of crime prevention. Politics washes through crime prevention in all sorts of ways – from strategy setting to the delivery of specific measures. The chapter does not pretend to cover all the politics of crime prevention. Instead, it focuses specifically on the politics of *effective* crime prevention. It begins by arguing that effective crime prevention targets preventive interventions on concentrated crime harms; that it enlists those who are competent to deliver effective crime prevention measures; and that it delivers ethical interventions that are effective in preventing or reducing specific crime problems. A generic framework is proposed, suggesting which groups are typically involved in the politics of decisions over priorities, responsibilities, and interventions, and how these groups interact with one another. Effectiveness and ethics are not necessarily prioritised. Chicago's 'stop and frisk' strategy to address shootings and homicides is used as a case study (see Skogan, 2023) to populate the framework. The chapter then goes on to look specifically at decision-making as it relates to prioritisation, responsibilisation, and choice of interventions, as well as how they relate to effectiveness. The chapter ends with a discussion of the politics of research and data construction, as strong research and good data are necessary, though not sufficient, for decision-making in favour of effective crime prevention.

Chapter 9 is overtly Whiggish. It begins by looking back at an informed but critical guide to crime control for honest politicians published some 50 years ago. It shows that much has improved since then. Many of the specific identified needs have been met, with reductions in crimes that were then prevalent. It also acknowledges some continued failures, especially relating to weapon control. It reveals, nevertheless, how much progress has been made.

The remainder of the chapter highlights the need for, as well as importance of, a continuous improvement agenda. It then sets out an unending agenda for better (and better) crime prevention. Moreover, the 'Red Queen' evolutionary processes noted earlier in this chapter suggest that such improvement will be needed even to stand still in relation to the production and control of crime harms!

Exercise: Identify the main differences and similarities between human crime prevention and 'crime' prevention by another species.

References

Armstrong, E. (2008). Research note: Crime, chemicals and culture: On the complexity of khat. *Journal of Drug Issues, 38*(2), 631–648. doi:10.1177/002204260803800021

Carroll, L. (1871). *Through the looking glass.* Many Editions.

Curra, J. (2000). *The relativity of deviance.* Thousand Oaks, CA: SAGE.

Davies, N., Krebs, J., & West, S. (2012). *An introduction to behavioural ecology.* Oxford: Wiley-Blackwell.

Ge, D., Chesters, D., Gómez-Zurita, J., Zhang, L., Yang, X., & Vogler, A. (2011). Anti-predator defence drives parallel morphological evolution in flea beetles. *Proceedings of the Royal Society B, 278,* 2133–2142. doi:10.1098/rspb.2010.1500

Gilbert, S., & Green, S. (2021). *Vaxxers.* London: Hodder and Stoughton.

Hobbes, T. (1651). *Leviathan.* Many Editions.

Skogan, W. (2023). *Stop & frisk and the politics of crime in Chicago.* New York: Oxford University Press.

2   Crime prevention examples

This chapter outlines several examples of crime prevention. These address different problems using a range of methods. They also cover 'primary,' 'secondary,' and 'tertiary' prevention, which is prevention aimed respectively at everyone; at those at heightened risk; and those already exhibiting crime problems as offenders, targets, or victims (see Brantingham & Faust, 1976, who draw on similar distinctions from health). These examples will give you an idea of what is done to try to prevent crime. They will also be drawn on at various points in the following chapters.

Vehicle theft

Vehicle theft has been a major focus for crime prevention initiatives. Theft of and from vehicles comprised around a quarter of all recorded crime in England and Wales in the early 1990s (27% in 1993, see Home Office, 2012). Numbers had risen steadily and consistently over the previous 30 years (thefts from motor vehicles grew from 144,602 incidents in 1963 to 925,819 in 1993, and thefts of motor vehicles from 11,713 in 1963 to 592,660 in 1993). Vehicle-related theft was a nuisance to motorists and a headache for police services. Rates of detection were low and appear to remain low, especially for theft from motor vehicles where the prospects of identifying offenders are poor (for the most recent year when figures were published, overall detection rates for theft from a vehicle were 8% and for theft of a vehicle 13%, Home Office, 2013). Because of the high volume of vehicle thefts, they became a focus for research and for crime prevention measures. Rates of vehicle theft in England and Wales have fallen since the early 1990s and, by the early 2020s, had numerically become a minor problem, making up only 6% of recorded crime in the year ending March 2022 (ONS, 2023).

There were sundry efforts to reduce vehicle crime at its height, and the fall in thefts since the early 1990s is the consequence of preventive measures that have been introduced. These preventive efforts have focused on:

DOI: 10.4324/9780429356155-2

1. The locations where vehicles are parked and may be especially vulnerable – in car parks, for example by installing CCTVs, improving lighting, adding services to increase natural surveillance, using barriers at entrances/exits, and avoiding the use of stickers showing how long it's likely that the car will be left in the car park.
2. Motorists, who are encouraged to take care to leave their cars as secure as possible (e.g. by locking them and by avoiding leaving goods liable to attract thieves on show), to reduce the accessibility of their keys at home, and to obstruct remote copying of electronic keys by keeping them in Faraday cages.
3. Vehicles themselves – for example with steering wheel locks; improvements to door locks; installation of mechanical and electronic immobilisers, alarms, and trackers; the redesign of windows to reduce the chances that they can be opened from outside the vehicle; the distribution of audio equipment within a vehicle such that it can no longer be stolen from one vehicle for installation in another; the use of wheel nuts that cannot easily be removed; the presence of automatically folding wing mirrors; and the use of lockable fuel caps or fuel caps that can only be opened from inside the vehicle.

Although measures, such as CCTV in car parks (Tilley, 1993a; Poyner, 1991), have been shown to have some local impacts on the levels of vehicle theft, the major source of the sustained drop since the early 1990s has been increases in vehicle security (Farrell, Tseloni, Mailley, & Tilley, 2011; Farrell, Tseloni, & Tilley, 2011). Farrell et al. look at the vulnerability of cars to theft with differing combinations of security devices, at the patterns of vehicle theft drop, and at the timing of drops in thefts. Their research shows that security improvements in general and electronic immobilisers in particular have been the main engines of the sustained falls in vehicle thefts.

The police had recognised that vehicle insecurity was a problem as rates of theft rose in the years up to the early 1990s, but manufacturers were reluctant to incur the expense involved in improving security: they did not themselves bear the costs of the thefts. These were borne by owners, drivers, insurance companies, and the police (alongside other members of the criminal justice system) who had to devote scarce resources to responding to thefts. Manufacturers took notice, however, when third parties began to show the weaknesses in vehicle security and the consequences these had for rates of theft, especially when the vulnerability of specific makes and models was demonstrated.

A range of governmental organisations at local, national, and international levels eventually made the installation of electronic immobilisers mandatory. The Australian case is especially illuminating. Electronic immobilisers were required in Western Australia before they were required in the rest of the country. Thefts fell first in Western Australia and then in the remainder of Australia in accordance with the timing of the introduction of immobiliser requirements (Kriven & Ziersch, 2007; Farrell, Tseloni, Mailley, et al., 2011; Farrell, Tseloni, & Tilley, 2011).

Although thefts of and from vehicles have fallen with the increase in the use of security measures, they have not been eliminated, and new theft problems have emerged. This follows from the ability of offenders to both adapt to new security measures and overcome them (such as the cloning of keys) and the emergence of new crime opportunities with new designs of cars, for example the use of catalytic converters that can be quickly removed and sold (HLDI, 2021; Pertsev, 2021).

Domestic burglary

Domestic burglary has also been a major focus of research and of crime prevention initiatives over a sustained period (Clarke & Hope, 1984; Laycock & Tilley, 2018). This is partly to do with the relatively high volume of burglaries and partly to do with the anxiety experienced by victims when their homes are broken into.

The Kirkholt burglary prevention project ran in the late 1980s when the numbers of domestic burglaries were high on a national level and had been increasing over the preceding decades. In England and Wales, 14,182 domestic burglaries were recorded in 1940, rising to 41,898 in 1960 and 504,702 in 1986 (see Home Office, 2012). 'Kirkholt,' a housing estate in Rochdale, a town within Greater Manchester in the North-West of England, had particularly high levels of domestic burglary. There were 231 burglaries per 1,000 dwellings in March 1986 to February 1987, which was ten times the national rate at the time (Pease, 1991; Tilley, 1996). Given that not all burglaries are reported and of those reported not all are recorded, the real rate of burglary both nationally and on the Kirkholt estate will have been higher.

The Home Office funded the Kirkholt project to try to bring the rates down with lessons for others to emulate elsewhere if the project succeeded. Reflecting the severity of domestic burglary there, and the absence of proven ways of reducing burglary, the Home Office made substantial funds available for the project (almost £300,000 between 1985–1986 and 1989/1990). Researchers from Manchester University were at the heart of the project. They played a pivotal part in both its development and its evaluation. The project began with an open agenda for the choice of interventions. It was run through a multi-agency group, led by a police officer.

The idea was to begin by developing an evidence-based understanding of the local burglary problem and to formulate responses in the light of that understanding. Accordingly, 76 burglars, 237 victims, and 137 neighbours of victims were interviewed about the burglaries in the area (Forrester, Chatterton, & Pease, 1988). Results were important in shaping responses. One finding was that 49% of the burglaries involved the loss of cash from prepayment meters for gas and electricity. Another was that burglars found it easy to gain entry to the dwellings targeted, given some specific security weaknesses. A third was that victims of burglary were four times more likely to experience a second or subsequent burglary than non-victims and to do so within a short period of time (Pease, 1991).

Phase 1 interventions were tailored to these findings about burglary on the estate (Forrester et al., 1988; Pease, 1991). Hence, with the agreement of householders, utility companies were persuaded to replace prepayment coin meters with ones that used cards, to deny burglars the rich cash pickings they could otherwise expect from breaking into the meters. The Housing Department made prompt security upgrades to victimised dwellings which were tailored to the weakest entry points used by burglars on the estate. Victims were offered postcode property marking. Neighbours were mobilised to create cocoons (six or seven neighbouring homes) around victimised dwellings to provide support, surveillance, and guardianship to victims at heightened risk of revictimisation.

Phase 2 involved further interrogation of local offenders and more detailed analysis of vulnerability to burglary (finding, for example, that movers were at heightened risk). Additional measures were put in place. These included group work with offenders, a school-based prevention programme, a 'crime prevention festival,' work with disaffected pupils, the creation of a credit union (a low-cost savings and loan scheme) for local residents, and improved probation services (officers were able to provide courts with better-informed reports) (Forrester, Frenz, O'Connell, & Pease, 1990; Pease, 1991).

The short-term results from Phase 1 of the Kirkholt project were dramatic. There was a cliff-edge drop in the number of burglaries in year one, and repeats were eliminated. In the year immediately before the project (March 1986 to February 1987), there had been 526 burglaries, but in the first year of the project, this fell by 58% to 223 incidents. The trend continued but at a slower rate for the next two years. In Year 2 of the project, burglaries fell by a further 25% to 167 incidents compared to the previous year and in the third year by another 21% to 132 incidents (Forrester et al., 1990; Pease, 1991).

The annual falls in Kirkholt far exceeded those in the local police subdivision. In the calendar year 1987, compared to 1986, the fall in Kirkholt was 38% in contrast to an increase of 1% in the rest of the subdivision; in 1988, compared to 1986, there was a fall of 67% in Kirkholt but a much smaller drop of 19% in the rest of the subdivision; and in 1999 compared to 1996, there was a fall of 72% in Kirkholt but of only 24% in the rest of the subdivision (Pease, 1991).

Because of the apparent cumulative and dramatic successes in Kirkholt, its emulation was widely advocated elsewhere. Initially, this was through the Home Office 'Safer Cities' programme, which provided 20 cities with staff and funding to try to reduce crime. Burglary was a key issue at the time. It was a focus of much Safer Cities work (Tilley & Webb, 1994). Several Safer Cities attempted to replicate the Kirkholt project, but the results were generally disappointing. Those running the attempted replications decided to pick up on different facets of Kirkholt. It was difficult for them to determine which elements were crucial in general, or for them, in their own areas (Tilley, 1993b, 1996).

Globally, what has turned out to be most influential about the Kirkholt project was its identification of repeat victimisation as a key pattern around which crime prevention initiatives can be delivered effectively, efficiently, and equitably. We will return to this, as well as to other aspects of Kirkholt, in later chapters.

Many other measures to prevent the problems of burglaries have been tried. These include, for example property marking, alleygates, Neighbourhood Watch, and burglar alarms. Box 2.1 summarises some research findings relating to these. It also notes the effects of 'WIDE' *combinations* of security devices: Window locks plus Internal lights on a timer plus Double doorlocks plus External lights on a sensor.

Box 2.1 Some measures used to reduce domestic burglary

Property marking: Laycock (1985, 1992) found that although the use of property marking in the South Wales villages where it was trialled led to a drop in burglary, the supposed mechanisms through which this was to occur (identifying stolen property and catching offenders with marked property) were inactive. Rather, the active ingredient of the experiment seems to have been the publicity and credibility given to property marking by the razzamatazz surrounding its introduction and then later reports of its apparent initial effects! (Laycock, 1992).

Alleygates (gates at the ends of pathways running to the rear of dwellings): these were trialled in Merseyside, where much terraced (row) housing includes such alleyways which gave access to burglars entering dwellings from the back. The introduction of alleygates led to falls in the rates of domestic burglary in the areas covered, compared to those without them, and to nearby areas (Bowers, Johnson, & Hirschfield, 2004).

Neighbourhood Watch: Bennett (1990) reports the effects of the introduction of Neighbourhood Watch in areas matched for the presence or absence of Neighbourhood Watch. The results he reported did not provide support for Neighbourhood Watch as a crime/burglary prevention intervention.

Burglar alarms: a retrospective study of burglar alarms, drawing on annual victimisation surveys in England and Wales, found that although in early waves of the survey (1992 to 1996), alarms reduced burglary risk, in later waves (2008/2009 to 2011/2012), the opposite was the case – alarms increased risks of burglary (Tilley, Thompson, Farrell, Grove, & Tseloni, 2015).

Security measures and the crime drop since the 1990s: the study of burglar alarms formed a small part of a much larger project examining the role of security measures in the sustained and widespread falls in domestic burglary since the mid-1990s. Victimisation surveys have estimated that numbers of incidents in England and Wales fell from an estimated total of 2,430,000 in the calendar year 1993 to 582,000 in the year April 2019 to March 2020 (victimisation surveys provide much better estimates of the real levels of crime than recorded crime, given failures to report and record incidents in the latter). The larger study found that the growth in extent and increase in quality of security measures explained the dramatic and steady falls in overall burglary rates. It also found that a 'WIDE' combination of Window locks, Internal lights on a timer, Double doorlocks, and External lights on a sensor was the most effective and economical package of security measures (Thompson, Tseloni, Tilley, Farrell, & Pease, 2018; Tseloni, Thompson, Grove, Tilley, & Farrell, 2017).

Commercial robbery

Commercial robbery can be traumatic for those on the premises at the time. They face threats from offenders with weapons. The cash losses are far being from the only (or most serious) harms from commercial robberies. What follows is an account of a targeted preventive initiative in London.[1]

In the Metropolitan Police Area, there were 403 robberies of bookmakers in the year 2009/2010. This represented a 62% increase from 2006, when there were 248 incidents. The attraction of bookmakers as targets for robberies lies in the fact that they hold large amounts of cash, and they are readily accessible.

Given the high and rising numbers of bookmaker robberies in London in 2009/2010, the Flying Squad (part of the Metropolitan Police Service), in conjunction with the bookmaking industry, attempted to put in place a preventive strategy to address the problem. They looked at five years of recorded crime data on bookmaker robberies. They found that there were consistent temporal patterns. Robberies peaked at the end of the working day, presumably because at that time cash holdings would be highest, and there would be fewer people on the premises. When opening hours were extended in 2007, peak hours changed accordingly. They also found that most offences involved demanding money at the counter, yielding an average of £1,228 per incident in 2006/2007.

The Flying Squad coordinator visited premises where robberies had taken place to try to work out what had made them vulnerable. He identified nine characteristics putting them at heightened risk:

1. Shop fronts completely covered (reducing risk for offenders).
2. Poor CCTV or no CCTV (reducing risk for offenders).
3. Large amounts of cash on hand (offering rich pickings for offenders).
4. No warning signs relating to security measures in place (feeding offender confidence).
5. No safe or safe not used (ready cash quickly available to offenders).
6. No means of entry control at vulnerable times (making access for offenders easy).
7. Policies and procedures not adhered to (potential preventive activities missed).
8. Staff not properly trained (potential preventive activities missed).
9. Poor communication with local police (potential preventive responses missed).

Few premises were found to have exhibited all these failings, but no company had got everything right.

The findings relating to bookmaker robberies were presented to the industry group in 2008. They agreed to set standards with the help of a multi-agency group, identify good practices, and apply them in all bookmakers' premises in London.

The standards developed included:

- Training for staff, to ensure premises' managers embraced measures and other workers understood what they should do.
- Operating requirements for CCTV equipment.
- Standards for cash office doors.
- Requirements for security screens.
- Safe and time delay system requirements.
- Opening and closing procedures.
- Banking procedures.
- Customer service requirement.
- Management and security procedures' requirement.
- Police liaison recommendations.
- Suspicious incident recording and reporting.

The draft standards were accepted and endorsed by all major bookmakers, and the police licencing officers were alerted to them (bookmakers' premises needed licences to operate).

There was no immediate impact: incidents rose to the high number of 403 in 2009/2010. However, 2010/2011 saw a 46% fall in numbers of book-maker robberies compared to the previous year. This may reflect the time taken for the new standards to bed in and become operational.

A notable feature of this example of an effort to tackle commercial robbery was its use of informed advice on crime pattern analysis and on intervention possibilities, including from Matthews, Pease, and Pease (2001), Clarke and Eck (2003), Ekblom (1987), Great Britain Crime Reduction Centre (2003), and the Home Office Crime Reduction Centre (2007).

Gang-related shootings

According to the Centres for Disease Control and Prevention (CDC), the leading cause of death among young black men in the United States in 2018 was homicide (31.5% of deaths among 1–19 year olds and 26.1% of deaths among 20–44 year olds) (CDC, 2022). Petrosky et al. (2020) report that in 2017, firearms were used in 72.9% of homicides in the United States; that among males, homicide rates were highest for 20–24 year olds; that non-Hispanic black males accounted for 57.7% of male homicide victims, which was the highest rate for any racial/ethnic group; and that among males, 11.4% of homicides were gang related. This suggests that the prevention of gang-related homicides involving young gang members and firearms is important for public health as well as crime prevention purposes.

One of the first projects to tackle gang-related shootings successfully was the Boston Gun Project (Operation Ceasefire). This was tightly focused on the use of firearms in youth gangs in Boston in the mid-1990s (Braga, Kennedy, Piehl, & Waring, 2001; Braga, Kennedy, Waring, & Piehl, 2001; Kennedy, Braga, & Piehl, 2001). Following a decade when yearly numbers fluctuated between the low 20s and high 30s, the number of homicide victims aged 24 or less grew rapidly from 22 in 1987 to 73 in 1990. Between 1991 and 1995, after the 1990 peak, there was an average of 44 per annum. These deaths were concentrated on a small number of young people involved in gangs: around 1,300 members of gangs, most with extensive criminal records, were found to be responsible for some 60% of youth homicides in the city. The gangs were involved in chronic conflicts with one another. Both victims and offenders tended to be gang members.

Operation Ceasefire worked with the support of a pre-existing well-functioning interagency group already concerned with gangs. This group included the police, streetworkers employed by the city council, and a 'Ten Point Coalition' made up of police, clergy, and probation officers. Alongside this group, staff from Harvard University developed and implemented the strategy, with support from prosecutors and the Federal Bureau of Alcohol, Tobacco and Firearms (ATF). The Harvard group undertook a detailed analysis of gangs and shootings using qualitative and quantitative methods, for example to look at gang membership, gang functioning, gang conflicts, locations of incidents and of gang territory, and pathways to gun acquisition. Their work was crucial to the development of Ceasefire.

Ceasefire was put in place in late Spring 2006 to try to bring down the numbers of gang-related youth homicides in the city. Two main methods were used. First, an effort was made to reduce the supply of firearms to youth gangs. This involved a variety of enforcement activities aimed at firearms trafficking, for example by focusing on intrastate as well as interstate trafficking and by attending specifically to types of trafficked firearms most used in gangs (newish semiautomatic pistols). Second, strong deterrence, specifically aimed at reducing homicides, was used to target the gang use of firearms. This 'focused deterrence,' as it came to be called, was initially referred to as 'pulling levers.'

A core element of the Operation Ceasefire strategy was to convey to gang members explicitly and consistently the hard line that would be taken in relation to firearms offences and the broader enforcement consequences that would be incurred by gangs and gang members if any member carried or used firearms. Publicity and direct, targeted communications to gangs were therefore a key element. The effects could only be brought about if all members of all gangs came to know the score. Police officers, probation officers, and streetworkers, for example, all took the message to gang members. Semi-formal meetings, where the message was driven home, were also held with selected gangs. Streetworkers encouraged member attendance although it was sometimes also made a probation requirement. Once the strategy was in place, further publicity for it targeted gang members, for example through meetings, leaflets, and posters. This publicity highlighted the severe consequences of firearms crimes, both for the perpetrator and for the gang to which he was attached.

The deterrence measures were directed neither at particular individuals nor at the general population. The aim was not to dissolve gangs but rather to reduce their most harmful behaviours. Concentrated enforcement activities kicked in if any gang member used firearms. These would be directed at the whole gang, not only at those using firearms. Gang members typically engaged in a wide range of illicit activities. It would not be practicable for the police to attend to all of these all the time. The police, however, had ample enforcement opportunities to disturb normal (non-firearm using) criminal and antisocial behaviour among gang members if any member used firearms. The gangs had an interest in members not behaving in ways that attracted police enforcement activities that would jeopardise their everyday criminal behaviours, which largely took place under the police radar. All members thus had an interest in inhibiting firearms' use by any member. The strategy enjoyed widespread community support, given that no one welcomed large numbers of youth homicides. It is important to stress that gang members were not immune from normal police enforcement activities, only that these would be intensified if firearms were used by a member, taking every opportunity any enforcement body had (thus, for example, including probation as well as police).

It transpired that although gang gun use might have begun in relation to drugs, it had come to have its own dynamic as young people, including gang members, carried guns for self-protection. The reduction of gun violence would in turn reduce that anxiety and hence the motivation to carry firearms.

Complementing the focused deterrence, mediation services and offers of support for members to exit gangs were provided in the wake of the enforcement activities to disrupt gang functioning and reduce gang conflicts.

Sophisticated statistical methods were used to assess the effectiveness of Operation Ceasefire. The headline finding was that in the 54 months before the full implementation of the project, the mean number of youth homicide victims in Boston was 3.5, and in the following year the monthly mean fell by 62% to 1.3. Of course, Ceasefire was not the only aspect of Boston that was changing: other local factors may thus have produced the fall in youth homicides. Moreover, the fall may have reflected national reductions in youth homicides, which were occurring for altogether different reasons. More complex statistical analyses, attempting to take these possibilities into account, however, suggested that the falls observed were not attributable to other factors. Moreover, the steep and sustained falls following the May 1996 start date seem to suggest that it was something then that produced the drop in numbers.

Domestic violence

Historically, domestic violence (DV) was neglected for either enforcement or crime prevention purposes. It was treated as a private matter, where incidents mostly took place behind closed doors. This is no longer the case. Domestic abuse as a criminal issue has come to encompass a wide range of behaviours, from physical violence to coercive control. Victims and perpetrators can include males and females and anyone from the very young to the very old. It can take place in same sex as well as heterosexual relationships. Much remains unreported. The relationship between perpetrators and victims can make reporting difficult, especially when the victim is dependent on the perpetrator. This dependency has also meant that victims may return to those who have abused them and may therefore also be reluctant to act as witnesses in criminal trials. The private settings where the violence takes place also make criminal convictions difficult when allegations are easily rebutted, and there is a lack of independent evidence. All this is to say that domestic violence has some special features that pose distinct problems for those trying to deal with it effectively.

The 'Killingbeck' project, based on an area in Leeds of that name, focused on DV involving violence perpetrated by men on women (Hanmer, Griffiths, & Jerwood, 1999). It operated in 1997. Its focus was on repeat victimisation, because domestic violence incidents are seldom isolated, with the same perpetrators repeatedly abusing the same victims. The interventions focused equally on the men and women involved. The project involved the police as well as relevant partner agencies. The core idea of the project was to intensify interventions, on perpetrators, and on victims, as successive incidents occurred. Hence, there was more enforcement attention on the perpetrator and greater protection for the victim with successive incidents. This cumulative intervention approach was informally termed the 'Olympic model.'

The approach was intended to make efficient use of limited resources. If a relatively light intervention is not followed by further incidents, either the initial incident was a one off or the intervention was sufficient to prevent further incidents. If repeat incidents persisted, lighter interventions were not sufficient to stem repeats, and heavier inputs, requiring greater resources, would kick in. The Olympic model, however, was not operated mechanically. If the details of a specific case suggested that a heavier intervention was needed earlier, discretion allowed that to be provided.

A second idea behind the approach was that it would not allow repeat incidents to be downgraded. While the discretion to jump to more intensive intervention was permitted if the specifics of the situation suggested this was needed, discretion in the other direction was not allowed. Repeat incidents always required an intensified response. This prevented the risk of officers saying, for example, that 'It's just a domestic, again involving Fred and Marge. It's not worth going. She never follows through with her allegations.'

A third important feature of the model's application was that it was overt and that awareness of it was made clear to those involved in incidents. Both perpetrators and victims knew about measures taken in relation to the other. Perpetrators were told of the consequences for them in the event of repeat incidents.

A fourth crucial feature was the quite detailed specification of what must be delivered at successive incidents, which was made clear to all officers involved in attending incidents. All knew what was required of them.

Table 2.1 shows the model used and the types of intervention that were put in place: level 1 for the first, level 2 for the second, and level 3 for any subsequent incidents (Hanmer et al., 1999, p. 4).

It should be clear that the Killingbeck project involved not only the police but also prosecutors, courts, community members, and victim support organisations. The one-year period for the implementation of the Killingbeck model used prior experience of domestic violence as the basis for the level of intervention selection. A great deal of effort was put into maximising the fidelity to the model, which required extensive training, data cleaning,

Table 2.1 The DV Olympic model.

Intervention level	Victim	Perpetrator (common law offences*)	Perpetrator (criminal offences)
Level 1	Gather information Information letter 1 Police watch	Reiterate force policy First official warning Information letter 1	Magistrates – conditional bail/ checks Police watch Information letter 1
Level 2	Information letter 2 Community constable visit Cocoon and police watches**	Reiterate force policy Second official warning Police watch Information letter 2	Magistrates – bail opposed/checks Police watch increased Information letter 2 Prosecutor file jacket and DV history
Level 3	Information letter 3 Police watch Domestic violence officer visit Agency meeting Panic button/cell phone	Reiterate force policy Third official warning Police watch Information letter 3	Magistrates – bail opposed/checks Police watch increased Information letter 3 Prosecutor file jacket and DV history and contact prosecutor office
Emergency intervention	Implement – log reasons for selection	Not applicable	Implement and log level of action taken

Notes: * Common law offences are primarily breaches on the peace.
** Cocoon watch involves asking neighbours, family, etc., to protect the neighbours by promptly contacting the police in the event of further incidents (used with informed victim consent). Police watch involves providing visible police presence to both victim and offender through police patrols in the vicinity of incidents, twice weekly for six weeks following the incident.

monitoring, and management, although the operation of the model required few additional resources.

As implemented in Killingbeck, the approach seems to have been successful in that the proportion of one-off incidents rose from the pre-project quarter, when 66% of incidents were not repeated (April to June 1996) to the final quarter for which project entry data were analysed (October to December 1997), when 85% of incidents were not repeated. Moreover, the time interval between repeat attendances at incidents increased to over one year for half the men.

Drink-driving

Unlike most offences, those involving drink-driving do not create deliberate harms to third parties. The harms produced are inadvertent and are either to the perpetrator or to others caught up in accidents which result from the drivers' reduced abilities occasioned by their intoxication. The main pay-off from reduced offences of drink-driving are fewer injuries or deaths from road traffic accidents.

In New South Wales, an initiative was introduced involving random breath testing (RBT) applied to large numbers of drivers (Homel, 1994, 2004). It began on December 17, 1982. The law enabling RBT was widely publicised and was vigorously applied. It was not construed as a temporary crackdown but as a new form of policing. The arrest rate for those tested, following the introduction of RBT was 0.4%. There was an instant precipitous drop of 19.5% in all fatal crashes, of 30% in holiday periods (Homel, 1994, pp. 147, 150), and of 36% in those that were alcohol-related (Homel, 2004). The falls were maintained for a decade. Homel (2004) estimates that by mid-1991, there had been a cumulative sum of at least 2,000 fewer fatal accidents than would have been expected on the basis of previous trends.

Homel (2004) suggests that the RBT rate needed to produce the preventive outcomes observed in New South Wales had to be high. In the first year of the initiative, there were around one million tests, where the population of licenced drivers was around three million. The randomness of the breath test made it impossible for the driver to reduce risk by attempting to drive carefully. The rate of stops meant that being caught, if drinking and driving, appeared a real possibility. Over time, non-drinking and driving have become the norm. Driving after drinking alcohol had previously been widely accepted as normal.

Graffiti

Graffiti in itself is not a serious problem. Indeed, artistic graffiti, most obviously for example the work of Banksy, may be highly valued. However, graffiti can also be highly harmful. It may be obscene. It may be provocative, for example as used at times and in places in Northern Ireland to celebrate unionist or republican causes. It may also signal general disorder and create a permissive attitude towards other, more serious crime.

Graffiti was (rightly or wrongly) deemed a serious problem in the New York City subway in the 1970s and early 1980s. Sloan-Howitt and Kelling (1990) describe an initiative that removed the graffiti and prevented its reappearance.

Beginning as random name scratching, subway graffiti had blossomed into a 'subculture that included hundreds of youths . . . emblazoning subway cars with murals that covered entire trains, obscuring windows and subway maps' (Sloan-Howitt & Kelling, 1990, p. 131). This was a problem due to the ways in which those using the subway were believed to read the graffiti as unconscious signals of more serious crimes such as 'robbery, rape, assault and murder' and as signs that the control of the environment and of offenders within it had been lost (ibid.). Furthermore, Sloan-Hewitt and Kelling quote Glazer (1979), stating that 40% of graffiti writers went on to more serious offences, making the graffiti subculture 'a training ground for future adult offenders.'

The approach that eventually led to the elimination of subway graffiti involved cleaning the graffiti off the subway cars immediately and not returning the cars into service again until the graffiti had been removed. The idea was to deprive the graffiti 'artists' of the reward of seeing their graffiti on show or being able to show it to others. The programme began small: two cars were taken out of service, cleaned of all graffiti and returned. If any graffiti reappeared, the car was again taken out of service within two hours, and the graffiti was cleaned off before returning to service. Further cars were gradually added to the cleaning regime: they too were cleaned and again taken out of service if graffiti reappeared and were recleaned. No new graffiti added to any car in the programme remained on display to allow the artists to enjoy their work.

The cleaning programme began in May 1984, and all 6,245 cars were included by May 1989, five years later. All were clean. Sloan-Howitt and Kelling report that the resources needed to maintain the programme went down, as fewer cars needed to be removed for recleaning. Indeed, the cleaning crews that had been put in place for rapid cleaning were no longer needed by 1987 (Sloan-Howitt & Kelling, 1997, p. 249).

Criminality

The examples discussed so far in this chapter have all related to efforts to prevent specific crimes. A different approach has been to try to prevent criminality, which, if successful, would prevent the wide array of crimes that would otherwise be committed by those whose potential criminality had been averted. The approach is very appealing. It speaks to what are often assumed to be the 'root causes' of crime: the family, community, or individual conditions that produce criminal dispositions.

One of the most extensive, most documented, and most systematically evaluated programmes that has attempted to prevent criminality was the Cambridge-Somerville Youth programme which was run in the industrialised Massachusetts towns of Cambridge and Somerville. The programme was developed in the late 1930s and ran from 1939 to December 1945 (with recruitment of members from 1937). It was the brainchild of a physician, Dr Richard Clarke Cabot. As intended by Dr Cabot, who was determined to bring evidence to treatment decisions, evaluation followed up potential effects after the programme came to an end to determine if it had, indeed, reduced or prevented criminality among participants.

The initiative was set up as a controlled experiment, allocating a matched sample of 325 boys to the treatment to be trialled and the same number who would not be provided with that special treatment. The boys were matched in pairs based on a combination of statistical measures and 'clinical syndromes' (Powers & Witmer, 1951, p. 7). One of each pair of boys was allocated to treatment and the other to control, based on the flip of a coin. The average age of the boys in December 1939 was 11, slightly older than had been intended by Cabot. The samples were supposed to have equal numbers of proto delinquent boys believed to be potential beneficiaries of the intervention and boys who were 'average' or 'normal' – the mix was used to avoid labelling the boys taking part. The later involvement of the two groups in criminal behaviour was compared to determine if the treatment had been effective in preventing criminality. Major, book-length follow-up evaluations were published in 1951 (Powers & Witmer, 1951) and 1959 (McCord & McCord, 1969).

The ambitious programme conceived by Dr Cabot planned ten years of interventions, although the programme came to an end after only six years. Sadly, Cabot had a heart attack in 1939 and died before the programme became fully operational. The basic idea behind the project was to provide each of the boys with a counsellor with whom he could develop and maintain a close and trusting relationship so that the boys in the treatment group could be supported and guided away from delinquency.

McCord and McCord summarise what was actually delivered to members of the treatment group:

> In some cases, it meant a close, intimate friendship between boy and counsellor. In most cases, however, treatment consisted of talks between the family and counsellor, trips for the children, and medical, dental and welfare aid whenever it was required. Some counsellors, emphasising educational assistance, tutored the boys in reading and arithmetic. Others acted primarily as coordinators for welfare and family agencies, the Y.M.C.A., and summer camps. Religion formed an important part of the treatment: boys and their families were encouraged to attend church, priests and ministers were alerted to their problems. Police departments, particularly juvenile bureaus, kept in close touch with the project. . . . Counsellors avoided making structural changes within the community.
>
> McCord and McCord (1969, pp. 3–4)

Thus, what happened departed from Cabot's vision both in what was delivered and the period over which the boys received the treatment. This was in part due to the war which meant it was often not possible to maintain the same counsellor for the boys; many counsellors also drifted into other jobs making continued involvement impossible. What McCord and McCord say of the actual programme as delivered, however, is that,

> (I)ts methods were similar to those used by the Big Brother Association, progressive probation officers, family welfare agencies, and some mental health clinics. Thus, the Cambridge-Somerville project can illuminate the effectiveness of treatment used by many social agencies concerned with the problem of crime.
>
> McCord and McCord (1969, p. 4)

Unsurprisingly, there was some attrition in the sample. By the time of McCord and McCord's work, 253 pairs were left. Table 2.2 presents McCord and McCord's overall findings.

These findings suggest that the programme had no discernible overall effects. The treatment group shows slightly more crimes under some measurements and slightly fewer under others: the differences are small as well as inconsistent. More detailed analyses, for example relating to the differences at different ages, were no more suggestive of outcome effectiveness up to 1955.

Table 2.2 Overall outcomes of the Cambridge-Somerville programme.

Type of crime	Treatment group	Control group
Number of convictions to 1955		
Non-traffic	315	344
Traffic	171	127
TOTAL	486	471
Boys convicted for selected crimes, 1938–1955		
Property	86	77
Person	14	15
Sex	12	13
Drunkenness	46	37
Traffic	70	67
Number of convictions for selected crimes, 1938–1955		
Property	212	214
Person	17	20
Sex	14	17
Drunkenness	72	83
Traffic	171	127

Joan McCord followed up the participants to middle age, finding 98% of them between 1975 and 1981. Her findings are sobering. Although most of those in the treatment group felt the programme had helped them, harder data from mental hospitals, alcoholism treatment facilities, courts, and death records told a different story. For most of the pairs, there was no difference between those in the treatment and control groups, but for 103 pairs, the contrast was significant. This, though, did not favour the treatment group. McCord summarises the overall picture as follows:

> For the 103 pairs who had different outcomes, those who had been in the treatment program were more likely to have been convicted for crimes indexed by the Federal Bureau of Investigation as serious street crimes. Those who had been in the treatment program had died an average of five years younger. And those who had been in the treatment program were more likely to have received a medical diagnosis as alcoholic, schizophrenic, or manic depressive.
> McCord (2003, pp. 20–21).

These findings suggest that, insofar as the Cambridge-Somerville programme had any effects, it backfired for a proportion of the boys who participated. Greater intensity of treatment produced worse outcomes than less intense treatment. Greater cooperation with the treatment produced worse outcomes. Summer camps seemed to be especially harmful, particularly with repeat visits: comparing the numbers of matched boys attending once, twice, or three times, those attending had increasingly elevated chances of 'bad outcomes' (28 versus 25 for one attendance, 16 versus 12 for two attendances, and 20 versus 2 for three attendances (McCord, 2003, p. 22)).

Conclusion

This chapter should have given you a good idea of the wide range of methods used to prevent crime and of the diverse crime types that have been the focus of preventive attention. You should also have realised that well-meaning crime prevention efforts do not always produce their intended benefits. Measures aiming to prevent crime can inadvertently backfire, producing unintended negative outcomes. Later chapters will pick up on and discuss the significance of the examples sketched here and introduce additional examples as appropriate.

Exercise: Find and summarise a published example of a crime prevention initiative targeting human trafficking.

Note

1 It was an entry to a police problem-solving competition of which I was a judge. Unfortunately, no published version is available.

References

Bennett, T. (1990). *Evaluating neighbourhood watch*. Aldershot: Gower.

Bowers, K., Johnson, D., & Hirschfield, A. (2004). Closing off opportunities for crime: An evaluation of alley-gating. *European Journal on Criminal Policy and Research, 10*, 285–308. doi:10.1007/s10610-005-5502-0

Braga, A., Kennedy, D., Piehl, A., & Waring, E. (2001). Part II. Measuring the impact of operation ceasefire. In *Reducing violence: The Boston gun project's operation ceasefire* (pp. 55–71). Washington, DC: US Department of Justice Office of Justice Programs.

Braga, A., Kennedy, D., Waring, E., & Piehl, A. (2001). Problem-oriented policing, deterrence and youth violence: An evaluation of Boston's operation ceasefire. *Journal of Research in Crime and Delinquency, 38*(3), 195–225. doi:10.1177/0022427801038003001

Brantingham, P., & Faust, F. (1976). A conceptual model of crime prevention. *Crime and Delinquency, 22*, 284–296. doi:10.4324/9781439817803-21

Centre for Disease Control and Prevention (CDC). (2022). *Leading causes of death – males – non-Hispanic Black – United States, 2018*. Retrieved July 29, 2022, from www.cdc.gov/healthequity/lcod/men/2018/nonhispanic-black/index.htm

Clarke, R., & Eck, J. (2003). *Become a problem-solving crime analyst*. London: Jill Dando Institute Crime Science.

Clarke, R., & Hope, T. (Eds.). (1984). *Coping with burglary*. Dordrecht: Springer.

Ekblom, P. (1987). *Preventing robberies at sub-post offices: An evaluation of a security initiative* (Crime Prevention Unit Paper 9). London: Home Office.

Farrell, G., Tseloni, A., Mailley, J., & Tilley, N. (2011). The crime drop and the security hypothesis. *Journal of Research in Crime and Delinquency, 48*(2), 147–175. doi:10.1177/0022427810391539

Farrell, G., Tseloni, A., & Tilley, N. (2011). The effectiveness of vehicle security devices and their role in the crime drop. *Criminology and Criminal Justice, 11*(1), 21–35. doi:10.1177/1748895810392190

Forrester, D., Chatterton, M., & Pease, K. (1988). *The Kirkholt burglary prevention project, Rochdale* (Crime Prevention Unit Paper 13). London: Home Office.

Forrester, D., Frenz, S., O'Connell, M., & Pease, K. (1990). *The Kirkholt burglary prevention project: Phase II* (Crime Prevention Unit Paper 23). London: Home Office.

Glazer, N. (1979). On subway Graffiti in New York. *The Public Interest, 54*, 3–11.

Great Britain Crime Reduction Centre. (2003). *Passport to crime reduction: An introduction to crime reduction*. London: Home Office Crime Reduction Centre.

Hanmer, J., Griffiths, S., & Jerwood, D. (1999). *Arresting evidence: Domestic violence and repeat victimisation* (Police Research Series, Paper 104). London: Home Office.

Highway Loss Data Institute (HLDI). (2021). Toyota Prius theft losses. *Bulletin, 38*(8).

Home Office. (2012). *Official statistics: Historical crime data*. Retrieved July 26, 2022, from www.gov.uk/government/statistics/historical-crime-data

Home Office. (2013). *National statistics: Crimes detected in England and Wales, 2012 to 2013*. Retrieved July 24, 2022, from www.gov.uk/government/statistics/crimes-detected-in-england-and-wales-2012-to-2013

Home Office Crime Reduction Centre. (2007). *Your business keep crime out of it* (2nd ed.). London: Home Office.

Homel, R. (1994). Drink-driving law enforcement and the legal blood-alcohol limit in New South Wales. *Accident Analysis and Prevention, 36*(2), 247–255. doi:10.1016/0001-4575(94)90084-1

Homel, R. (2004). Drivers who drink and rational choice: Random breath testing and the process of deterrence. In R. Clarke & M. Felson (Eds.), *Routine activity and rational choice: Advances in criminological theory* (Vol. 5, pp. 59–84). New Brunswick, NJ: Transaction Publishers.

Kennedy, D., Braga, A., & Piehl, A. (2001). Part 1. Developing and implementing operation ceasefire. In *Reducing violence: The Boston gun project's operation ceasefire* (pp. 5–53). Washington, DC: US Department of Justice Office of Justice Programs.

Kriven, S., & Ziersch, E. (2007). New car security and shifting vehicle theft patterns in Australia. *Security Journal, 20*, 111–122. doi:10.1057/palgrave.sj.8350026

Laycock, G. (1985). *Property marking: A deterrent to domestic burglary?* (Crime Prevention Unit Paper 3). London: Home Office.

Laycock, G. (1992). Operation identification or the power of publicity? In R. Clarke (Ed.), *Crime prevention: Successful case studies*. New York: Harrow and Heston.

Laycock, G., & Tilley, N. (2018). A short history of the England and Wales national burglary security initiatives. In A. Tseloni, R. Thompson, & N. Tilley (Eds.), *Reducing burglary* (pp. 21–44). Cham, Switzerland: Springer.

Matthews, R., Pease, C., & Pease, K. (2001). Repeated bank robbery: Theme and variation. In G. Farrell & K. Pease (Eds.), *Repeat victimization: Crime prevention studies* (Vol. 12, pp. 153–164). Boulder, CO: Lynne Rienner Publishers.

McCord, J. (2003). Cures that harm: Unanticipated outcomes of crime prevention programs. *Annals of the American Association of Political and Social Science (AAPSS), 587*, 16–30. doi:10.1177/0002716202250781

McCord, W., & McCord, J. (1969). *Origins of crime: A new evaluation of the Cambridge-Somerville youth study*. Montclair, NJ: Patterson Smith. (Original work published in 1959 by Columbia University Press).

Office for National Statistics (ONS). (2023). *Crime in England and Wales: Appendix tables*. Retrieved July 25, 2022, from www.ons.gov.uk/peoplepopulationandcommunity/crimeandjustice/datasets/crimeinenglandandwalesappendixtables

Pease, K. (1991). The Kirkholt project: Preventing burglary on a British public housing estate. *Security Journal, 2*(2), 73–77.

Pertsev, R. (2021). International experience in anti-theft of catalytic converters installed in cars. *Archives of Criminology and Forensic Science, 3*, 67–73. doi:10.32353/acfs.3.2021.06

Petrosky, E., Ertl, A., Sheats, K. J., Wilson, R., Betz, C. J., & Blair, J. M. (2020). Surveillance for violent deaths – national violent death reporting system, 34 states, four California counties, the District of Columbia, and Puerto Rico, 2017. *MMWR Surveillance Summaries, 69*(SS-8), 1–37. doi:10.15585/mmwr.ss6908a1

Powers, E., & Witmer, H. (1951). *An experiment in the prevention of delinquency*. New York: Columbia University Press.

Poyner, B. (1991). Situational crime prevention in two parking facilities. *Security Journal, 2*(2), 96–101.

Sloan-Howitt, M., & Kelling, G. (1990). Subway Graffiti in New York City: "Getting up" vs. "Meanin' it and cleanin' it". *Security Journal, 1*(3), 131–136.

Sloan-Howitt, M., & Kelling, G. (1997). Subway Graffiti in New York City: "Getting up" vs. "Meanin' it and cleanin' it". In R. Clarke (Ed.), *Situational crime prevention: Successful case studies* (pp. 242–249). New York: Harrow and Heston.

Thompson, R., Tseloni, A., Tilley, N., Farrell, G., & Pease, K. (2018). Which security devices reduce burglary? In A. Tseloni, R. Thompson, & N. Tilley (Eds.), *Reducing burglary* (pp. 77–104). Cham, Switzerland: Springer.

Tilley, N. (1993a). *Understanding car parks, crime and CCTV: Evaluation lessons from safer cities* (Crime Prevention Unit Paper 42). London: Home Office.

Tilley, N. (1993b). *After Kirkholt: Theory, method and results of replication evaluations* (Crime Prevention Unit Series Paper 47). London: Home Office.

Tilley, N. (1996). Demonstration, exemplification, duplication and replication in evaluation research. *Evaluation, 2*(1), 35–50. doi:10.1177/135638909600200104

Tilley, N., Thompson, R., Farrell, G., Grove, L., & Tseloni, A. (2015). Do burglar alarms increase burglary risk? A counter-intuitive finding and possible explanations. *Crime Prevention and Community Safety, 17*, 1–19. doi:10.1057/cpcs.2014.17

Tilley, N., & Webb, J. (1994). *Burglary reduction: Findings from safer cities schemes* (Crime Prevention Unit Series Paper 51). London: Home Office.

Tseloni, A., Thompson, R., Grove, L., Tilley, N., & Farrell, G. (2017). The effectiveness of burglary security devices. *Security Journal, 30*, 646–664. doi:10.1057/sj.2014.30

3 Targeting crime prevention
Costs, harms, and concentrations

This chapter is about deciding how to focus crime prevention resources. Chapter 1 stressed that this book is about crime prevention as harm reduction rather than as stopping lawbreaking as an end in itself. However, it is not feasible to do all that might be done to prevent all crimes that would otherwise occur, even if we confine attention to those that cause harm. Here, we consider measures of cost-effectiveness, efforts to compare harms, and findings about patterns of crime concentration as sources of evidence that can be drawn on to inform the allocation of crime prevention resources.

Costs of crime and cost-effectiveness

Resources are always limited, and can be put to alternative uses. Economics is sometimes defined as the science that studies just this (Robbins, 1935, p. 16). Optimal resource distribution is achieved where no change would yield an increase in overall utility. This goes for us as individuals and for those in business, as well as for policymakers and practitioners in the public sector.

The absence of crime prevention, as Roman and Farrell (2002) note, comprises a missed opportunity to reduce crime costs that are otherwise incurred. Where bearers of costs of prevention (say manufacturers of cars) are different from the bearers of the costs of crime (say motorists), the state may need to intervene to motivate (increase the costs of failures to prevent) those who are in a position to prevent but are not the direct beneficiaries of the preventive outcomes. Crime costs in these circumstances are akin to those from pollution: unintended (but preventable) harmful consequences of actions that profit those producing them but who do not suffer the harms they create.

The overall costs of crime to a community comprise the number of incidents multiplied by the average cost of each, including both tangibles and intangibles. This should inform decision-making orientated towards harm reduction. As Roman and Farrell put it,

> Counting crimes will never go out of fashion. It is easy, and everyone can understand how many crimes have occurred. However, research on crime

DOI: 10.4324/9780429356155-3

requires a common metric via which crimes can be compared. It is likely that the overall social cost of crime is the best common metric. . . . A common metric that incorporates non-monetary costs allows the impact of crime prevention to be discussed and evaluated on the same terms. This should allow crime policy to move towards an overall harm reduction approach.

Roman and Farrell (2002, p. 82)

Economists undertake a variety of forms of analysis to work out and compare the costs and pay-offs from alternative uses of resources (see Manning, Johnson, Tilley, Wong, & Vorsina, 2016). These analyses focus, for example, on *cost-effectiveness* (at what costs are specific outputs or outcomes produced and how do interventions differ in their cost-effectiveness, so that the more cost-effective can be selected over the less?) and *cost–benefit* (at what total cost are what utilities generated, normally monetised so that a common unit of account is used to measure the costs of the intervention and the utilities produced?). Cost–benefit analysis is the most advanced. It is also trickiest to do properly, given that all costs need to be included and monetised (e.g. volunteers, capital costs, vehicles, and space as well as staff time from all agencies involved) as do all benefits (changed tangible and intangible crime harms and other side effects[1]). Moreover, the estimates of costs and benefits need to take account of 'discounting,' the greater valuation of costs borne and benefits enjoyed now as against at some future date. Conventions about discount rates (how to estimate for now future costs and benefits) vary quite widely.

'What Works Centres' were established in the UK to try to establish intervention effectiveness, costs, and benefits in different areas of public policy, including crime prevention (the What Works Centre for Crime Reduction – WWCCR). One of the offshoots of a research programme to support the WWCCR was the formation of the 'Manning tool' for undertaking economic analyses, which readers might like to look at and use, alongside the book that was produced in tandem with it (Manning et al., 2016).[2] Another output of the research programme supporting the WWCCR was a review of all systematic reviews that had attempted to assess different crime prevention interventions (Tompson et al., 2021). This review of systematic reviews scored those reviews across different dimensions, including economic analysis. The results are sobering: of the 70 systematic reviews that were found following a comprehensive search, 64 included no economic analysis and none scored more than 2 on a scale from 0 to 4 (see Chapter 7 for more detail). In brief, there had been little economic analysis and that which had been undertaken was rudimentary. Given the practical challenges of robust economic analysis in relation to crime, this is not surprising!

Costing intangibles that relate to the effects on quality of life of crime prevention interventions is tricky. The inclusion of intangibles is, however, crucial if we are concerned with crime prevention as harm reduction, given that intangible costs refer to real harms but are omitted from tangibles. Widespread techniques used in relation to estimating intangible costs include 'willingness to pay' (How much would you be prepared to pay to reduce the chance of a given crime?) and 'willingness to accept' (How much would you need to be paid to tolerate the risk of a given crime?). Both have obvious flaws. The first is bounded by how much a respondent has. The second is affected both by the resources a respondent has and by the fact that for some crimes, such as murder or rape, no amount might be accepted, rendering calculations impossible. Both are obviously entirely hypothetical and do not capture the real intangible harms experienced and their respective monetised levels.[3] Economists have, however, used a variety of proxy measurements to estimate intangibles, notably victim compensation awards. Better than nothing, but obviously far from being perfect.

Heeks, Reed, Tafsiri, and Prince (2018, pp. 34–37) drew on a wide range of literature and data to estimate and monetise the emotional and physical harms of a wide range of crime types in England and Wales. Their findings are summarised in Table 3.1, where intangibles are included alongside losses under 'Consequence.' For England and Wales, according to Heeks et al., the crime with the highest total cost was violence with injury. After homicide, rape had the highest incident cost. Heeks et al.'s estimates are widely and uncritically used in British crime prevention cost–benefit analyses, although some economists fret over the use of such confected numbers (see Kay & King, 2020).

Miller, Cohen, and Wiersema (1996) attempted to estimate the overall tangible and intangible costs of several crime types in the United States, as shown in Table 3.2. They note that, when multiplied by the number of incidents, rape was the costliest crime overall. They also note that intangible costs dwarf tangible ones for all those offence types listed, except for burglary.

Economic analysis has a lot to say about the theory of targeting crimes and interventions in the interests of harm reduction. But such analysis is difficult and, hence, rare. More could be done in the future, both in the theory and practice of cost–benefit analysis. There is a rich methodological and practical agenda, as well as a strong demand for more and better work. The Manning Tool is a promising start. Moreover, in a recent development building on the Manning Tool, Manning, Wong, Mahony, and Vidanage (2023) have devised a method for more nuanced cost–benefit analysis that promises a means to distinguish subsets with varying costed outcomes providing more fine-grained analysis. This could improve the targeting of preventive interventions, taking account of the ways in which interventions work differently among varying subgroups.

Table 3.1 Estimated costs of crime in England and Wales, 2015/2016.

Crime	Anticipation	Consequence	Response	Total unit cost	Estimated total costs	Estimated total number of crimes
Homicide	£61,070	£2,343,730	£812,940	£3,217,740	£1.8bn	570
Violence with injury	£340	£11,220	£2,500	£14,050	£15.5bn	1,104,930
Violence without injury	£120	£3,750	£2,060	£5,930	£5.1bn	852,900
Rape	£980	£31,450	£6,940	£39,360	£4.8bn	121,750
Other sexual offences	£160	£5,220	£1,150	£6,520	£7.4bn	1,137,320
Robbery	£330	£6,310	£4,680	£11,320	£2.2bn	193,470
Domestic burglary	£710	£3,420	£1,800	£5,930	£4.1bn	695,000
Theft of vehicle	£1,730	£4,670	£3,900	£10,290	£0.7bn	68,000
Theft from vehicle	£120	£580	£180	£870	£0.5bn	574,110
Theft from person	£30	£930	£430	£1,380	£0.6bn	459,240
Criminal damage – arson	£320	£3,110	£4,980	£8,420	£0.2bn	22,620
Criminal damage – other	£70	£770	£510	£1,350	£1.4bn	1,007,160
Fraud	£220	£840	£230	£1,290	£4.7bn	3,616,460
Cybercrime	£290	£260	£0	£550	£1.1bn	2,021,330
Commercial robbery	£2,300	£8,020	£4,680	£15,000	£2.0bn	136,150
Commercial burglary	£8,030	£4,660	£2,770	£15,460	£1.6bn	102,570
Commercial theft	£210	£510	£250	£970	£4.2bn	4,312,970
Theft of commercial vehicle	£5,920	£25,370	£3,900	£35,180	£0.3bn	8,400
Theft from commercial vehicle	£240	£1,460	£180	£1,870	£0.1bn	59,890
Commercial criminal damage – arson	£1,840	£4,110	£4,980	£10,930	£0.1bn	6,910
Commercial criminal damage – other	£320	£590	£510	£1,420	£0.4bn	303,790

Table 3.2 Costs of crime per victimisation in the United States, 1987–1990.

Crime	Tangible costs	Intangible costs	Total costs
Murder	$1,030,000	$1,910,000	$2,940,000
Rape/sexual assault	$5,100	$81,400	$86,500
Robbery/attempt with injury	$5,200	$13,800	$19,000
Assault or attempt	$1,550	$7,800	$9,350
Burglary or attempt	$1,100	$300	$1,400

Source: Miller et al. (1996).

Harms and harm indexes

Rather than monetising tangible and intangible benefits to compare with the costs of preventive measures, crime harm indices try to develop alternative quantitative approaches to assess different offences' harms. The Cambridge Harm Index (CHI) is the leading example (see Sherman, Neyroud, and Neyroud (2016) and University of Cambridge Institute of Criminology (2023)), although there are others as well (Ignatans & Pease, 2016; Ratcliffe, 2015). The CHI uses recommended sentence starting points as an indicator of the relative harms caused by different offences. It allows the prospective benefits of preventive investment to be compared across crimes.

The CHI, developed initially in Britain, has been emulated in other jurisdictions. Sherman et al. (2016) mention Uruguay and Western Australia (House & Neyroud, 2018). More recently, it has been picked up in Denmark (Andersen & Mueller-Johnson, 2018) and Sweden (Karrholm, Neyroud, & Smaaland, 2020).

The original CHI and others devised in its wake are clever and address a real problem. As already suggested, simply counting prevented crimes, no matter of what type, is a poor basis for allocating preventive resources. The social value of preventing one type of crime is different from that of preventing another. The idea of developing some metric to compare the values of preventing one rather than another type of crime is a sensible one. Using sentencing is a neat way of capturing the varying negative values attached to different crimes in a society, and that in turn obviously enables quantification and hence comparison of the benefits from their prevention.

Table 3.3 shows Sherman et al.'s findings for selected offences in the UK in 2011/2012. There are, however, good reasons to use the index with caution.

As described in Sherman et al. (2016), recorded crimes are used to work out overall harm. We know that reporting and recording levels vary by crime types. This makes the total CHI result misleading, albeit that this could,

Table 3.3 Cambridge Crime Harm Index for the UK.

Crime type	Total number	Starting point sentence days	Total CHI sentence days
Homicide	553	5,475	3,027,675
Rape	16,038	1,825	29,269,350
Robbery	74,688	365	27,261,120
Theft of vehicle	85,803	20	1,716,060
Dwelling burglary	245,312	20	4,906,240
Shop theft	308,326	2	616,652
Fraud	181,023	20	3,620,460

Source: Sherman et al. (2016, p. 179).

in principle, easily be fixed with victimisation survey data for most crime types. Subjectivity is clearly not removed from the Cambridge Harm Index. It depends on what is defined as a crime. Moreover, sentencing guidelines in part reflect subjective (albeit commonly accepted) judgements about the weights to attach to different crimes, not all of which necessarily focus on the harms produced. These judgements of crime seriousness are apt to change and to vary by jurisdiction, making them applicable only within jurisdictions and only at specific times. Some corporate offences, such as those to do with pollution, may produce very serious and extensive harms to people and places within and across national borders, which are not reflected in the sentences applied to offenders. This is not to say that harm indices are of no value, only that there are inbuilt limitations and that the need for contestable judgements by decision-makers cannot be avoided by the use of such a formulaic scale.

Although the remainder of this chapter does not add to the discussion of different offence-type harms and their relevance to resource allocation decisions, it does go on to describe the findings of empirical research on crime patterns, which have an important role to play in informing decisions as to how to focus preventive efforts. These findings relate to ways in which crimes are concentrated and hence where preventive efforts might most fruitfully be directed.

Concentrations

What is sometimes referred to as the '80/20 rule' (more formally the Pareto Principle, named after the classic Italian sociologist Vilfredo Pareto) applies to several forms of crime concentration. The 80/20 rule has it that a large proportion of outcomes come from a small proportion of potential sources. It applies in many contexts. As we will see later in the chapter, the 80/20 rule applies to crime victims, theft targets, crime locations, offenders, facilities, and systems. Moreover, these forms of concentration often overlap. Identifying concentrations provides useful information for targeting scarce crime prevention resources.

Victims

Victim support volunteers, as well as attending police officers, used to console those who had suffered domestic burglary with the adage that, 'Lightning doesn't strike in the same place twice.' The victim had had their turn. There was a diminished chance that they would become victims again. The Kirkholt burglary prevention project, outlined in Chapter 2, found the opposite. Experience of a burglary increased the chances of another burglary. Allocating preventive efforts to victims is thus an efficient way of drip-feeding scarce victim-focused burglary prevention resources (Pease, 1998). Moreover, the finding that these repeat incidents tended to happen quickly added to the resource-efficiency of acting promptly (ibid). At the same time, this way of allocating limited resources seems distributionally fair: victims deserve priority, given the crime harm they have experienced.

The findings relating to repeat victimisation in Rochdale confirmed the findings of an early crime victimisation survey in Britain (Sparks, Genn, & Dodd, 1977), although the significance for crime prevention allocation decisions was not then realised. It was the Rochdale project that again found the repeat pattern, which first used the phenomenon as a basis for prioritising preventive interventions on households that had recently experienced burglary.

The findings for Kirkholt and domestic burglary were soon replicated in other places in Britain. They were also repeated for domestic burglary in other countries (e.g. Kleemans, 2001 for the Netherlands; Morgan, 2001 for Australia). They were again found for diverse crime types, for example for commercial as well as domestic burglary in Britain (Tilley, 1993) and for business extortion in Mexico (Estevez-Soto, Johnson, & Tilley, 2021). Farrell and Pease (2001) brought together similar early findings, including ones related to fraud and robbery.

Measuring repeat victimisation poses several challenges, especially where recorded crime data are used. Only a proportion of crimes are reported and recorded; victim and target details are often recorded inconsistently and inaccurately; and there are varying time periods available for repeats to occur where data are drawn from a given period (typically a year). All these tend towards repeat incidents being missed and hence levels of repeats underestimated. At a subjective level, within police services, it is likely that different officers attend successive incidents and hence will not have a sense that there are repeats. Moreover, following the pioneering work in Kirkholt, some police services, crunching through crime records, were unable to find repeat patterns, but it turned out that this was due to limitations in the recorded data.

My own experience relates to estimating the rate and time course of repeat commercial burglaries using police records (see Tilley, 1993). Records of all incidents over two years were assembled in order that each incident over one year could be followed up for the following 12 months to see if there had been repeats (if we use only one year, an incident on January 1 has 12 months for a repeat but that on December 31 has no time!). Extensive data cleaning was required to make sure that repeats were not missed due to recording inconsistencies. Generating the required data involved a researcher and police officer sitting side by side over several weeks to go through records manually!

Although victimisation surveys have their own limitations (to do for example with respondent recall, the formulation of the questions, and the number of repeat incidents included in the analysis), they generally provide more robust data on repeat patterns than recorded crime.

Crime surveys can distinguish between incidence and prevalence in measuring crime rates. Incidence (I) refers to the number of crimes in relation to a given population over a given period, for example 100 robberies per 100,000 people or 100 burglaries per 100,000 households or 100 vehicle thefts per 100,000 owners of cars over a year. Prevalence (P) refers to the proportion of those that have suffered one or more crimes of a particular type over a given period; for example 2% of households have suffered one or more burglary; or 1% of individuals have suffered a robbery; or 3% of drivers have had their vehicles stolen over a year. Knowing the prevalence and incidence rates allows the level of concentration (C) to be calculated – the average number of crimes per victim per year. Basically, 'C' equals 'I' divided by 'P,' provided that both are expressed in the same way, for example in absolute numbers or fractions using the same denominator $(C = I/P)$. Concentration gives us a metric for estimating the levels of repeats. Recorded crime rates cannot normally be used for this calculation as the figures only report incidence levels. However, if there are consistently used unique identifiers for individuals and addresses then calculations do become possible, albeit that problems of partial reporting and recording remain.

Table 3.4 shows findings from the Crime Survey of England and Wales for 2019 to 2020 for selected offences, based on survey estimates of total numbers of selected offence types (the sample for the survey included 33,427 respondents). It shows that levels of concentration were highest for violence, followed by fraud and computer theft, then domestic burglary, and finally personal theft where repeats were relatively uncommon.

Two different broad mechanisms producing repeats are mooted. The 'flag' (or 'state dependency' or 'risk heterogeneity') mechanism refers to fixed attributes of the victim that will tend to attract offenders (say the appearance of rich pickings and/or low risk of being caught). The 'boost' (or 'event dependency') account, on the other hand, refers to ways in which the occurrence of one offence heightens the vulnerability to another (e.g. when the knowledge gleaned by a given offender of further goods that could be stolen

Table 3.4 Estimated incidents, victims, and concentration for selected crime types in England and Wales, April 2019 to March 2020.

	Number of incidents	Number of victims	Concentration (average incidents per victim over one year's recall)
Violence	880,000	548,000	1.606
Fraud and computer misuse	4,491,000	3,723,000	1.206
Domestic burglary	534,000	462,000	1.156
Robbery	98,000	94,000	1.043
Theft from the person	347,000	346,000	1.033

Source: ONS (2023).

or the knowledge of safe ways to commit the crime against the repeated target is used in a repeat incident, or when the offender tips off other offenders about the crime opportunity).

There is some evidence that the same offenders return, and that these are often prolific criminals (Pease, 1998). It is unlikely, however, that either the flag or boost mechanism alone fully explains the observed repeat patterns. There may also be interactions between them whereby flags lead to boost: an attractive target (due say to location) is selected by offenders, but they (or an associate) then return to it because of known further crime opportunities there.

A project ran in Huddersfield that built on the achievements of the Kirkholt initiative (Chenery, Holt, & Pease, 1997). Huddersfield pioneered the Olympic model of intervention, whereby response intensity increases and changes with successive crimes against the same target. The initial focus was on target hardening to try to put offenders off, and then in the event of further incidents, the focus switched to detection, using measures (such as silent alarms) that would increase the prospects of detecting prolific offenders. We referred to a further application of a tiered approach to intervention in the domestic violence prevention project in Killingbeck as outlined in Chapter 2.

Research building on the findings relating to repeats of crimes against the same targets has found that the increased risk faced by those who have experienced a crime spreads also to those nearby (known as 'near repeats'). Moreover, it reveals a similar time course of increased risk. Bowers, Johnson, and Pease (2004) report that for up to two months after a burglary at a particular address, other properties within 400 metres were also at higher risk of burglary. This pattern can inform predictions of when and where future burglaries are most likely to take place and hence the deployment of preventive efforts such as police patrol. For a summary of experience in identifying repeats and near repeats and preventive responses, see Farrell and Pease (2017).

The discussion of repeats and near repeats takes us neatly to crime concentrations by place and to hotspots more particularly.

Places

Spatial concentrations of crime are found at every level of geography, from region to city to area within the city to police beat to zip or postcode to street segment to address. Concentrations at lower levels partly explain concentrations at higher levels. A large volume of research has been devoted to the identification, measurement, and explanation of crime concentrations as well as to the development and trialling of interventions to reduce crime where it is concentrated. Chainey (2021) provides a comprehensive account of the geography of crime.

Location matters because 'traditional' crimes take place in physical places (cybercrimes are rather different). One of the earliest and most influential studies of spatial concentration examined the distribution of crimes in Minneapolis, using police dispatch data covering the period of December 15, 1985 to December 15, 1986 (Sherman, Gartin, & Buerger, 1989). Sherman et al. estimated that there were 109,000 street addresses and 6,000 intersections, together making up the 115,000 places to which a crime could be located. Similar problems for location definition faced Sherman et al. as those found in studies of repeat victimisation.

Sherman et al. found a relatively small number of hotspots within the city. They report that 50.4% of all calls to the police for which cars were dispatched went to only 3.3% of all addresses/intersections: in half of these, there was only one call. The top 5% had an average of 24 calls each over the year. Concentration was even greater for the subset of calls to predatory crimes, including criminal sexual conduct (rape, molestation, and exposure), robbery, and auto theft: 4,166 robbery calls were to only 2.2% of all possible places; 3,903 vehicle theft calls were made to 2.7% of possible places; and 1,729 sexual conduct calls were made to 1.2% of possible places. Combining data on all three calls to predatory crimes, Sherman et al. report that there were 230 hotspots with five or more calls and 67 with at least 10. Turning to calls to crimes inside premises, including burglary, domestic disturbances, and assaults, Sherman et al. again found that the level of concentration by place was far greater than would be expected by chance.

Sherman et al.'s findings for Minneapolis suggest that substantial overall reductions in crime could in principle be achieved by targeting its hotspot locations. Similar patterns of spatial crime concentration in hotspots to those reported for Minneapolis have been widely found elsewhere. The identification of hotspots thus provides some empirical evidence to inform the allocation of scarce crime prevention resources. In a systematic review, Lee, Eck, SooHyun, and Martinez (2017) identified 44 studies examining empirically the spatial concentration of crime. They consistently found it. Wilcox and Eck (2011) refer to an 'iron law of crime concentration,' and Weisburd (2015) to a 'law of crime concentration.'

Cross-cutting the concentration of crime by place, there is concentration in the times when crimes occur. Crimes do not tend to occur randomly by season, day of week, or time of the day. Of course, identifying time of the day for many types of offence is tricky. Victims don't necessarily know when a crime was committed, and police records tend therefore to provide ranges of times when it might have occurred or to pin them to one temporal marker such as midnight or midday. Say, someone arrives to find that their car has been broken into, they know when they left the car and they know when they found that it had been broken into, but within that time frame they don't know exactly when the offence was committed. There are some smart techniques for making estimates, but these do not fully obviate the problem. Ratcliffe and McCullagh (1998) propose an 'aoristic' method of analysing event time patterns, better to understand crime concentrations in places. This involves taking the population of records of crimes covering the period when a crime might have taken place as a way of estimating an incident time, rather than allocating the mid-point of start to finish, which may be convenient but there is no special reason to use it (for an explanation of the method and a statistical package in R to undertake it, see Ratcliffe, 2022).

One study looking at place and time, in this case looking at offences where timing is not uncertain – theft and violent crime around Wembley soccer stadium on match days – was able to identify specific times and places when crime was elevated (Kurland, Johnson, & Tilley, 2013). This, like other studies looking at time and place (including the time for repeat and near-repeat victimisation), was able to suggest where and when preventive interventions were most needed and offered most scope for impact, again empirically informing the allocation of scarce preventive resources.

Where specific locations are at issue for frequent victimisation, two major types of mechanisms have been produced: 'generation' and 'attraction' (see Chapter 4). 'Generation' refers to the ways in which some crime-target rich places are attended by many people. Among the attendees, those open to criminal temptation are liable to exploit crime opportunities they come across (Brantingham & Brantingham, 1995). 'Attraction' refers to the ways in which offenders may be attracted to some places because of the plentiful crime opportunities they throw up. Offenders go to those places because of the known crime opportunities they furnish, intending to exploit them. Busy railway stations may largely be crime attractors in that those offenders wishing to commit personal thefts can expect plentiful opportunities. Supermarkets and amusement parks probably combine attraction and generation.

Products

Some 'hot' products are stolen much more than others, but there are also changes in hot products over time. Using data from the British Crime Survey/ Crime Survey of England and Wales (a high-quality victimisation survey with sweeps going back to 1982), Thompson (2017) ranks goods stolen from the person from 1993 to 2001. She shows that cash, and purses, and wallets consistently took the top two places (each being taken in around 35% to 70% of offences). Next came credit/debit cards, though they rose from 1993 to 1995 and then remained in third or fourth place till 2001 (each being taken in around 7% to 35% of offences). Documents, briefcases, and handbags took fifth and sixth places (each being taken in around 7% to 10% of offences). Thompson notes some significant changes. The proportion of thefts involving the loss of a mobile phone rose between 1996 and 2010, while the proportion involving cash and chequebooks fell.

In relation to shop theft in 1975, Walsh (1978, p. 73) reported that in Exeter, some goods tended to be targeted by shoplifters. Examples, from retailers experiencing overall high levels of shop theft, are shown in Table 3.5.

What makes a product hot? Clarke (1999) uses the acronym CRAVED to capture attributes of goods that make them especially attractive to thieves. CRAVED refers to 'Concealable' (items that easily hidden), 'Removable' (items that can be easily taken from where they are located), 'Available' (items that are accessible and abundant), 'Valuable' (items that are of relatively high value), 'Enjoyable' (items whose consumption is likely to be rewarding to the thief), and 'Disposable' (items for which there is a ready market). The more a product has these attributes the more likely it is to be stolen. The CRAVED acronym has been applied in relation to many theft targets, including livestock in Malawi (Sidebottom, 2013), parrots in Mexico (Pires & Clarke, 2012), cell phones (Whitehead et al., 2008), drugs (Natarajan, 2012), and even sexual homicide (Beauregard & Martineau, 2015).

Table 3.5 Types of shop and items shoplifted in Exeter in 1975.

Shop type	Most stolen items
Department stores	Most small items
Food shops	Pre-packaged foodstuffs
Confectioners	Cigars, chocolate bars
Ladies clothing	Tights
Booksellers	Stationery

Source: Walsh (1978, p. 73).

Thompson's findings about theft targets, as identified in the Crime Survey of England and Wales and Walsh's on items stolen from retailers in Exeter, accord well with CRAVED.

The practical value of CRAVED for the efficient targeting of preventive resources lies in identifying future as well as existing products in need of designs that will counter their attractiveness to offenders. The failure to anticipate the most theft-prone products and take pre-emptive action means not only that those who are victimised need not have been, but also that more resources need to be used later to retrofit preventive measures (Pease, 1997).

The attributes of CRAVED targets for thieves make them attractive for paying customers too. Products' attractiveness to thieves is in that sense a by-product of attributes most of us welcome because they contribute to our expected enjoyment from our purchases. The case of car theft, discussed in Chapter 2, brings this out. Certain makes and models were especially hot (such as hot hatches) because they were fun to drive. Their CRAVED attributes made them highly vulnerable to theft. Before manufacturers built in an array of measures to reduce their vulnerability, owners had to bear the costs of retrofitting preventive measures if they wanted to reduce risks of theft.

Another acronym sometimes used to capture attributes of crime targets (and therefore not exclusively items that are stolen) is VIVA, which refers to 'Value,' 'Inertia,' 'Visibility,' and 'Access' (Cohen & Felson, 1979; Felson & Cohen, 1980). 'Value' refers to the monetary or symbolic value of the target; 'Inertia' to any feature of the potential target that is difficult to overcome for illegal purposes, such as weight, bulk, or capacity for physical resistance; 'Visibility' to exposure of theft targets to the offender; and 'Access' to the suitability of the site for the offender to commit crime against the target. VIVA has some overlaps with CRAVED and has implicit suggestions for reducing target suitability (decrease value, increase inertia, reduce visibility, reduce access). VIVA also helps explain why targets change over time. For example once the ownership of a given product approaches saturation and becomes very cheap, its value as a target diminishes and thefts will decline. The steps leading up to saturation are sometimes referred to as the 'product life-cycle,' where 'innovation' (expensive products bought only by enthusiasts) is followed by 'growth' (more goods, lower prices), then 'mass market' (including a market for stolen goods, when theft becomes 'endemic'), and finally 'saturation' (when almost all wanting to have the product have it, so thefts decline) (Felson, 1997).

Facilities

Facilities describe, 'special purpose structures operated for special functions. Examples of place facilities include high schools, taverns, convenience stores, churches, apartment buildings, and public housing projects' (Eck & Weisburd, 1995, p. 8). Other examples include libraries, hospitals, car parks, railway stations, and shopping centres (Eck, Clarke, & Guerette, 2007). Different types of facility, of course, have different crime profiles: for example although shop theft might feature significantly in convenience stores, this will not be the case for churches! What is more significant here, however, is the finding that within the population of types of facility in each area, rates of crime vary widely: crimes are concentrated on a small proportion of them. The 80/20 rule applies (Eck et al., 2007).

Reviewing research on crime concentration in facilities, Eck et al. (2007) give examples at the local level, citing calls to the police from bars in Shawnee, Kansas; shoplifting from stores in Danvers, Connecticut; crime incidents from apartment complexes for the over 50s in Jacksonville, Florida; and calls to the police from motels in Chula Vista, California. In all cases, a small number of the facilities of the given type account for a large proportion of incidents. Eck et al. summarise findings of 37 studies of concentration in different types of facility, including apartment complexes (1 study); banks (2 studies); bars, pubs, and clubs (n = 3); bus stop shelters (n = 1); businesses of various kinds (n = 10); construction sites (n = 1); convenience stores (n = 1); fast food outlets (n = 1); gas stations (n = 3); healthcare facilities (n = 1); hotels (n = 1); parking lots (n = 3); schools (n = 5); sports facilities (n = 1); telephone kiosks (n = 1); and young offender institutions (n = 2). These studies were undertaken in different countries including Australia, England, Scotland, Sweden, and the United States. The results consistently point to crime concentration within populations of similar facilities.

Eck et al. give four possible causes of crime concentration in facilities: 'random variation' (at a particular time it may be that crime is concentrated, but this reflects random ups and downs in numbers of crimes at each within the population of facilities); 'reporting processes' (some may simply report incidents at a higher rate than others); 'targets' (some may have more targets than others); offenders (some may attract, be known to, or be more convenient for offenders than others); and 'place management' (how the people owning or controlling the facility run it). They suggest that causes of facility concentration need further investigation and analysis to find out the sources of concentration as a basis for working out whether they are real and what might be done to reduce crimes in facilities where they are concentrated.

There will most clearly be scope to make changes in place management aimed at reducing crime in those facilities where crime occurs at disproportionately high rates (see Eck, Linning, & Herold, 2023).

Facility crime concentration is relevant to crime prevention resource allocation. Knowing about crime concentration can help owners or managers of chains of any given type of facility (say supermarkets, hospitals, car parks, or restaurants) decide how to focus preventive efforts. For those who are not themselves targets but bear costs from crime events, for example police agencies or insurance companies, knowing which facilities are disproportionately targeted can help decide where to target crime prevention support or leverage. The betting shops, discussed in Chapter 2, provide an example.

Systems

Formally speaking, systems comprise 'any set of organised or consciously developed habitual human behaviours' (Sidebottom & Tilley, 2017, p. 254). Examples make it easier to get a feel for what they are: arrangements for vehicle registrations and change of ownership, procedures through which bank payments are made, processes through which businesses order goods and pay for them, forms of tax payment and collection, arrangements for student assessment, forms of welfare claims and benefit payments, arrangements for the delivery of goods to customers, systems for the payment for fuel at service stations, car park payment systems, systems for the reimbursement for goods returned to stores, and so on all comprise systems which are apt to vary in ways relevant to the production of crime.

Knutsson and Kuhlhorn (1997) show how banking systems unintentionally fostered cheque fraud in Sweden. Homel, Hauritz, McIlwain, Wortley, and Carvolth (1997) show how systems for running nightclubs could foster drunkenness and violence in Australia. As we saw in Chapter 2, Sloan-Howitt and Kelling (1997) show how changing the system for cleaning graffiti off subway cars could reduce the rate at which graffiti was (re)produced in the United States.

Many systems are now embedded electronically. Concentration in relation to such systems can be assessed by looking at the distribution of crime by different suppliers of the same service. Sidebottom and Tilley (2017) do just this in relation to dating sites and reported romance scams in the UK. They take City of London Police counts of numbers of online frauds per dating site, where there had been at least one reported incident. Figure 3.1 shows counts over two years (2013 and 2014) ranging from the highest to the lowest. Figure 3.2 uses the same incident data but shows rates per one million visitors to each site, again ranged from highest to lowest. Both show the same basic pattern. Scams are heavily skewed to a few sites with large numbers or high rates of reported occurrences. The top five sites accounted for 78% of all reported incidents. Something about some sites seems to make them much more vulnerable than others. Sidebottom and Tilley describe high crime systems as 'leaky.'

Finding where crimes are concentrated in systems providing similar services but showing high variations in crime level (rates or numbers) is helpful in directing the efficient allocation of crime prevention resources to understand what lies behind the high levels in some and what might be done to reduce their vulnerability.

We turn now to offenders themselves and the concentration of criminal behaviour on a subset of them.

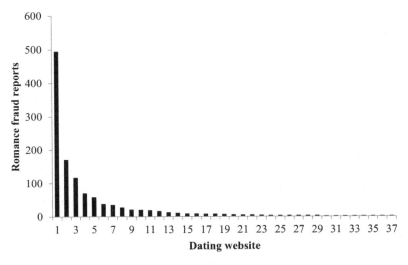

Figure 3.1 Online romance frauds by dating website.

Source: City of London Police recorded crime data, January 2013 to December 2014; Sidebottom & Tilley (2017).

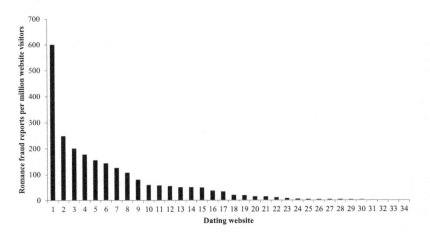

Figure 3.2 Online romance frauds per one million visitors to online dating website.

Source: City of London Police recorded crime data, January 2013 to December 2014; Sidebottom & Tilley (2017).

Note: the numbers in Figures 3.1 and 3.2 do not denote the same sites.

Offenders

As Thomas Gabor memorably put it in the title to his book, *Everybody Does it!* (Gabor, 1994). Gabor assembled an array of evidence showing that crime is not the preserve of the aberrant few but is an activity pretty much all of us have engaged in or will engage in. For example he presented striking findings from a survey of New Yorkers, conducted soon after the Second World War by Wallerstein and Wyle (1947), as illustrated in Table 3.6. The average number of offences admitted by each respondent (referring to the 49 offence types covered in the survey) was 18 for men and 11 for women. Gabor quotes many other research findings relating to self-reports of criminal activity. Although the findings are often not so stark as those for New Yorkers, the overall pattern is quite consistent. There is nothing out of the ordinary about offending, especially by men, who consistently report participation in more criminal activity than women.

The finding that participation in crime is the norm is important in reminding us that criminals are not a pathological few, set apart from the normal, law-abiding many. However, recognising this does not mean that there are not enormous variations in rates of criminal activity. In accordance with

Table 3.6 Members of the public in New York admitting lawbreaking – selected offences.

Offence	Men (N = 1,020)	Women (N = 678)
Larceny	89%	83%
Falsification and fraud	46%	34%
Tax evasion	57%	40%
Assault	49%	39%
Indecency	77%	74%
Concealed weapons	35%	3%
Auto theft	26%	8%
Burglary	17%	4%
Robbery	11%	1%
Disorderly conduct	85%	76%

Source: From Wallerstein and Wyle (1947), as reported in Gabor (1994, p. 55).

findings about other forms of crime concentration, it seems that rates of criminal activity vary widely and that a large proportion of all crimes are committed by a small proportion of offenders.

Following a systematic literature search, Martinez, Lee, Eck, and SooHyun (2017) identified 73 studies of crime concentration among offenders. They found evidence of crime concentration among male and female offenders, among young and old offenders, and among offenders in different countries. They quote, for example, Sampson and Laub's finding in 2003 that less than 3% of Boston male offenders accounted for 51% of arrests of those aged under 31 and Ambihapathy's finding in 1983 that among female offenders in Ottawa, 8% of them accounted for 36% of their arrests. Findings of this general kind go back a long time (at least to 1950) and continue to be repeated.

Martinez et al. (2017) found 15 studies where the data provided would enable them to graph cumulative percentages of numbers of offenders according to their frequency of offending against the cumulative percentage of the total of their offences. These graphs produce 'J curves' which allow the user to read off the proportion of all offenders up to a given offending frequency, who are accountable for the cumulative percentage of all offences for which they are responsible (as measured, for example, by arrests) over a given time for a given population of offenders and for given types of crime. The systematic review found consistent and similar patterns of crime concentration across offender groups.

The recurrent findings on crime concentration suggest that although involvement in criminal behaviour appears to be near ubiquitous, concentrating limited offender-focused preventive resources on prolific offenders, provided that effective measures can be identified, will be more efficient than focusing on all offenders.

Overlapping concentrations

The different forms of concentration described in this chapter often overlap and interact. High rates of repeat victimisation contribute to local area crime concentrations, for example, such that targeting repeat victims would bring down crime levels in high crime neighbourhoods (Trickett, Osborn, Seymour, & Pease, 1992).

Repeat (and near-repeat) victimisation is often a function of repeat offenders, most clearly in the case of domestic violence. Highly victimised and high offending populations sometimes overlap, as in the case of violent gang conflicts. It seems likely that among populations of similar facilities, the more highly victimised will include those using the leakiest systems.

Farrell (2005, p. 166) uses a Venn diagram, shown in Figure 3.3, to represent the intersection between hotspots, repeat victimisation, repeat offending, and hot products as the most fruitful points of intervention to concentrate preventive resources.

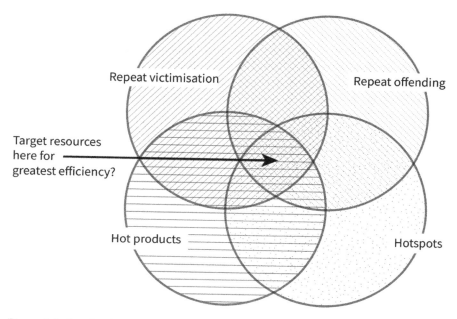

Figure 3.3 Overlap between repeat victimisation, hotspots, repeat offending, and hot products.

Source: Farrell (2005).

Spelman and Eck (1989) distinguish between 'sitting ducks,' 'ravenous wolves,' and 'dens of iniquity.' They highlight studies producing the kinds of finding mentioned in this chapter: that crime is concentrated by places (referring to a study finding that 60% of crimes were committed in 10% of areas), by offenders (55% of crimes committed by 10% of offenders, Blumstein, Cohen, Roth, & Visher, 1986), and by victims (10% of victims accounting for about 40% of all crimes, Nelson, 1980). They argue that different problems of concentration need to be identified to determine the appropriate local strategy: high crime areas could be reduced by reducing sitting duck vulnerability, the supply of ravenous wolves, or the conduciveness to crime of dens of iniquity. Where sitting ducks, ravenous wolves, and dens of iniquity overlap in hot spots, they obviously comprise a strong focus for preventive attention.

Conclusion

The optimal allocation of limited crime prevention resources in the interests of harm reduction is clearly tricky. In practice, allocations are often made as a matter of routine, with changes in priority made in response to mass media commentary following high-profile cases or to political pressure. However, better judgements could be informed both by the findings about characteristic forms of concentration outlined so far in this chapter and by a critical appreciation of patterns of harms caused by those crimes.

This chapter has described a range of types of crime and criminality concentration, covering victims, places, product targets, facilities, systems and offenders, and interrelationships between these forms of concentration. In each case, there is ample evidence to inform decisions about how to allocate limited preventive resources. However, the issue of harm and harm reduction is not resolved by these findings. Notwithstanding difficulties in economic cost calculations and in crime harm indices, they highlight the importance of variations in harms caused by different crimes and of taking these into account in prioritisation.

Finally, we need to recognise that some crime harms have tended to be neglected and that changing crime patterns can create new patterns of crime harm which need to be recognised in crime prevention resource allocation.

Neglected harms: Decisions over the allocation of preventive efforts have tended to neglect crime-related harms produced by white collar workers and corporations. Gabor provides a sobering account of the routine criminality that has pervaded corporate life in North America (Gabor, 1994, pp. 116–133). This is not reflected in the kinds of statistics generally used in analyses of crime concentration or in the work of those charged with providing local crime prevention services. Corporate crime does not figure, for example, in Heeks et al.'s estimates of the costs of different types of crime, as shown in Table 3.2.

Gabor gives some examples of corporate criminal harms:

(T)he Ford Motor Company . . . poured millions of Pintos off its assembly lines although Ford executives knew the gas tanks were defective and could rupture after a rear-end collision, burning passengers alive. There is the Johns-Manville Corporation, producer of asbestos products, which for decades failed to inform its workers that inhaling asbestos can be lethal – about 10,000 people die each year of asbestos-related cancer. There is A.H. Robins, manufacturer of the Dalkon Shield, an inter-uterine contraceptive device. Despite the fact that women using the device were dying, having still births and babies with birth defects in large numbers, as well as suffering from internal injuries on a large scale, the company for years tried to cover up the product's dangers. There have also been countless cases of illegal dumping of hazardous materials resulting in fatalities, chromosomal damage, and chronic illnesses on the part of significant segments of the population.

Gabor (1994, pp. 116–117)

Gabor also cites systematic studies that give an idea of how widespread corporate crime is, even if the examples are of less harm-producing offensive behaviour. He refers, for example, to a neat study by a Canadian journalist, Robert Sikorski, who went on a road trip coast-to-coast in Canada. Sikorski went to 152 repair shops (covering both independents and chains), having first made sure that his car was in tip-top condition. Before each stop at the repair shop, he disconnected a connector at the idle air control that automatically led to a 'Service engine soon' warning message. The dangling lead would make the source of the fault obvious. Fifty seven per cent of the repair shops 'overcharged, performed unnecessary work, tried to sell unneeded parts, or fixed the car and lied about what work had been done' (Gabor, 1985, p. 120). This would suggest that unrecognised and repeated scams can be a routine feature of some businesses' practices.

Change, harm, and cybercrime: Crime patterns change. The advent of cyber-related crime clearly marks a sea change in the source and nature of crime-related harms. The Crime Survey of England and Wales for 2022 (ONS, 2023a, 2023b), which deals with crimes against individuals and households, found that there were as many crimes of fraud and computer misuse as there were of all other personal and property crimes measured by the survey. Furthermore, according to the Commercial Victimisation Survey, a third of all businesses experienced at least one incident of debit or credit fraud, and a quarter experienced 'people impersonating your organisation for emails, online, for payment' in 2022 (Home Office, 2023).

Figures 3.1 and 3.2 showed the concentration of cyber-enabled romance scams – their tendency to be found on some dating sites but not others. For preventive purposes, much greater detail will be needed on the harms produced by romance scams and on ways in which they are concentrated.

Voce and Morgan (2023) make a good start in measuring different types of cybercrime and their harms in Australia. They conducted a survey of 13,887 computer users and found a 47% one-year prevalence rate for all cybercrimes. They distinguish among 'online abuse and harassment' (27% prevalence), 'identity crime and misuse' (20%), 'malware' attacks (22%), and 'fraud and scams' (8%). They note the cumulative growth in harms according to the number of types of cybercrime suffered, as shown in Table 3.7.

As Voce and Morgan also say,

> A growing body of evidence shows victims of cybercrime experience trauma and hardship in response to their victimisation. Victims of cyber-enabled crimes can experience financial hardship, emotional distress (e.g. feelings of embarrassment, shame, anger, sadness and distress), loss of confidence in other people, physical symptoms (e.g. difficulty sleeping,

Table 3.7 Cybercrime harms.

Harms	Number of types of cybercrime experienced			
	One type (%)	Two types (%)	Three types (%)	Four types (%)
Practical	32.8	45.4	62.0	63.0
Social	12.1	20.8	31.7	39.0
Health	10.0	16.6	30.0	48.5
Financial	8.6	16.8	31.6	46.8
Legal	0.6	1.6	4.3	10.4
N	3,558	1,708	704	324

Source: Australian Crime Survey (weighted data) in Voce and Morgan (2023).

weight loss and nausea), relationship and family conflict, and, at the extreme end of the spectrum, suicidal thoughts and ideation. Victims of cyber-dependent crime also report problems communicating with friends and family, financial strain, problems dealing with businesses, and even mental or emotional distress requiring treatment.

(Voce and Morgan, p. 80)

Exercise: Write a guide to the local police or local crime prevention partnership, setting out a method for selecting priorities for the allocation of limited preventive resources.

Notes

1 All positive and negative side effects ideally need to be identified, measured, and costed. For obvious reasons, delivering on this counsel of perfection is very difficult! Moreover, the choices may reflect the interests of stakeholders commissioning the work or the interests of those conducting the analysis.
2 Other extensions can be found at Manning (2020); College of Policing (2023); and Manning, Christen, Wong, Ranbaduge, and Vidanage (2019).
3 This is not to say that nothing can be learned from willingness to pay estimates. Johnson, Blythe, Manning, and Wong (2020), for example report an ingenious experiment aiming to estimate what extra people would be prepared to pay to improve the security of various items falling within the Internet of Things (smart TVs, wearable devices, smart thermostats, and security cameras).

References

Ambihapathy, C. (1983). *Criminal career research in the City of Ottawa* (Unpublished doctoral dissertation). University of Ottawa, Ottawa.

Andersen, H., & Mueller-Johnson, K. (2018). The Danish Crime Harm Index: How it works and why it matters. *Cambridge Journal of Evidence-Based Policing, 2,* 52–69. doi:10.1007/s41887-018-0021-7

Beauregard, E., & Martineau, M. (2015). An application of CRAVED to the choice of victim in sexual homicide: A routine activity approach. *Crime Science, 4,* 24. doi:10.1186/s40163-015-0036-3

Blumstein, A., Cohen, J., Roth, J., & Visher, C. (1986). *Criminal careers and career criminals* (Vol. 1). Washington, DC: National Academy Press.

Bowers, K., Johnson, S., & Pease, K. (2004). Prospective hotspotting: The future of crime mapping. *British Journal of Criminology, 44*(5), 641–658. doi:10.1093/bjc/azh036

Brantingham, P., & Brantingham, P. (1995). Criminality of place: Crime generators and crime attractors. *European Journal on Criminal Policy and Research, 3*(3), 5–26. doi:10.1007/BF02242925

Chainey, S. (2021). *Understanding crime: Analysing the geography of crime.* Redlands, CA: Esri Press.

Chenery, S., Holt, J., & Pease, K. (1997). *Biting back II: Reducing repeat victimisation in Huddersfield* (Crime Detection and Prevention Paper 85). London: Home Office.

Clarke, R. V. (1999). *Hot products: Understanding, anticipating and reducing demand for stolen goods* (Police Research Series, Paper 112). London: Home Office.

Cohen, L., & Felson, M. (1979). Social change and crime rate trends: A routine activity approach. *American Sociological Review, 44,* 588–608. doi:10.2307/2094589

College of Policing. (2023). *Practical evaluation tools.* Retrieved July 3, 2023, from www.college.police.uk/research/practical-evaluation-tools

Eck, J., Clarke, R., & Guerette, R. (2007). Risky facilities: Crime concentration in homogenous sets of establishments and facilities. In G. Farrell, K. Bowers, S. Johnson, & M. Townsley (Eds.), *Imagination for crime prevention: Essays in honour of Ken Pease. Criminal justice studies 21* (pp. 225–264). Monsey, NY: Criminal Justice Press.

Eck, J., Linning, S., & Herold, T. (2023). *Place management and crime: Ownership and property rights as a source of social control.* Cham: Springer.

Eck, J., & Weisburd, D. (1995). Crime places in crime theory. In J. Eck & D. Weisburd (Eds.), *Crime and place: Crime prevention studies 4* (pp. 1–32). Monsey, NY: Criminal Justice Press.

Estevez-Soto, P., Johnson, S., & Tilley, N. (2021). Are repeatedly extorted businesses different? *Journal of Quantitative Criminology, 37,* 1115–1157. doi:10.1007/s10940-020-09480-8

Farrell, G. (2005). Progress and prospects in the prevention of repeat victimisation. In N. Tilley (Ed.), *Handbook of crime prevention and community safety* (pp. 143–170). London: Willan.

Farrell, G., & Pease, K. (Eds.). (2001). *Repeat victimization: Crime prevention studies 12.* Monsey, NY: Criminal Justice Press.

Farrell, G., & Pease, K. (2017). Preventing repeat and near repeat crime concentrations. In N. Tilley & A. Sidebottom (Eds.), *Handbook of crime prevention and community safety* (pp. 143–156). London: Routledge. doi:10.4324/9781843926146

Felson, M. (1997). Technology, business, and crime. In M. Felson & R. Clarke (Eds.), *Business and crime prevention.* Monsey, NY: Criminal Justice Press.

Felson, M., & Cohen, L. (1980). Human ecology and crime: A routine activity approach. *Human Ecology, 8*(4), 389–406. doi:10.1007/BF01561001

Gabor, T. (1994). *Everybody does it! Crime by the public.* Toronto: University of Toronto Press.

Heeks, M., Reed, S., Tafsiri, M., & Prince, S. (2018). *The economic and social costs of crime* (Research Report 99, 2nd ed.). London: Home Office.

Home Office. (2023). *Crime against businesses: Findings from the 2022 commercial victimisation survey.* Retrieved July 3, 2023, from www.gov.uk/government/statistics/crime-against-businesses-findings-from-the-2022-commercial-victimisation-survey/

Homel, R., Hauritz, M., McIlwain, G., Wortley, R., & Carvolth, R. (1997). Preventing drunkenness and violence around nightclubs in a tourist resort. In R. V. Clarke (Ed.), *Situational crime prevention: Successful case studies* (2nd ed.). New York: Harrow and Heston.

House, P., & Neyroud, P. (2018). Developing a crime harm index for Western Australia: The WASHI. *Cambridge Journal of Evidence-Based Policing, 2,* 70–94. doi:10.1007/s41887-018-0022-6

Ignatans, D., & Pease, K. (2016). Taking crime seriously: Playing the weighting game. *Policing, 10*(3), 184–193. doi:10.1093/police/pav029

Johnson, S., Blythe, J., Manning, M., & Wong, G. (2020). The impact of IoT security labelling on consumer product choice and willingness to pay. *PLoS One, 15*(1), e0227800. doi:10.1371/journal.pone.0227800

Karrholm, F., Neyroud, P., & Smaaland, J. (2020). Designing the Swedish Crime Harm Index: An evidence-based strategy. *Cambridge Journal of Evidence-Based Policing, 4,* 15–33. doi:10.1007/s41887-020-00041-4

Kay, J., & King, M. (2020). *Radical uncertainty: Decision-making for an unknowable future.* London: The Bridge Street Press.

Kleemans, E. (2001). Repeat burglary victimisation: Results of empirical research in the Netherlands. In G. Farrell & K. Pease (Eds.), *Repeat victimization: Crime prevention studies 12* (pp. 53–68). Monsey, NY: Criminal Justice Press.

Knutsson, J., & Kuhlhorn, E. (1997). Macro measures against crime: The example of check forgeries. In R. V. Clarke (Ed.), *Situational crime prevention: Successful case studies* (2nd ed., pp. 113–121). New York: Harrow and Heston.

Kurland, J., Johnson, S., & Tilley, N. (2013). Offenses around stadiums: A natural experiment on crime attraction and generation. *Journal of Research in Crime and Delinquency, 51*(1), 5–28. doi:10.1177/0022427812471349

Lee, Y., Eck, J., SooHyun, O., & Martinez, N. (2017). How concentrated in crime at places? A systematic review from 1970 to 2015. *Crime Science, 6,* 6. doi:10.1186/s40163-017-0069-x

Manning, M. (2020). *SmartCBT tool.* Retrieved July 3, 2023, from https://manningcba.digital/

Manning, M., Christen, P., Wong, G., Ranbaduge, T., & Vidanage, A. (2019). *Economic support and reporting tool (ESRT).* Retrieved July 3, 2023, from https://dmm.anu.edu.au/ESRT/

Manning, M., Johnson, S., Tilley, N., Wong, G., & Vorsina, M. (2016). *Economic analysis and efficiency in policing, criminal justice and crime reduction: What works?* London: Palgrave Macmillan.

Manning, M., Wong, G., Mahony, C., & Vidanage, A. (2023). A method and app for measuring the heterogeneous costs and benefits of justice processes. *Frontiers in Psychology, 14*, 1094303. doi:10.3389/fpsyg.2023.1094303

Martinez, N., Lee, Y., Eck, J., & SooHyun, O. (2017). Ravenous wolves revisited: A systematic review of offending concentration. *Crime Science, 6*, 10. doi:10.1186/s40163-017-0072-2

Miller, T., Cohen, M., & Wiersema, B. (1996). *The extent and costs of crime: A new look.* Washington, DC: U.S. Department of Justice.

Morgan, F. (2001). Repeat burglary in a Perth suburb: Indicator of short-term or long-term risk. In G. Farrell & K. Pease (Eds.), *Repeat victimization: Crime prevention studies 12* (pp. 83–118). Monsey, NY: Criminal Justice Press.

Natarajan, M. (2012). A rational choice analysis of organized crime and trafficked goods. In N. Tilley and G. Farrell (Eds.), *The reasoning criminologist* (pp. 194–204). London: Routledge.

Nelson, J. (1980). Multiple victimisation in American cities. *American Journal of Sociology, 85*, 870–891. doi:10.1086/227092

Office for National Statistics (ONS). (2023a). *Crime in England and Wales: Year ending December 2022.* Retrieved August 7, 2023, from www.ons.gov.uk/peoplepopulationandcommunity/crimeandjustice/bulletins/crimeinenglandandwales/yearendingdecember2022

Office for National Statistics (ONS). (2023b). *Crime in England and Wales: Appendix tables.* Retrieved August 7, 2023, from www.ons.gov.uk/peoplepopulationandcommunity/crimeandjustice/datasets/crimeinenglandandwalesappendixtables

Pease, K. (1997). Predicting the future: The roles of routine activity and rational choice theory. In G. Newman, R. Clarke, & S. Shoham (Eds.), *Rational choice and situational crime prevention: Theoretical foundations* (pp. 233–245). Aldershot: Dartmouth Press.

Pease, K. (1998). *Repeat victimisation: Taking stock* (Crime Detection and Prevention Series Paper 90). London: Home Office.

Pires, S., & Clarke, R. V. (2012). Are parrots CRAVED? An analysis of parrot poaching in Mexico. *Journal of Research in Crime and Delinquency, 49*(1), 122–146. doi:10.1177/0022427810397950

Ratcliffe, J. (2015). Towards an Index for harm-focused policing. *Policing, 9*(2), 164–183.

Ratcliffe, J. (2022). *Aoristic analysis.* Retrieved August 7, 2022, from www.jratcliffe.net/aoristic-analysis

Ratcliffe, J., & McCullagh, M. (1998). Aoristic crime analysis. *International Journal of Geographical Information Science, 12*(7), 751–764. doi:10.1080/136588198241644

Robbins, L. (1935). *An essay on the nature and significance of economic science* (2nd ed.). London: Macmillan.

Roman, J., & Farrell, G. (2002). Cost-benefit analysis for crime prevention. In N. Tilley (Ed.), *Evaluation for crime prevention* (pp. 53–92). Monsey, NY: Criminal Justice Press.

Sampson, R., & Laub, J. (2003). Life-course desisters? Trajectories of crime among delinquent boys followed to Age 70. *Criminology, 41*(3), 555–592. doi:10.1111/j.1745-9125.2003.tb00997.x

Sherman, L., Gartin, P., & Buerger, M. (1989). Hotspots of predatory crime: Routine activities and the criminology of place. *Criminology*, 27(1), 27–55. doi:10.1111/j.1745-9125.1989.tb00862.x

Sherman, L., Neyroud, P., & Neyroud, E. (2016). The Cambridge Crime Harm Index: Measuring total harm from crime based on sentencing guidelines. *Policing*, 10(3), 171–183. doi:10.1093/police/paw003

Sidebottom, A. (2013). On the application of CRAVED to livestock theft in Malawi. *International Journal of Comparative and Applied Criminal Justice*, 37(3), 195–212. doi:10.1080/01924036.2012.734960

Sidebottom, A., & Tilley, N. (2017). Designing systems against crime: Introducing leaky systems. In N. Tilley & A. Sidebottom (Eds.), *Handbook of crime prevention and community safety* (2nd ed., pp. 254–273). London: Routledge.

Sloan-Howitt, M., & Kelling, G. (1997). Subway Graffiti in New York City: "Getting up" vs. "Meanin' it and cleanin' it". In R. Clarke (Ed.), *Situational crime prevention: Successful case studies* (pp. 242–249). New York: Harrow and Heston.

Sparks, R., Genn, H., & Dodd, D. (1977). *Surveying victims*. Chichester: Wiley.

Spelman, W., & Eck, J. (1989). Sitting ducks, ravenous wolves, ad helping hands: New approaches to urban policing. *Public Affairs Comment*, 35(2), 2–9.

Thompson, R. (2017). Portable electronics and trends in goods stolen from the person. *Journal of Research in Crime and Delinquency*, 54(2), 276–298. doi:10.1177/0022427816660743

Tilley, N. (1993). *The prevention of crime against small businesses: The safer cities experience* (Crime Prevention Unit Paper 45). London: Home Office.

Tompson, L., Belur, J., Thornton, A., Bowers, K. J., Johnson, S. D., Sidebottom, A., Tilley, N., & Laycock, G. (2021). How strong is the evidence-base for crime reduction professionals? *Justice Evaluation Journal*, 4(1), 68–97. doi:10.1080/2475197 9.2020.1818275

Trickett, A., Osborn, D. R., Seymour, J., & Pease, K. (1992). What is different about high crime areas? *The British Journal of Criminology*, 32(1), 81–89. doi:10.1093/oxfordjournals.bjc.a048181

University of Cambridge Institute of Criminology. (2023). *The Cambridge Crime Harm Index (CCHI)*. Retrieved August 5, 2022, from www.crim.cam.ac.uk/research/thec ambridgecrimeharmindex#:~:text=The%20Cambridge%20Crime%20Harm%20 Index%20%28CCHI%29%20is%20the,not%20just%20the%20number%20 of%20officially%20recorded%20crimes

Voce, I., & Morgan, A. (2023). *Cybercrime in Australia* (AIC Statistical Report 43). Canberra: Australian Institute of Criminology.

Wallerstein, J., & Wyle, C. (1947). Our law-abiding law breakers. *Probation*, 25, 107–112.

Walsh, D. (1978). *Shoplifting: Controlling a major crime*. London: Macmillan.

Weisburd, D. (2015). The law of crime concentration and the criminology of place. *Criminology*, 53(2), 133–157. doi:10.1111/1745–9125.12070

Whitehead, S., Mailley, J., Storer, I., McCardle, J., Torrens, G., & Farrell, G. (2008). In safe hands: A review of mobile phone anti-theft designs. *European Journal on Criminal Policy and Research*, 14, 39–60. doi:10.1007/s10610-007-9040-9

Wilcox, P., & Eck, J. E. (2011). Criminology of the unpopular. *Criminology and Public Policy*, 10(2), 473–482. doi:10.1111/j.1745–9133.2011.00721.x

4 Crime prevention theories

This chapter will show that theory is unavoidable in crime prevention, that good theories are invaluable, and that poor theories can lead to waste and harm. Many practitioners may be suspicious of theory, but there is no escape!

The chapter proceeds as follows. It begins with an account of what we mean by 'theory.' It goes on to show the role of theory in some of the examples of crime prevention outlined in Chapter 2, and how this helps us learn lessons from them. We then turn to some theoretical perspectives that have been developed to inform crime prevention or that can be drawn on in crime prevention, again referring, where possible, to examples given in Chapter 2. The practical application of theory in working out what to do in trying to address crime problems on the ground is discussed in Chapter 6.

What is 'theory'?

When we take action to try to prevent crime, we take that action in the expectation that it will be effective. Our expectation comprises a basic theory (or hypothesis) that the action in question will produce the intended crime prevention outcome. Generally, the outcome takes the form of less crime or less criminality. Tests of such hypotheses are designed to establish whether, or not, our expectations are warranted. As in health, much that is done conventionally may turn out to be ineffective or even harmful, notwithstanding the best intentions of the practitioners. The point of articulating and testing hypotheses is to sort the effective from the ineffective and harmful. This sounds straightforward, though in practice it can be technically very demanding.

Stronger theories not only comprise expectations that a given crime prevention outcome will be brought about by our intervention but also explain why we hold that expectation. What is it about what we do that leads us to expect that the crime prevention outcome will be produced? We use the term 'mechanism,' or more strictly 'causal mechanism,' to refer to how we expect our intervention to produce the intended outcome. Mechanisms are often 'tacit,'

DOI: 10.4324/9780429356155-4

in that practitioners and policymakers take them for granted and so do not spell them out. Indeed, in some instances the mechanisms may appear so common-sense that articulating them would seem to be redundant. As we'll see in due course, however, the mechanisms assumed to be activated by preventive interventions are sometimes not activated. Moreover, mechanisms that had not been anticipated are activated and lead to unintended consequences.

Best of all are theories that specify not only the expected preventive outcomes from the crime prevention intervention and the causal mechanisms through which they are supposed to produce those outcomes but also the conditions that are needed for those causal mechanisms to be activated. Such theories also ideally identify conditions that will lead to the unintentional activation of causal mechanisms that produce unintended – negative as well as positive – outcomes.

The ideal theory of any crime prevention (or for that matter health-related) intervention takes the general form. 'Intervention A is expected to produce outcome B (or outcomes B1–n) by activating mechanism C (or mechanisms C1–n), in conditions D.' The general question across all interventions dealt with in such theories is, 'What works for whom in what circumstances and how?' (see Pawson & Tilley, 1997).

Although this may seem tricky and complicated, it accords well with the sentiments of many crime prevention practitioners and policymakers. They know they want to prevent crime. They mostly have reasons to believe that their chosen interventions will work for them. They appreciate, however, that sometimes conditions may mean that the intended outcome is not achieved and or that the intervention backfires. They have a strong interest in an improved understanding of what works for whom in what circumstances to produce better (less crime or less crime harm) outcomes.

Examples of theory in crime prevention practice and what we learn from them

Using examples taken from Chapter 2, 'basic theories,' 'better theories,' and 'best theories,' as characterised earlier, are briefly described.

Immobilisers and global reductions in car theft

- Basic theory: electronic immobilisers reduce levels of car theft.
- Better theory: electronic immobilisers reduce car theft by making cars fitted with them more difficult to steal.
- Best theory: electronic immobilisers reduce car theft (by making cars more difficult to steal) to the extent to which offenders have not yet devised techniques to overcome them.

Criminal behaviour generally takes place in groups. As we saw in Chapter 3, involvement in criminality is normal although some go on to become prolific criminals, albeit often only during adolescence. Car theft for joyriding is one type of early collective criminal behaviour, which is associated with an increased risk of progression to prolific criminality (Svensson, 2002; Owen & Cooper, 2013), as offenders learn to find crime rewarding and find friends with whom to co-offend. The electronic immobiliser put a stop to car theft for joyriding, hence that common avenue into high-rate offending. Best theory would articulate and test this out (Farrell, Laycock, & Tilley, 2015).

Kirkholt and domestic burglary

- Basic theory: removing cash prepayment meters for electricity and gas, upgrading the security of dwellings that have been burgled, and establishing cocoons around properties that have been burgled reduce the levels of repeat burglary and burglary levels overall.
- Better theory: removing cash prepayment meters reduces the temptation to burgle a property by removing a preferred target (cash); upgrading the security of a burgled dwelling makes it more difficult to break and enter properties to commit burglary and hence discourages some burglars; and establishing (well-publicised) cocoons increases the risk burglars perceive they will incur if they attempt burglary, so some decide against doing so.
- Best theory: in a small housing estate, with few entry and exit points, where burglars are local and alternative courses of action are offered to them, the removal of local, convenient, readily available, low-risk, high-reward local targets which can be repeatedly exploited is sufficient to lead to a reduction in repeat burglaries and overall burglary rates.

As we saw in Chapter 3, the risk of a repeat burglary at a particular address also increases the risk, for a short period, to those nearby (because active offenders learn that there are nearby suitable – high-reward, low-effort, low-risk further potential targets there). Cocoons may, thereby, have sensitised neighbours to increased risk and led them to improve their security and/or watch over one another as well as the property at the centre of the cocoon. This provides the basis for further strong and testable theory about how to reduce burglary risks to properties close to the ones where burglaries have taken place, when those properties are at heightened risk.

Boston and gang-related shootings

- Basic theory: well-publicised and prompt crackdowns on gangs across all offences reduce the number of youth homicides in the event of any firearms offence by one of their members.

- Better theory: the prospect of immediate crackdowns against all gang members, backed by publicity and follow-up action, deters the illegal use of firearms by all gang members who have an interest in not being shot and in being able to maintain other aspects of gang life without any disruption from concentrated attention from law enforcement bodies. Gang members appreciate that criminal and antisocial behaviour figures routinely in their individual and collective everyday lives, permitting law enforcement bodies always to be able to find infractions of one kind or another warranting action. All gang members have an interest in none of their fellow members attracting that kind of police attention, and they therefore encourage one another to avoid firearms use. As firearm use in gang conflicts diminishes, the perceived need to carry firearms for self-protection falls. Therefore, firearms cease to be carried routinely, reducing firearms offences and the need for law enforcement officers to allocate resources to crackdowns. The number of firearms offences, the related youth homicides, and the resources needed for law enforcement bodies to devote to the crackdowns all drop in the medium term.
- Best theory: where the patterns of gang membership and intergang relationships are well understood by law enforcement and where local well-respected community organisations and law enforcement bodies trust one another and are agreed on the need to de-normalise firearms use in the interest of reducing youth homicide, congruent messages reinforcing and embracing the crackdown strategy can be consistently transmitted. In these conditions, the crackdown strategy will be delivered without significant resistance or subversion from influential members of the community. Thus, the strategy and targeted messaging can be delivered and received in ways most likely to be accepted and acted on in the intended way by gang members.

Killingbeck and domestic violence

- Basic theory: tiered interventions of increasing intensity, focusing on both offenders (moving from deflection towards enforcement) and victims, lead to falls in repeat domestic violence.
- Better theory: among perpetrators, the realisation that if they continue their domestic violence they will face increasingly punitive and humiliating responses from the police deters them from further domestic violence. Among survivors, the realisation that there will be cumulative, continuous, and consistently applied protective responses to them and, likewise, cumulative enforcement responses to perpetrators, empowers those survivors to call authorities in the event of further abuse and, if it persists, to leave the perpetrator.
- Best theory: if the responses by the police do not consistently increase in intensity in ways that are clearly explained to victims and perpetrators, the change mechanisms producing reductions in repeat victimisation will

fade and lose credibility, and impact will diminish (see Hanmer, 2003). The tiered approach used in the Killingbeck initiative requires that police officers, who are normally expected to use their discretion in dealing with incidents, are no longer permitted to use it in these cases. The approach requires that records of incidents and actions taken in response to them are kept assiduously so that shortcomings can be corrected promptly.

New South Wales and drink-driving-related deaths

- Basic theory: high rates of randomised breath tests (RBTs) of drivers for exceeding the permitted alcohol consumption lead to lower rates of drink-driving and fewer deaths associated with driving under the influence of alcohol.
- Better theory: because the rates of random breath testing are high enough for all to be at high risk of it, remember it, and hear of it among friends and family, drivers perceive the risk of being caught for drink-driving to be high. Moreover, they understand that they will be unable to sidestep the prospect of an RBT stop by slow or especially careful driving (they cannot control their risk of RBT: on any occasion, it might be high or low). They therefore decide no longer to drink and drive. Behavioural adaptation follows whereby, for example, a 'designated driver' agrees not to drink on occasion so that others can. Over time, the norm of drinking and driving fades and that of sharing occasional duties as the designated driver takes hold.
- Best theory: high levels of perceived legitimacy of RBT (and hence support for its introduction and maintenance) is required for its introduction, its acceptance, and hence citizen cooperation with it. Any widely known possibility of drivers eliminating the risk of RBT will reduce its perceived legitimacy and its potential effects on drink-driving and the road casualties associated with drink-driving.

Cambridge-Somerville and criminality

- Basic original theory: the provision of sustained, trusting relationships with a caring adult prevents the development of criminality among early adolescent boys who would otherwise be at high risk of becoming criminals.
- Better theory for what was delivered in practice: discontinuous provision of advice, educational support, and recreational opportunities is insufficient effectively to address the underlying problems that lie behind the emergence of criminality among some boys who are statistically at relatively high risk of becoming offenders.
- Best theory: supporting adolescent boys by sending them away for group recreational holidays leads them to reinforce one another's incipient criminality, leading to higher risks of becoming criminal than among boys who did not go on these holidays (McCord, 2003; McCord & McCord, 1969).

The Cambridge-Somerville example shows how implementation often departs from intention and that in doing so what is tested ceases to be the original basic theory. The extensive secondary literature in this case describes in detail what was delivered in practice, and the data collected are used to test theories relating to what was done by taking advantage of variations within the programme.

Box 4.1 adds further comments on recreational schemes and how they may be implemented with preventive effects.

Box 4.1   Recreational schemes

Recreational schemes do not have a strong track record in preventing crime, perhaps due to the mechanism mentioned here under 'best theory.' An example where it does seem to have produced positive effects on criminal behaviour is a scheme where summertime criminal and antisocial behaviour was reduced from its expected level based on previous years' records. Here boys were put into a summer league where the winning team was to be presented with medals by the celebrity manager of the highly successful local premier division football club. Points were deducted if any member of a team came to the attention of the police for criminal or antisocial behaviour. This led members to put pressure on one another not to behave in ways that threatened their chances of winning the league. The conjectured mechanism was, therefore, informal social control by peers, activated by the terms of the league, and the effect was specific to the period when the competition was in place.

Routine activities as a general framework for crime prevention theories

The 'routine activities theory' (RAT), or approach, forms a convenient starting point for describing theories that speak to differing crime prevention mechanisms and their activation. Once stated, routine activities theory seems obvious or tautologous (rather like Darwin's evolutionary theory). That's the genius of the theory.

RAT states, simply, the three necessary conditions for a direct-contact predatory crime to take place: there needs to be a 'likely' or 'motivated' offender and a 'suitable target,' and there must not be a 'capable guardian' of the suitable target. These three conditions must converge in space and time. Absent any of these, a crime will not take place. RAT specifies at a high level of abstraction the necessary contextual conditions for crimes to occur.

RAT was first formulated to explain the rise in crime in the years following the end of the Second World War (Cohen & Felson, 1979). At this time, there was an increase in the supply of suitable targets (especially cars and lightweight, high value, goods such as many electrical devices); a reduction in capable guardianship (e.g. more women in paid employment away from home); and an increased availability of likely offenders (e.g. young men freed from domestic chores and able to travel around on motorcycles). The self-service shop provided an ideal venue for theft: admitting all, presenting attractive goods for anyone to pick up, and relatively few staff to watch what was going on. Changes in everyday life, or 'routine activities,' created conditions for rising levels of crime by widening crime opportunities. There was no need to invoke changes in criminality to explain the crime rise. Changes in opportunity as a side effect of developments in everyday life were enough.

Since the original application of the routine activities approach to explain the rise in crime in the United States after the Second World War, there have been some modifications. Felson (1986) refers to 'intimate handlers' who must also be missing if a crime is to take place. Intimate handlers comprise significant others for otherwise likely offenders, whose presence inhibits commission of the offence due to their actions or known disapprobation. Mothers, sisters, girlfriends, teachers, and known clergy, for example, may all act as intimate handlers. 'Intimate handlers' and 'capable guardians' both comprise crime-preventive intermediaries between likely offenders and suitable targets.

According to routine activities theory, *patterns of crime* are a function of the supply, distribution and movement of likely offenders, intimate handlers, suitable targets and capable guardians, and the convergences between them that are thereby produced. *Changes in crime patterns* are similarly a function of alterations in the supply, distribution and movement of likely offenders, intimate handlers, suitable targets and capable guardians, and the convergences between them that are produced. Box 4.2 refers to RAT and the explanation of changes in crime pattern associated with the COVID-19 pandemic.

Box 4.2 Application of RAT to explain crime falls associated with the COVID-19 pandemic

Shutting shops, stay-at home rules, advice on maintaining physical distance from others and the reduced use of public transport for a period, applied in different ways in different countries, have tended to lead to drops in several crime types, for example personal robbery, personal theft, and domestic burglary (see, e.g. Halford, Dixon, Farrell, Malleson, & Tilley, 2020; Nivette et al., 2021).

Theories for crime prevention have tended to focus on different necessary contextual conditions for crime identified in RAT – suitable targets, capable guardians, offenders, handlers, or factors leading to the convergence of necessary conditions. One set of theories focuses on situations that are conducive to crimes by providing opportunities, and how those situations can be changed. Another set focuses on the supply, availability, and capacity of likely offenders to take advantage of crime opportunities and how this supply, availability, and capacity can be contained. I turn to each next, although as will become clear there are some overlaps. I then go on to the possibilities for drawing on other theories that have not explicitly attended to crime prevention.

Theories for crime prevention focused on opportunity

Situational crime prevention

The idea that focusing on reduction in opportunity could comprise a promising general approach to the prevention of crime was first laid out systematically in a Home Office Research Study, *Crime as Opportunity*, in 1976 (Mayhew, Clarke, Sturman, & Hough, 1976). This drew together a range of previous research in which opportunity had been 'acknowledged in passing' (p. 4) as important to understanding what people do. One reference is to research in Birmingham finding that incidents of self-gassing dropped from 87 in 1962 to 12 in 1970 as the toxic content of the gas supply fell, which explained almost entirely the reduction in overall rates of suicide in that city over the period. Mayhew et al. refer to the 'power of opportunity in determining behaviour' (p. 6) and the variety of ways in which it may do so. They classify opportunities into those relating to people and those to objects. People's opportunities to commit crime vary by their age, sex, and lifestyle. As potential victims, people generate variations in opportunity for offenders. People's opportunities for crime can, the authors say, also be affected by 'patterns of daily activity' that follow from 'forms of social organisation' (p. 6). In regard to the 'properties of objects,' they refer to the 'abundance of goods,' 'environmental opportunities,' 'physical security,' and to 'surveillance and supervision.'

Crime as Opportunity gave a couple of worked examples: one an account of the effects on car theft of putting steering column locks in cars, and another relating to the effects of supervision on bus vandalism. Steering column locks were fitted to all new cars in Britain from 1971. Mayhew et al. examined the change in numbers of thefts and unauthorised takings in the Metropolitan Police District between 1969 and 1973, as shown in Table 4.1. The data suggest no change overall but a substantial fall in the number and proportion of the new and a corresponding increase in the number of older vehicles taken. The authors conclude that the introduction of the steering column locks may have led to some displacement of thefts from newer to older vehicles.

Table 4.1 Steering wheel locks and car thefts in London.

	1969	1973
All cars taken	917	918
New cars taken	192	47
Old cars taken	725	871
% of all cars stolen that were new	20.9	5.1

Source: Adapted from Mayhew et al. (1976) who originally made a distinction between cars stolen and those taken without the owner's consent, a distinction that was hard to make in practice then and no longer made now. The figures have been combined in this table.

Regarding vandalism on buses, Mayhew et al. report a study in Manchester finding that levels varied very substantially by the amount of supervision. One-person operated buses had much higher levels of vandalism than those operating with two people in all locations on the buses. On all types of buses, seat damage on the top deck was much higher that on the bottom deck. These differences, the authors find, could not be explained by variations in passenger types using the upper and lower decks of buses.

Crime as Opportunity concludes with an argument that opportunity reduction comprises a promising new approach to crime prevention but one that required a stronger research basis. The authors say,

Finally, it is hoped that this report has begun to illustrate that physical prevention is not simply a matter of intensive policing and crude security, but that it can, in imaginative and unobtrusive ways, utilise technological and architectural expertise to protect vulnerable property from theft and vandalism, curtail the means of committing crime (for instance by restricting the availability of dangerous weapons), and take advantage of the natural supervision of the environment by ordinary individuals. Hopefully, it has illustrated too that if physical prevention implies a different form of 'social engineering' from that of social prevention, it does not necessarily involve a greater degree of behavioural control. These are small beginnings, however . . . [t]here is also a need to test the notion of 'general' displacement (i.e. the displacement of one type of criminal activity to disparate forms of crime), though this may prove . . . elusive . . . Thereafter perhaps, the most pressing need will be for research which will allow the importance of opportunity relative to other factors in criminal behaviour, to be more precisely determined. Only then will it be clear whether opportunity merits as central a place in criminological explanation as it is given in the title of this report.

Mayhew et al. (1976, p. 30)

On the issue of displacement, Clarke and Mayhew (1988) show how a specific change in opportunity produced a large and sustained fall in the number of suicides in Britain. Building on the Birmingham study mentioned in *Crime as Opportunity*, they tracked the number of suicides from 1958 to 1977 and the number of suicides committed using domestic gas. Figure 4.1 shows the results. They are striking. What happened over that period is that the composition of the gas supply changed. Highly toxic coal gas was replaced by non-toxic natural gas. Of course, this did not mean that suicide was no longer possible at all. There are plenty of alternative methods of taking one's own life. Only rarely will some specific individual, perhaps because of a disability, be incapable of taking their own life other than through using the domestic gas supply. The change in the gas supply, however, removed one especially convenient, painless, and non-disfiguring means of doing so that many (particularly women) chose to use. The removal of this method was sufficient to lead to a substantial reduction in the total number of suicides. Although some may have switched methods, the figures strongly suggest that many did not do so. A side effect of changing the composition of the gas piped to homes for heating and cooking was a reduction in the opportunity for suicide and a real reduction in the number of suicides. Decisions to commit suicide are not taken lightly. Even here, however, the removal of one opportunity (of many others that are available) produced a substantial drop in overall numbers. Clarke and Mayhew suggest that the same will be true of crime where, presumably, the actions reflect less deep-rooted motives.

The fact that situational crime prevention was developed within the Home Office is significant. The Home Office is the government department

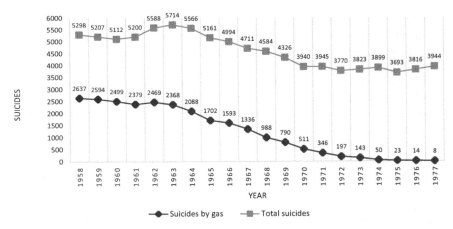

Figure 4.1 Trends in suicides in England and Wales, 1958–1977.

for England and Wales responsible for policing and crime prevention. The research undertaken within the department was orientated to informing policy and practice, rather than with theoretical development for its own sake. We return to the significance of government-office based research in Chapter 8.

Crime as Opportunity was produced to inform crime prevention, when the confidence in the effectiveness of traditional approaches was waning. 'Nothing works!' was a widely parroted slogan, following a review by Lipton et al. published in 1975 (see also Martinson, 1974 and Brody, 1976). *Crime as Opportunity* marked the start of a research, policy, and practice agenda that continues to develop. The focus of *Crime as Opportunity* was on crime events, the role of opportunity structures in producing patterns of crime events, and on the scope for practical measures to reduce criminal opportunities.

The example of car theft discussed in Chapters 2 and 3 illustrates the significance of opportunity and its reduction for achieving long-term falls in specific crimes. Cars are fun to steal and drive. Cars are also of high monetary value either to be sold complete with their identity changed or broken up to sell parts. Cars are left in public car parks for much of the day. Goods are sometimes left on display. Cars often have valuable parts that are easily removed, such as audio systems or, introduced more recently, catalytic converters. Security of cars has been weak in the past: they could be hot-wired to be driven away, windows were easily opened from the outside, and so on. The result was high and rising car crime rates up to the early 1990s.

Improvements in the security of cars (alarms, better door and window locks, mechanical and electronic immobilisers, etc.) and car parks (CCTV, gates, patrols, etc) led to plummeting levels of vehicle crime. This occurred without attending to the motivation of those involved in vehicle crime. Only opportunity was reduced. The measures introduced did not eliminate car theft, of course, but were sufficient to prevent most opportunist vehicle crimes, notably those where the vehicle was stolen and later recovered. Professional car thieves, targeting high-value luxury cars, could still steal them. Over time, new methods of car theft can be devised to overcome security and gradually become more widely available.

Developments of situational crime prevention

Since the original publication of *Crime as Opportunity*, there have been several developments in situational crime prevention theory.

1. Classification of mechanisms through which opportunities can be lessened and the kinds of interventions that can activate these mechanisms (Clarke, 1992, 1995; Cornish & Clarke, 2003)

The initial classification referred to ways in which interventions could reduce rewards, increase efforts, and increase risks (Clarke, 1992, 1995). This implied *rational choice* by potential offenders, who could be deterred at the margin by changing the balance between expected reward, as against the efforts required to commit the crime, and the risk of adverse consequences if caught. Some, but not necessarily all prospective offenders, would make a different decision about whether to commit a crime if the expected pay-offs were reduced. Changes in expected pay-offs can be achieved both by changing the *real* prospects of reward in relation to risk and effort and by changing the *perceived* prospects. Given that in the longer term, the perceived and real pay-offs are liable to converge, if offenders come to realise what changes in real risk amount to the latter may have a relatively short effectiveness shelf life unless propped up with persuasive publicity.

The initial classification of situational crime prevention techniques has since been expanded to include other preventive mechanisms and the measures that may trigger them. One mechanism relates to the excusability of the criminal act. If the would-be offender sees the criminal act as on balance likely to produce instrumental pay-offs for them, they may still be discouraged if they see the behaviour as inexcusable on other grounds, for example that it would put others at risk of serious harm or would in some other way breach a moral or legal code to which the potential offender adheres. Rule reminders prevent criminal behaviour by prompting rule-recognition when and where a crime is liable to be committed. A second mechanism relates to provocation, which has to do with non-instrumental reasons for criminal acts: for example some people may 'see red' if they are angered in a fit of jealousy and as a consequence commit an assault.

The columns in Table 4.2 show the five major mechanisms that have been identified. The three to the left are clearly to do with rational choice, and the two on the right less so. Cornish and Clarke have argued that rational-choice underpins all situational crime prevention, albeit that the rationality is 'bounded' (Simon, 1955). Others sympathetic to situational crime prevention are sceptical (see, e.g. the essays in Reynald & Leclerc, 2018).

2. The formulation of 'crime scripts' (Cornish, 1994)

Crime scripts capture the steps involved in committing an offence. They can be illuminating especially in relation to complex crimes which may involve different people in different places and take place over a period of time. Preparation to commit a crime, the conduct of the crime event (including getting there, the act itself, and then getting away), and realisation of the benefits from crime comprise different stages and may all involve different acts and different people, who must interact directly or indirectly. The preventive purpose of devising crime scripts is to enable the most promising 'pinch-points' to be identified: the most tractable elements in the script that might be open to interventions to increase the difficulty, increase the risk, and/or reduce the rewards for at least some of those involved. Table 4.3 shows a crime script devised by Cornish, and how it may fail at different points. Crime scripts help identify those features of the script most open to thwarting an offender.

3. Recognition of the independent importance of publicity (Laycock, 1992)

   Initially, changes in risk, effort, and reward were stressed. The importance of perception and in particular the use of *publicity* to alter *perceptions* of risk, effort, and reward as mechanisms of change have since been stressed (see, e.g. Laycock's 1992 study which highlighted the importance of publicity in effecting reductions in burglary in a study that was ostensibly about property marking). Changed perceptions of crime opportunity also lie behind the diffusion of benefit effects mentioned later in the chapter (effects found beyond the operational range of interventions), and these changes can be brought about deliberately by the way interventions are presented.

4. Offender resources (Ekblom & Tilley, 2000)

   Offender resources are touched on in the bottom left cell of Table 4.2, which relates to 'control tools/weapons' under the general heading 'increasing effort.' However, the mechanism in this case does not relate to efforts and choice so much as possibility. Some crime prevention measures eliminate choices that would otherwise in principle be available by removing the (physical or human) resources needed to commit those crimes. Some crimes become possible when new resources become available to enable them (Ekblom & Tilley, 2000).

   Suppose I'd like to commit bank robberies! I could make better use of the money than the banks. However, I have no idea how to rob a bank. I don't know what resources I would need. I lack the contacts to access resources that may be needed to commit bank robberies. I don't commit bank robberies because I can't do so.

5. Place management (Eck, 2015)

   Crime is concentrated by place, and there is scope in high crime locations to reduce it by attending to the conditions there that foster it. Place managers can change the contingencies at work in the places where crime is concentrated. These contingencies provide opportunities or stimuli for crime. They may offer low-risk, low-effort, and high-reward crime opportunities; they may make crime seem permissible; and they may provoke crimes. Place managers may prevent crime in some places, and their lack of action may explain why it is high in others. Introducing effective place management in high crime places (and their equivalents for high

Table 4.2 A classification of types of situational crime prevention.

Instrumental rational choice mechanisms			Affective choice mechanisms	Normative choice mechanisms
Increase the Effort	Increase the Risks	Reduce the Rewards	Reduce Provocations	Remove Excuses
1. Target harden • Steering column locks and ignition immobilisers • Anti-robbery screens • Tamper-proof packaging **2. Control access to facilities** • Entry phones • Electronic card access • Baggage screening **3. Screen exits** • Ticket needed for exit • Export documents • Electronic merchandise tags **4. Deflect offenders** • Street closures • Separate bathrooms for women • Disperse pubs **5. Control tools/weapons** • 'Smart' guns • Restrict spray paint sales to juveniles • Toughened beer glasses	**6. Extend guardianship** • Go out in group at night • Leave signs of occupancy • Carry cell phones **7. Assist natural surveillance** • Improved street lighting • Defensible space design • Support whistle-blowers **8. Reduce anonymity** • Taxi driver IDs • 'How's my driving?' decals • School uniforms **9. Use place managers** • CCTVs for double-deck buses • Two clerks for U.S. convenience stores • Reward vigilance **10. Strengthen formal surveillance** • Red light cameras • Burglar alarms • Security guards	**11. Conceal targets** • Off-street parking • Gender-neutral phone directories • Unmarked armoured trucks **12. Remove targets** • Removable car radio • Women's shelters • Prepaid cards for pay phones **13. Identify property** • Property marking • Vehicle licencing and parts' marking • Cattle branding **14. Disrupt markets** • Monitor pawn shops • Controls on classified ads • Licence street vendors **15. Deny benefits** • Ink merchandise tags • Graffiti cleaning • Disabling stolen cell phones	**16. Reduce frustrations and stress** • Efficient queues • Polite service • Expanded seating • Soothing music/muted lights **17. Avoid disputes** • Separate seating for rival soccer fans • Reduce crowding in bars • Fixed cab fares **18. Reduce temptation and arousal** • Controls on violent pornography • Enforce good behaviour on soccer field • Prohibit racial slurs **19. Neutralise peer pressure** • 'Idiots drink and drive' • 'It's OK to say No' • Disperse troublemakers at school **20. Discourage imitation** • Rapid repair of vandalism • V-chips in TVs • Censor details of modus operandi	**21. Set rules** • Rental agreements • Harassment codes • Hotel registration **22. Post instructions** • 'No Parking' • 'Private Property' • 'Extinguish camp fires' **23. Alert conscience** • Roadside speed display boards • Signatures for customs declarations • 'Shoplifting is stealing' **24. Assist compliance** • Easy library checkout • Public lavatories • Litter receptacles **25. Control drugs and alcohol** • Breathalysers in bars • Server intervention programmes • Alcohol-free events

Table 4.3 Script for the temporary use of a stolen vehicle for driving fast for fun.

Scene/function	Script action	Failure explanation
1. Preparation	Gather tools	Forget scaffold tube
2. Entry	Enter car park	Car park closed
3. Precondition	Loiter unobtrusively	Noticed by security
4. Instrumental precondition	Select the vehicle	No Vauxhall Astra GTEs
5. Instrumental initiation	Approach the vehicle	Driver returns
6. Instrumental actualisation	Break into the vehicle	Vehicle impregnable
7. Doing	Take the vehicle	Vehicle immobilised
8. Postcondition	Reverse out of bay	Crash into wall
9. Exit	Leave car park	Gates closed for night

Source: From Cornish, (1994, p. 164).

crime facilities and systems) may prevent crime by their activation of situational crime prevention mechanisms.

6. Future crime anticipation and crime pre-emption (Pease, 1997; Johnson et al., 2019)

Crime problems change over time. New opportunities emerge, for example as side effects of technological developments that provide new targets or new resources for crime. The invention of the 'CRAVED' acronym, as described in Chapter 3, was important in capturing the characteristics of frequently stolen products. CRAVED can be used to anticipate new products that are likely to be targeted and into which crime pre-emptive design may be built, rather than having to retrofit preventive measures in response to a high rate of theft (see Pease, 1997). Likewise, new facilities and systems that can be expected to attract or generate crime may be configured in ways that provide more or fewer opportunities for crime in terms of rewards, effort, risk, provocation, and apparent excusability.[1]

7. Evolution and co-evolution (Ekblom, 1997)

Chapter 1 referred to the Red Queen in biological evolution. Ekblom (1997) pointed out that similar processes of co-evolution occur in crime prevention. Mutual adaptation involves see-saw innovations by offenders and preventers. New situational measures may thwart offenders, but offenders can adapt and new successful adaptations by some eventually spread undermining the effectiveness of the situational measure.

Preventers then make adjustments to take account of new offender capabilities. This explains the history of lock-development and lock-picking. Two implications follow. First, single preventive measures, even if highly sophisticated and initially effective, are risky if widely used: once overcome, the innovative offender (and those learning from them) can come prepared and be able to commit multiple crimes. Hence, diversity in measures may produce greater preventive effects than depending on the best available, in that the offender will not so easily be able to anticipate what they will need to complete an offence successfully. Second, early-warning arrangements and continuous refinement and development in situational preventive measures will always be necessary to respond quickly when offenders innovate.

8. Convergence between situational crime prevention and problem-oriented policing (POP) (Clarke, Goldstein, Eck)

   The problem-focused action research methods advocated early in the development of situational crime prevention (Ekblom, 1988; Clarke, 1992) complement Goldstein's independently developed ideas about POP (Goldstein, 1979, 1990; Eck & Spelman, 1987). Chapter 6 will show the theoretical and practical convergence between SCP and POP.

9. The discovery of diffusion of benefits (Clarke & Weisburd, 1994)

   This notes that situational measures may have a positive preventive effect beyond their operational reach. Their types are the same as those for displacement, of which more is said later in the chapter.

10. Applications of situational crime prevention to the prevention of the onset of criminal careers and the continuation of criminal careers that have started (Farrell et al., 2015, Shaefer, Cullen, & Eck, 2016).

    When we turn to crime prevention approaches that focus on offender supply, we will find ways in which opportunity-enabled induction into criminality can be prevented through situational measures. Likewise, when we come to treatment to prevent repeat offending, we will discuss ways in which interventions focused on opportunity reduction can help those who are subject to probation orders to discontinue their criminal careers.

Advantages of situational crime prevention

Situational approaches to crime prevention focused on opportunity reduction have several advantages:

- There are plenty of studies that show the effectiveness of opportunity-reducing measures, pre-empting and reducing crime problems.
- Situations are generally easier to change than criminal dispositions.
- The preventive pay-off from changing situations is quick.

- Theories focusing on situational contingencies apply to all crime types. Table 4.4 (taken from Clarke & Bowers, 2017) lists a variety of crimes to which situational crime prevention has successfully been applied, in addition to high-volume crimes such as burglary and car theft, examples of which are given in Chapter 2.
- Situational prevention avoids labelling sections of the population, particular communities, and sets of people as inherently criminal.
- Remedying community, family, or individual deficits or injustices matters more as an end in itself than any crime saving the side effects it might have.
- There is evidence that situational contingencies for crime among adolescents induct some of them into criminality that then persists, for example by labelling them, making crime seem rewarding, or creating pro-crime bonds among co-offenders.

The example of Internet crimes, at the top of the list in Table 4.4, deserves special mention. As shown in Chapter 3, cyber and cyber-enabled crime have become very widespread. The Internet features heavily in our routine activities. It is almost impossible to avoid engagement with it in everyday life. It has created or enhanced a vast array of crime opportunities: for example for stalking, bullying, trolling, romance scams, frauds of varying kinds, extortion, pornography, and intellectual theft as well as malicious infection with computer viruses. These crimes are all rewarding to those committing them, are relatively easy to perpetrate, and present low risk, given the difficulties of detecting the crimes and the scope for committing them in one jurisdiction with the targets in others.

With Internet crime, there are plenty of vulnerable victims (some obliged to engage with the Internet even if they would rather not) who are ill-equipped to protect themselves. Frequent users are vulnerable because of the time they are exposed to risk and the diverse sites they visit, even if they are savvy enough to install software protecting them from viruses. Infrequent users are not only less exposed but also less likely to have installed protective software. The Internet can also tempt crime. Demetriou and Silke (2003) set up a site ostensibly offering access to games that are free. When at the site, the visitors found offers of access to illegally hacked games and to passwords for sites offering pornography. Demetriou and Silke found that of the 803 people visiting this site during their experiment, 38% tried to gain access to hacked games, 40% to pornographic images of women, and 9% to such images of men (in no case did links lead to actual pornography or hacked games!).

The Internet brings lots of benefits, but it is also criminogenic, presenting interesting challenges for prevention. It is unlikely that Internet crime will be controlled other than by focusing on reducing opportunities and temptations, along the general lines described above.

Table 4.4 A sample of studies showing the applications of situational crime prevention.

Authors	Application
Newman and Clarke (2003)	Internet crimes
McNally and Newman (2008)	Identity theft
Wortley and Smallbone (2006)	Child sexual abuse
Terry and Ackerman (2008)	Child sexual abuse in the Catholic Church
Cromwell, Alexander, and Dotson (2008)	Crime and incivilities in libraries
Graham (2009)	Bar-room violence
Guerette (2004)	Deaths of illegal immigrants on the United States/Mexico border
Lester (2009)	Suicide
Verma (2009)	Disrupting elections in India
Wortley (2002)	Disciplinary problems in prisons
Madensen and Knutsson (2011)	Crowd violence
Natarajan (2014)	Kerosene attacks on young women in India
Pires, Guerette, and Stubbert (2014)	Ransom kidnapping in Columbia
De Souza and Miller (2012)	Homicide in Brazilian favelas
Sidebottom (2012)	Domestic livestock theft in Malawi
Graycar and Sidebottom (2012)	Corruption
Clarke and Newman (2005)	Terrorism
Shane and Magnuson (2014)	Global piracy
Vollard (2015)	Marine oil pollution
Bullock, Clarke, and Tilley (2010)	Organised crime
Bichler and Malm (2015)	Disrupting criminal networks
Lemieux and Clarke (2009)	Elephant poaching in Africa
Moreto and Lemieux (2015)	Ranger patrols and poaching in Uganda
Pires and Clarke (2010, 2012)	Illegal trade in neo-tropical parrots
Petrossian and Clarke (2014)	Illegal oceanic fishing
Kim, Clarke, and Miller (2013); Clarke, Chetty, and Natarajan (2013)	Tiger poaching in India
Petrossian, Weis, and Pires (2015)	Illegal harvesting of crabs and lobsters

Source: From Clarke and Bowers (2017).

Criticisms of situational crime prevention

Situational crime prevention has been dismissed by some criminologists both as a theory and as an approach to reducing crime. The following are the main types of criticisms that have been levelled:

1. Rational choice

There are some paradoxes in rational choice which inevitably make it imperfect. Making a fully informed rational choice would involve an inordinate amount of effort to collect evidence about alternative courses of action and to calculate the expected relative returns from each of them. This would itself be a costly procedure, and the perverse effect of doing all this is that nothing would be done and the costs of the calculations would far outweigh the benefits. Moreover, most of us lack the ability to make good estimates. In practice, routines are needed, shortcuts taken, and good enough decisions made. In practice, we often use rules of thumb in decision-making. On top of this, a large volume of research has shown that we make many errors in the thinking that informs our decisions (Kahneman, 2011). All this is accepted by Cornish and Clarke. They refer to 'bounded' rationality, drawing on Simon (2000). The rationality of most action is limited. If we add choices that are affected by values and emotions rather than only utility maximisation, the rational-choice model of the offender becomes even less plausible.

Some remain committed to the bounded rational-choice model. It may be deemed a true reflection of offending decision-making. The decisions to offend or not to do so must, it is assumed, reflect rational utility-maximising choices: behaving according to moral scruples or disregarding them feeds into utility calculations (feelings of guilt are a cost; feeling that one has behaved well is a benefit); likewise, giving vent to feelings or bottling them up involves rational utility-maximising choices in that the emotional release from the provoked violence, for example, may exceed the expected costs in the heat of the moment. The problem with this way of propping up rational-choice assumptions is that in effect it inoculates rational choice from empirical test by defining action as that which reflects rational choice – we know it was rational choice because it's what was done! An alternative defence of adherence to the rational choice model is more pragmatic. The simplifying assumption of rational choice has been found to be invaluable in much social science, in particular in classical economics but also in much sociology. Thus, we should hold on to it, even if mindful of the need to be sensitive to exceptions and limitations in practice (see Popper, 1967; Weber, 1949; Tilley, 2004a).

Because of the implausibility of rational choice as strictly true for all decision-making, some have suggested jettisoning it as the general theory

of human behaviour to underpin situational crime prevention (Wortley &
Tilley, 2017). Choices may still have reasons, of course: 'I hit him because
I was angry'; 'I murdered her because I was jealous'; 'I stabbed him as
revenge for what he did to my friend'; 'They deserved it because of their
greed.' These are reasons but not in accordance with rational choice as
utility maximisation. The classical sociologist, Max Weber (1964), developed ideal types of four different reasons for action: means-ends (zweck-)
rationality (action in accordance with rational choice), value (vert-) rationality (action in accordance with values), affect (action in accordance with
emotions), and habit or tradition (action undertaken unreflectively and
routinely as a matter of course). In reality, these grounds for action will
often be mixed, but Weber is probably right to point out that decisions
(including those related to crime) are not adequately captured by reference
only to 'rational choice.'

For practical purposes, the veracity (or not) of rational-choice assumptions about human decision-making in criminal acts may matter little.
What is important is the identification of differing ways in which immediate conditions inform criminal choices and the scope there is for altering
these conditions in the interests of preventing or reducing crime. The risk
of holding on to an implausible rational-choice model, however, is first
that its weaknesses may discredit situational prevention more generally
and, second, that it may lead to the neglect of modifiable situational contingencies that could prevent some crimes other than by reducing their
means-ends rationality.

2. The creation of a fortress society

Situational crime prevention may be undesirable in leading to the creation of a fortress society which is ugly, exclusionary, and divisive. The
assumption of this criticism is that situational crime prevention puts prevention above all else and leads to the creation of a nasty social world of
mutual suspicion, the creation of spaces which exclude those who fail to
appear conventional and respectable, the prevention of crime against the
rich who can afford security devices at the expense of the poor who cannot, and the design of cities that are ugly and convey tacit messages that
citizens and citizen groups should mistrust one another. The dystopian
image is of a surveillance society where all are watched; where situational
crime prevention entails security measures that are ugly and intrusive;
where the rich, smug, and supposedly respectable are safe and kept at
arms-length from the poor, supposedly deviant and suspicious; and where
crime prevention aimed at protecting the crime-prone, relatively poor and
defenceless, is ignored or neglected. The examples given in Table 4.4 show
that this criticism is misplaced, at least as an account of what situational
crime prevention necessarily has done and can do. That is not to say that
situational or security measures are always desirable. Like any other types

of intervention, ethical issues are at stake in their choice and implementation. This issue is picked up in Chapter 5. Farrell and Tilley (2022) discuss what they take to be ethical design, and Tilley (2006a) outlines the radical potential of SCP.

3. Displacement

The Achilles' heel of situational crime prevention is supposed by some to lie in 'displacement' – the idea that if one crime is prevented, it inexorably leads to another. This is sometimes referred to as a 'hydraulic' theory of crime, according to which there is a fixed volume of crime that will occur come what may; the best we can do is to shift it around. The only way genuinely to prevent crime is to stop or reduce the supply of offenders. The hydraulic theory of crime is driven by the notion that offenders are different from the rest of us, driven to commit a certain amount of crime that will inevitably manifest itself one way or another. Because of the widely held assumption that the only effect of situational measures will be to displace crime, a substantial literature relating to displacement has been produced, distinguishing between displacement by place, time, target, crime type, technique, or offender (Reppetto, 1976). As noted earlier, Clarke and Weisburd have suggested that there may also be 'diffusion of benefits' effects, whereby crime-preventive effects extend beyond the operational range of control measures (Clarke & Weisburd, 1994). Any specific net effect will, of course, be a function of direct effects plus diffusion of benefits effects minus displacement effects.

A range of studies has attempted to estimate displacement and diffusion effects (for reviews of this literature, see Guerette & Bowers, 2009; Johnson, Guerette, & Bowers, 2014). Most of these studies have focused on short-term spatial impacts. The basic finding is that the fear of displacement is misplaced and that there can be diffusions of benefit. Of course, if displacement is taken as an article of faith, then the person committed to the inexorable displacement hypothesis can always find some form of displacement that hasn't been measured or has been measured inadequately. The displacement hypothesis is then in effect inoculated against empirical test.

Focusing studies on short-term spatial displacement (and also diffusion of benefits) has the practical advantage that its measurement is relatively straightforward. The findings are important and striking. They likely capture potential crime displacement/diffusion of benefit effects among the members of active cohorts of offenders who might otherwise commit a crime in a particular locality. It does not capture longer-term adaptation to situational measures across cohorts of offenders, which may mean that succeeding groups of otherwise similarly motivated offenders come to commit the same types of crime in different ways and/or to commit different types of crime. However, this does not invalidate situational crime prevention. It merely means that it must be continuously adaptive.

4. Root causes

Situational crime prevention does not focus on the root causes of criminality, which it is claimed must be addressed if crime problems are to be truly prevented. This is a traditional view of crime and crime prevention shared across political divides. Those on the right are liable to invoke individual wickedness, calling for repressive preventive responses disabling or incapacitating offenders. Those on the left are apt to invoke social inequalities and inequities that must be corrected before crime will be prevented by eliminating the basic social causes of criminality. Those somewhere in the middle (liberals or social democrats) are liable to invoke individual or social deficits that must be addressed to prevent criminality in the forms and places in which it is produced or expressed. Situational crime prevention does not sit well with any of these, in that it eschews concerns with root causes of criminality in favour of near causes and conditions for criminal events.

The 'fundamental attribution error' helps explain why theories stressing near causes in general and opportunity in particular face great difficulties in winning widespread acceptance. This scepticism persists even though we all conduct our everyday lives on the assumption that situational theories accurately capture causes of crime and preventive possibilities: we lock our doors, keep hold of our possessions in places we feel vulnerable, and avoid what we take to be dangerous places. The fundamental attribution error follows from a cognitive bias that favours explaining behaviour in terms of disposition (Ross & Nisbett, 2011; Kahneman, 2011). Our intuition is that people do what they do because of what they are like. Bad people do bad things. Good people do good things. To stop people doing bad things, we need to root out their badness or incapacitate them through imprisonment, capital punishment, or perhaps cutting their hands off.

We often exclude ourselves from embracing the fundamental attribution error when it comes to our own criminal acts (Pease & Laycock, 2012). We use 'techniques of neutralisation' to deny culpability (Sykes & Matza, 1957). These often involve invoking situational sources of our aberrant behaviour: 'I was provoked'; 'She started it'; 'It was hot'; 'I wasn't myself'; 'He should have locked his front door'; 'Everybody does it'; 'There was already lots of litter, so what I added didn't really make any difference'; 'They made me do it'; 'I had no choice'; and so on.

For the classic sociologist, Emile Durkheim, attaching blame and inflicting punishment on others who transgress are functional in collectively reasserting and reinforcing shared moral rules underpinning social order (Durkheim, 1933). It matters not whether the explanation of the behaviour is accurate. The collective condemnation of behaviours contributes to the reinforcement of shared moral sentiments and encourages behaviour that broadly conforms to them, even when those moral sentiments and associated rules are widely breached by others (as in Members of Parliament telling lies in the House of Commons in the UK!); even where they may tend to favour some at the expense of others (as was the case in the rights granted to slave owners in the treatment of their possessions in differing jurisdictions); and even when they prescribe or proscribe behaviours in ways that are harmful to some (as is the case with laws relating to abortion in some U.S. states).

The radicalism of focusing on situational measures and mechanisms to address crime problems, as well as the difficulties in gaining acceptance of them in public policy, lies in part in their challenge to taken-for-granted assumptions about crime and criminality that are widely shared across the political spectrum. Ironically, this widespread scepticism about focusing on situational contingences as a public policy measure persists, as already pointed out, despite our almost ubiquitous use of situational measures in our everyday, private lives!

5. An administrative criminology of the right

It is claimed that situational crime prevention comprises an intrinsically right-wing, administrative form of criminology that favours the rich and established. Although it is true that some security measures are costly and beyond the reach of the poor, it does not follow that the approach is inherently biased in favour of the better off when it comes to public policy. Indeed, the list of applications in Table 4.4 shows how situational crime prevention has been applied in relation to the otherwise disadvantaged and vulnerable (see also Tilley, 2016a). In so far as situational measures are applied to rule-breaking rather than harm reduction, they might be accused of a conservative bias in favour of whatever comprise existing laws. A focus on situational measures orientated to net harm reduction avoids this.

Complementary theories for crime prevention emphasising situations and opportunities

Crime pattern theory

Crime pattern theory focuses on the spatial distribution of crime. Its ideas align well with those of routine activities. It focuses on offender availability and awareness in relation to crime opportunities and the geographical patterns of crime that follow (Brantingham & Brantingham, 1981, 1984).

Crime pattern theory distinguishes between different types of activity 'nodes' between which we travel. Our main nodes typically comprise our homes, schools or places of work, and places where we shop or go to for entertainment. We are familiar with those nodes and the areas immediately around them and with the travel routes (or 'paths') between them. For offenders, these comprise 'awareness spaces' where they will know of better and worse crime opportunities. Crimes occur within these awareness spaces but at a distance from where we feel we are most likely to be recognised. There may be great opportunities elsewhere (rich rewards at low risk to offenders), but if those minded to commit crime don't know about them, they are unlikely to experience high rates of crime. Figure 4.2 illustrates the theory visually.

Some places are 'crime attractors' in that those who wish to commit crime go there with the intention of committing crime because they know of the criminal opportunities they can expect. Some places are 'crime generators' in that they provide plentiful crime opportunities that are exploited by some who go there for other reasons, and then are tempted to offend (see Brantingham & Brantingham, 1995). Many high crime locations are both crime attractors and crime generators, with offences committed both by those going there to commit crime and by those who come across and exploit crime opportunities while being there for other reasons. The addresses of drug dealers might be crime attractors

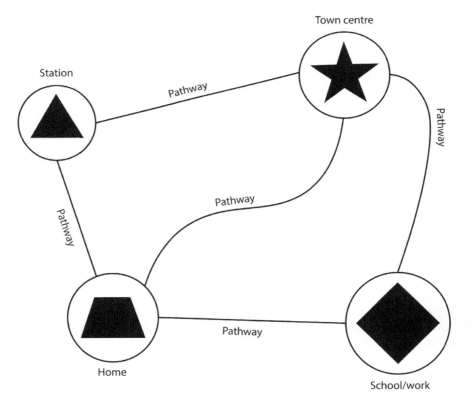

Figure 4.2 Crime pattern theory.

(known holdings of cash and low risk of the crime being reported to the police). Rock concerts might mainly be crime generators, with few going intending to commit crime but some open to temptation from the opportunities available. Shopping centres might be crime attractors and generators at the same time.

Potential victims' routine activities and crime risk awareness might be added to crime pattern theory (Hodgkinson & Tilley, 2007). Naïve individuals unaware of the crime risks in unfamiliar locations might be at enhanced risk from offenders out to victimise them. Tourists and travellers carrying cash and other high-value items in places with which they are unfamiliar and first-year undergraduates, living away from home in cities unknown to them and bringing with them new high-value goods, are examples where likely offenders can expect rich pickings.

Design against crime

A variety of theories focus on design and crime, with implications both for the modification of designs and for new designs to pre-empt future crime. Most of the work has related to the design of spaces and places. There are also literatures on products, facilities, and systems. Chapter 3 highlights ways in which crime is concentrated by place, product, facilities, and systems. Most design and crime theory aligns well with routine activities, crime pattern, and situational crime prevention, which have already been outlined in this chapter. Hence, treatment here will be brief.

PLACE DESIGN AND CRIME

Oscar Newman and defensible space (Newman, 1972): urban life tends to increase anonymity, which is conducive to crime (relatively low-risk and relatively little informal social control). Designs of space vary in the degree to which they foster anonymity. Resident 'territoriality' reduces anonymity. Territoriality can be designed into new developments (or developments can be modified to increase territoriality) by signalling both to residents and potential offenders, the association of spaces with residents (or other identifiable stakeholders). Residents/stakeholders assume (or are perceived to assume) some responsibility for the oversight of these spaces. It is this oversight that reduces anonymity and hence increases the perceived risk to the potential offender. Crime can, thus, be reduced at high crime locations by minimising the amount of space in which no identifiable stakeholder has a specific interest and responsibility for oversight.

Jane Jacobs and American cities (Jacobs, 1961): mixed-use areas provide for collective and complementary surveillance by different stakeholders in the neighbourhood, thereby reducing the risk of crime to themselves and to strangers. This surveillance can be done by residents on the 'stoop' looking out, noticing, and acting on predatory criminal behaviours in public places or by business owners who take a proprietary interest in the areas surrounding their businesses. Businesses and residents thereby act as guardians of potential crime targets by increasing risk to those who might otherwise offend. Single-use areas in cities lack such controls.

C. Ray Jeffery and *Crime Prevention through Environmental Design* (Jeffery, 1971): Jeffery adopted a behaviourist approach (as opposed to rational choice) to explain how crime concentrates by inadvertently reinforcing criminal behaviours in certain locations because of their designs. People (like any other organisms) adapt to their surroundings, and if their surroundings reward or reinforce some behaviours, for example those that are criminal, those behaviours are more likely to be reproduced. Changing the contingencies provided by surroundings leads to changed behaviours. The implication is that we can prevent crime where it has been concentrated by altering the contingencies there, making it less rewarding for offenders. Altering designs to reduce rewards prevents criminality in locations where criminal acts are common.

George Kelling and broken windows (Wilson & Kelling, 1982; Kelling & Coles, 1997): the term 'broken windows' refers to signs that an area is disorderly, which creates an impression that crime and antisocial behaviour are permissible and pose no significant risks to the offender. Moreover, further criminal acts make little overall difference to the area, so they hardly show and are easily excused in the eyes of the offender. The solution to the problem involves clean-ups that make the behaviours more obvious and less permissible to offenders. Clear strategies to enforce rules, for example by a crackdown, increases risks to offenders. Rewards may be removed (e.g. through the strategy to clean subway cars described in Chapter 2). Once 'broken windows' are removed, crime will no longer be reproduced. In crackdown and consolidation strategies, perceived permissibility of criminal behaviour and low risk to offenders are reduced in the longer term through successive crackdowns showing decreasing tolerance for criminal behaviours and reductions in the disorderly appearance of high crime neighbourhoods (Farrell, Chenery, & Pease, 1998; Tilley, 2004b). Crackdowns and their temporal diffusion of crime-preventive effects are used to build capacity for sustained collective control, as represented in Figure 4.3.

Robert Sampson and collective efficacy (Sampson, Raudenbush, & Earls, 1997): the literature on collective efficacy relates to the role of community conditions in the generation of crime patterns. Low social capital, weak informal social control, and poor access to external service supports produce neighbourhoods with high levels of crime, especially violence. There is relatively little to draw on for ways to increase collective efficacy. A concern with collective efficacy would not ordinarily be seen as a natural bedfellow of situational crime prevention and opportunity reduction. However, what the high collective efficacy community does is supply spontaneous neighbourhood

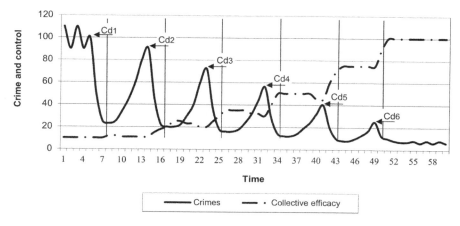

Figure 4.3 Crackdown and consolidation.

Note: Police crackdowns (Cd1 to Cd6) involve intensive attention in an area in relation to a crime problem. Such crackdowns tend to be successful for a limited period after which crime increases. The idea behind crackdown and consolidation is to repeat the crackdown before the previous high level has been reached and to do so repeatedly, gradually reducing the level at which a new crackdown is initiated. Between crackdowns, consolidation is attempted, for example by making physical changes to the area or by building community crime control capacities. Collective efficacy, described later in the chapter, comprises crime control capacities within communities to control crime, which are especially difficult to create during high crime periods.

surveillance and informal social control, which reduces crime opportunities as well, maybe, as criminal dispositions. In addition, the privileged access to external resources in communities with high collective efficacy enables them to draft in situational measures when they are needed, such as improved lighting, changes in road layout, or police support for Neighbourhood Watch. In this way, high collective efficacy communities are marked by greater scope for the use of situational measures to reduce crime opportunities than communities with low collective efficacy.

PRODUCT DESIGN AND CRIME

Technological developments have led to unintended crime consequences (Tilley, 2012). As we saw in Chapter 3, products have been developed and have evolved in ways that make them ideal targets of crime. Microelectronics have led to a proliferation of lightweight, high-value rewarding goods that are easily stolen, used, or resold. Modes of transport, including cars, motorcycles, and bicycles, are by their nature easily moved and may be resold or broken into separate components that can be sold. Mobile phones have comprised especially attractive targets for theft. Contactless payment cards are widely available and stolen for use to buy goods.

Technological developments have also provided resources that facilitate crime. Guns, cars, mobile phones, electronic screwdrivers, explosives, micro-computers, and presently the Internet are obvious examples.

Pease (1997) has referred to costly 'retrofitted' solutions in response to the emergence of new crime problems borne of new product developments. He notes the possibility of anticipating in advance their criminogenic potential. Recognising which new products are liable to be criminogenic can inform design-modifications to reduce the crime harvest that could otherwise be anticipated. The reduction in vehicle theft referred to in Chapter 2 comprises an example of what can be achieved economically and effectively by building a concern for crime prevention into the design of new products.

FACILITY DESIGN AND CRIME

As Chapter 3 showed, the same type of facility can be host to very differ-ent levels of crime. This is due largely to variations in 'place management,' referred to earlier in this chapter (Eck, 2015). Facilities of the same kind can be run in different ways, with varying crime consequences. Bars comprise a good example.

Within a city centre, bars vary widely in the amount of crime that occurs within and around them. Where there is competition between bars for the same young male clientele, each may make economies and adjustments in how they are run to attract customers and reduce costs. Typical strategies may include selling cut-price alcoholic drinks, having low staff levels, providing limited seating, and increasing the space for people to stand and drink, as well as minimising any spend on crime prevention measures. Running bars in this way at low cost will lead to a concentration of offending within local areas. Surfers Paradise, in Queensland's Gold Coast and Cardiff in South Wales, are well-documented examples (Homel, Hauritz, Wortley, McIlwain, & Carvolth, 1997; Maguire, Nettleton, Rix, & Raybould, 2003). Authorities in both inter-vened to encourage changes in place management to reduce crime problems.

The place management measures adopted in high crime facilities take us back to situational crime prevention. They relate mainly to reducing provo-cation (e.g. less crowding, more sitting) and increasing risk (e.g. more staff).

SYSTEM DESIGN AND CRIME

Internet services comprise archetypal systems. In relation to dating sites, Chapter 3 showed how crime is concentrated on some of them. Here, sys-tem rather than place management is at issue. What Ekblom (2011) refers to as 'troublesome trade-offs' will be at work. The design of systems that are attractive to users, cheap to access, cheap to produce and operate, and convenient and easy for clients to use and hence most profitable will be in tension with many measures that protect the Internet service itself, its customers, and third parties from exploitation and fraud.

System management practices orientated to reducing fraud (for example romance scams) and exploitation (e.g. children shown in child pornography sites) typically use situational measures. For instance online rule reminders/excuse removals are used in relation to those who might otherwise illicitly access digital sexual images on the Internet (Prichard et al., 2022), and two factor authentication is used to verify many payment orders. However, in troublesome trade-offs, prevention does not always win out. For example increasing the maximum amount covered by contactless payments is potentially criminogenic, but presumably financial services calculate that the losses will be more than compensated by the benefits to them (Farrell & Tilley, 2021).

* * *

So far, we have focused on opportunity reduction as applied mainly to the 'absence of capable guardianship' and 'availability of suitable targets,' which you will recall are identified as two of the necessary convergent conditions for crime in the routine activities approach. We turn next to likely offenders, the third element. We begin by discussing ways in which situational theories and interventions can reduce the supply and availability of offenders before moving to other offender-focused approaches.

Theories for crime prevention focused on the supply, availability, and capacity of offenders

Opportunity theory and offender supply and availability

Opportunity theories orientated to crime prevention have paid little explicit attention to the supply and availability of those disposed to commit crime, largely on the grounds that reducing opportunity is easier and has a strong track record of success.

It may be assumed in opportunity theory that disposition is normally distributed with saints at one tail, never taking advantage or tempted to commit crime, and sinners at the other, committing crimes whatever situational measures are in place to discourage them (see, e.g. Wilkins, 1967). The rest of us fall somewhere in between, some being more open to temptation than others, some reacting to provocation, some sometimes looking for opportunity, some routinely keeping an eye open for opportunity, and some looking to create opportunities.

Opportunities may, however, cause or reinforce dispositions. For behaviourists such as Jeffery, this was crucial in his ideas for *Crime Prevention through Environmental Design*. Other, more sociological accounts in accordance with opportunity theory would refer to the ways in which debut crimes induct some into groups supportive of criminal disposition (emphasised in 'differential association,' as noted by Sutherland, 1955). This may have happened with vehicle crime when car theft was easy and provided fun for young people (see Farrell et al., 2015). It was mentioned as one possibility for backfire effects mentioned in Chapter 2 in the Cambridge-Somerville experiment, where boys who went to summer camps may have been inducted into criminality through associations forged there. It is conceivable that cybercrime has become a recent debut crime, where some young people are drawn into crime through their collaboration with others. Opportunities for this are created, for example, through online gaming.

As noted in Chapter 3, offending is highly skewed. A small proportion of all offenders are prolific, and their careers as prolific offenders are often short. It seems plausible that those who become prolific offenders are less easily put off committing crimes by situational measures than occasional offenders. They are more likely to look for or try to create opportunities. Much preventive work has been orientated to reducing the supply of prolific offenders, curtailing their criminal careers, and deterring them from acting on their dispositions.

If you watch pre-school children playing, including siblings, you will see lots of assaults and thefts. Most seem to have a natural disposition to offend. Parents and other carers spend quite a lot of time trying to deal with this using situational measures (say keeping the children apart and issuing rule reminders), deterrence (say putting one or more of them on 'naughty' steps), and inculcation of rules requiring an adherence to social norms (say issuing instructions to them, reasoning with them, and conditioning them with rewards for 'good' behaviour).

Adolescent-limited and lifetime-persistent offenders

Looking at criminal careers, Moffitt (1993) distinguished between 'adolescent limited' and 'life-course persistent' offenders. Life-course persistent offenders begin offending early and continue past adolescence. Such people, she contends, carry a genetic potential to become life-course persistent offenders, which is activated if they experience adverse events (Moffitt, 2005). Neither the adverse experiences nor the generic attributes are sufficient to produce life-course persistent offenders. Rather, it is their interaction. Adolescent-limited offenders, in contrast, have short criminal careers that are curtailed naturally as they enter adulthood and take on adult responsibilities. Many people are involved in adolescent-limited offending. A painstaking American study tracked a cohort of male delinquents until they were 70, survivors among whom almost all eventually discontinued offending (Laub & Sampson, 2003).

The preventive implications of work on criminal careers are clear. Even if we cannot do much about the genetic potential of some to become life-course persistent offenders, programmes and policies that target the adverse childhood experiences liable to activate the potential are possible. We can also try to block routes into and hasten routes out of adolescent-limited offending. We can avoid responses to detected young offenders, which risk reinforcing their criminality or prolonging their involvement in it. For example prosecutions risk making employment more difficult by giving young people criminal records. Labelling some as 'criminals' may also bestow a deviant identity that is then appropriated and informs future involvement in crime.

Deficits and dispositions to commit crime

There is a substantial literature on risk and protective factors related to involvement in crime (see Farrington, 1996, 2007). Most risk factors relate to deficits of one kind or another: deficient intelligence, deficient care, a deficient family, a deficient community, a deficient education, a deficient social structure, or a deficient genetic constitution. Most protective factors are the obverse of the risk factors: strong and loving family; supportive community with high collective efficacy; and good, stable schools.

Programmes are put in place to try to ameliorate or remove risk factors and reinforce or introduce protective factors, in the hope that these will lessen deficits that otherwise are liable to dispose young people to become involved in crime. Early intervention, in particular, focuses on remedial work to lessen the chances that criminal careers will follow. In relation to those at risk of becoming life-course persistent offenders in particular, measures that remove significant stressors may help avert the activation of genetically determined susceptibility to early involvement, and then sustained participation, in criminal and antisocial behaviour.

Turning points

Homel (2013) and Laub and Sampson (2003) have written about 'turning points' which comprise contingencies that occur at critical points in our lives providing for different paths that may be followed, including ones that lead into crime careers and ones that lead to desistance and away from crime careers. Examples include changes in schools attended, changes in places lived in, being taken into care, coming out of care, finishing education, getting a job, entering and leaving military service, going to hospital, being prosecuted, being sent to prison, leaving prison, getting married, having children, losing a job, and getting divorced. These potential turning points provide both risks that pathways into crime are created and possibilities that pathways out are produced.

Some people's circumstances are conducive to successive turning points steering towards crime and others to successive turning points away from crime. For those on the crime path, there are intervention possibilities at potential turning points where nudges towards a non-crime pathway may be available. Also, for those bearing multiple risk factors, there may be a mandate for pre-emptive interventions at potential turning points towards a non-crime (and non-victimisation) pathway. For example girls in the care of the state as they begin to live independently are at risk of sexual exploitation, involving both offending and victimisation; intervention at that point may help steer some away from that pathway.

It seems likely that diverse mechanisms may be at work surrounding the contingences that may lead away from or towards criminal careers at turning points. Here are some candidates:

- Changed routines and changed encounters with crime opportunities.
- New peer group, providing changed norms or changed rewards for criminal or non-criminal behaviour.
- New sources of informal social control permitting, encouraging, or discouraging crime.
- New sources of formal social control.
- Changed significant other(s), either promoting criminal involvement or desistance from it.
- Changed opportunities to follow crime/non-crime paths.
- Changed perception of benefits/costs of criminal behaviours.
- New opportunity to choose a changed life course.
- Changed excuses available to commit/not commit crime.
- Changed perceived costs and benefits of criminal involvement.

Offender treatment

There is a long history of assuming that criminality reflects something pathological about offenders who need treatment to cure their criminal dispositions. Theft, for example, was diagnosed as 'kleptomania,' which called not so much for condemnation or punishment, as for understanding and professional care, and kleptomania is still used as a diagnosis for some repeat thieves for whom medical treatment is provided (Dannon, 2003). Stalking is often seen in the same general way (see, e.g. Civilotti, Sciascia, Zaccagnino, Varetto, & Acquadro Maran, 2020). Psychologists, psychiatrists, social workers, and probation officers provide diagnoses and treatments of various kinds that are orientated to dealing in an understanding way with the underlying causes of an individual's criminality. The idea is that criminal behaviour is abnormal, that the abnormality has a cause, that that cause should be sought, and that that cause of abnormal behaviour should then be the focus for informed professional responses. This treatment may be an alternative to punishment or may be provided as a complement to punishment. The notion of offenders as abnormal 'others' who are different from 'us' lies, however, at the heart of the fundamental attribution error discussed earlier.

Public health approaches attempt to forestall the development of criminality by putting in place measures that pre-empt causes that would otherwise lead some into criminality. This was the thinking behind the failed Cambridge-Somerville experiment described in Chapter 2, which was developed originally by a well-meaning physician for whom frameworks of pathology, treatment, and public health would come naturally.

Environmental corrections

Environmental corrections (Shaefer et al., 2016) have been proposed as a promising 'new paradigm' for the supervision of offenders in the community to try to prevent them from reoffending. The starting point for developing environmental corrections is the disappointing track record of treatments orientated to reducing disposition. It focuses instead on attempting to reduce the crime opportunities encountered by known offenders. Hence, unlike most other opportunity-reducing crime prevention efforts, it is not concerned with primary prevention but instead relates to tertiary prevention (the prevention of crime by known offenders). It tries to alter the situational contingencies met by known offenders rather than their criminal propensity. The practice of environmental corrections would begin with an effort to identify and understand the specific crime opportunities and temptations liable to be encountered by the individual offender under supervision. It would then go on to work out how those opportunities and temptations could practically best be removed or lessened. Measures might include, for example: mobilising those who might function effectively as handlers, occupying supervisees' time with prosocial activities, and helping those wishing to cease offending to learn how to avoid situations where they could be drawn into offending. The specifics would be tailored to each individual and their situation.

Cognitive behavioural therapy

Cognitive-behavioural therapy (CBT) has come to be widely used to deal with a range of problem behaviours, including those related to crime. It emerged in the mid-1970s, drawing on two contrasting and competing traditions in psychology, one relating to behaviour and behaviour modification and the other to cognition. Each tradition is internally very varied. In broad terms, however, the former tended to take little interest in internal processes: the emphasis was on the behaviour of animals and people. The latter was principally concerned with how people perceived and understood themselves and the world around them, with much less interest in what they did. The former tended to be self-consciously scientific, with a strong emphasis on observation. The latter was much more humanistic, emphasising hermeneutic methods. The former was sceptical of introversion and of anything that could not be seen and measured. The latter was sceptical of accounts of human beings that failed to recognise the obvious fact that there is an internal side to them: people do not just react mechanically; instead, crucially they are thinking, feeling beings. The therapeutic emphasis of the former was on changing the environment acting on people to elicit recurrent unwanted ('maladaptive') behaviours. The therapeutic emphasis of the latter was on improving unhappy people's sense of self by helping them change it.

Cognitive behavioural theory takes from behaviourism the notion that the environment affects behaviour and from cognitive psychology the notion that that influence is mediated by intra-psychic mechanisms. That is the environment is crucial, but the means by which it has its influence is a function of the ways it is processed by the subject. In simple terms, thoughts and feelings are at work in responding to experience.

Many chronic offenders will have learned in the past habits of responding to problem situations by committing crime, drinking heavily, and/or acting violently. In response to such criminals, cognitive behavioural approaches attempt to deal with the flawed and faulty reasoning which is deemed to explain their patterns of criminal behaviour. Offenders are taught, for example, how better to read the situations they encounter, problem-solving skills, and anger management in order that they respond more appropriately and, for example, less aggressively to circumstances they encounter. They learn thereby not to misconstrue others' actions as involving insults, to control anger before it spills over into aggressive behaviour, and to resolve difficult circumstances with strategies that do not involve the use of violence.

A variety of techniques are used in cognitive behavioural treatment of offenders. These include, for instance 'systematic desensitisation' which involves presenting the subject with arousing stimuli that provoke crime and then relaxing them in order that those stimuli no longer elicit feelings leading to the unwanted behaviour; teaching 'perspective taking,' an ability some offenders lack to understand how others may perceive situations so that this can be taken into account; 'modelling' appropriate responses to situations to which the subject has responded in inappropriate criminal ways (perhaps following earlier criminal modelling); and 'coaching' in what is suitable as against unsuitable behaviour and providing feedback to the subject on their responses.

Different offenders have different cognitive shortcomings, so the therapy needed to correct their faulty thinking would not be identical. It appears also that the levels of motivation vary in ways that are important to the receptiveness of subjects to the treatment provided. In practice in England and Wales, several standard programmes rooted in cognitive behavioural principles were put in place through the probation service during the Crime Reduction Programme (1999–2002). These included 'Think First,' 'Reasoning and Rehabilitation,' 'Enhanced Thinking Skills,' 'Priestly One-to-One,' and 'Addressing Substance-Related Offending' (Hollin et al., 2004). Most were for groups and included a standard number of sessions. For example Think First involved 22 two-hour sessions; Reasoning and Rehabilitation involved 38 two-hour sessions; and Enhancing Thinking Skills involved ten two-hour sessions. Priestly One-to-One was for individuals deemed unsuitable for group work (or in locations where no group work was available) but used the same kind of cognitive behavioural principles in 20 one-hour sessions. The completion rates were low for all group work programmes (from 21% to 38%), though reached 70% for the individual programme. The aggregate outcomes from comparing the 2,230 members of the experimental group with the 2,645 members of the comparison group across the five programmes were disappointing. The completers had only a marginally lower reconviction rate than the comparison group for males and a higher one for females (males 54% as against 60% and females 56% as against 50%). Non-completers had a much higher reconviction rate (68% for males and 77% for females). Overall findings for cognitive behavioural programmes are mixed (see Friendship & Debidin, 2006).

The summary of a Cochrane review of the use of the application of cognitive behavioural theory educational programmes concluded that,

> Research indicates that youth who join gangs are more likely to be involved in delinquency and crime, particularly serious and violent offences, compared to non-gang youth and non-gang delinquent youth. Research also has found that both delinquent youth and youth who join gangs often show a range of negative thoughts, feelings and beliefs compared to non-delinquent peers. Cognitive-behavioural interventions, designed to address these deficits, have had a positive impact on a variety of behavioural and psychological disorders among children and youth. This systematic review was designed to assess the effectiveness of such cognitive-behavioural interventions for preventing youth gang involvement. A three-part search strategy found no randomised controlled trials or quasi-randomised controlled trials of the effectiveness of cognitive-behavioural interventions for gang prevention; four excluded studies examining the impact of Gang Resistance Education and Training (GREAT) were of too poor a quality to be included in analysis. The only possible conclusions from this review, therefore, are the urgent need for additional primary evaluations of cognitive-behavioural interventions for gang prevention and the importance of high standards required of the research conducted to provide meaningful findings that can guide future programmes and policies.
>
> Fisher, Gardner, and Montgomery (2008)

A basic flaw in the cognitive behavioural approach may be the notion that repeated offending follows from flawed thinking. This may not be true in most cases, and even where it is the case changing it may be tricky, especially with standard sessions. The attraction of the cognitive behavioural approach is that it is relatively quick and inexpensive, though nothing much is gained if it is not effective.

Drug treatment

The theory behind drug treatment as a crime prevention strategy (as against other rationales for drug treatment) is that drug-taking drives crime in various ways. There are three basic drug-taking crime-generation mechanisms. The first relates to the way some drugs may dispose the individual to behave criminally, most particularly by being violent. The second relates to the need drug dependency creates for substantial sums of money to buy the drugs that can only be raised through crime. The third relates to the market supported by drug-takers, which produces drug trafficking and associated criminal activities, including serious violence to protect and pursue business and violence at the point of drugs sale.

Illicit drug-taking is quite commonplace among those at peak offending ages. The 2005/2006 BCS (British Crime Survey, since retitled 'Crime Survey of England and Wales') found that in England and Wales, some 45% of 16-to-24 year olds had taken one or more illicit drugs at some point in their lives, 25% in the last year and 15% in the last month. Notwithstanding this general pattern, there is also ample evidence not only in Britain but also in other countries of an association between illicit drug-taking and property crime (Flood-Page, Campbell, Harrington, & Miller, 2000; Makkai & Payne, 2003; ONDCP, 2000).

What is not quite so clear is that the relationship is a simple causal one, wherein drugs generate crime. Crime may also produce the drug-taking: the resources provided by crime provide the wherewithal to become involved in drug-taking, and regular drug-taking may be part of a general chaotic lifestyle for a minority that also includes involvement in crime – it is not the drugs per se that are responsible for the crime but a broader way of life that includes much else besides (McSweeney & Hough, 2006).

More complex drug–crime causal relationships are now widely believed to be at work (Makkai & Payne, 2003; McSweeney & Hough, 2006). Occasional drug-taking (especially cannabis) and property crime are quite normal in adolescence. More regular minor property crimes may lead to increased and more serious drug usage because drugs become affordable. High rates of drug usage eventually produce dependency among some individuals. Drug dependency brings with it a need to raise regular and large sums of money. One key method of raising this money may then include a high rate of property crime as well as participation in low-level drug trafficking. Many of those involved become members of peer groups with common deviant and self-destructive lifestyles which support, normalise, and reinforce high levels of drug-taking and the crime surrounding it. In addition, some of the drugs taken (including alcohol which is of course not illicit) may engender aggressiveness and hence violent crime. Moreover, the illicit drugs market, which is sustained by occasional and high-rate users, draws in serious criminals whose efforts to protect and take over supply routes involve major organised crime. The need to acquire drugs can also provoke violent behaviour towards suppliers. Once established, those benefiting from a local market have an interest in maintaining it with new cohorts of customers who can be attracted by cut-price offers that help foster dependency.

Those who are drug dependent have diverse attributes and needs (Audit Commission, 2002; National Institute on Drug Abuse, 2006; Marsden & Farrell, 2002). Motivation to stop, patterns of multiple drug use, medical and psychological problems, economic and social circumstances, and level of dependence all vary widely. There is no standard treatment that is believed to be appropriate for all. Tailoring to need is therefore crucial. Where treatment is offered and taken up among those who commit crime, levels of offending have been found to fall, though the 'same' treatment has been found to have widely varying outcomes (Audit Commission, 2002). Treatment has to be sustained if those receiving it are not to revert to their drug-taking and crime habits (Marsden & Farrell, 2002). What is required is often initial detoxification followed by maintenance (e.g. with methadone as a substitute for heroin), followed by dose reduction, and, after that, services aimed at relapse prevention since, for example, under the influence of peers, drug-taking may easily be resumed. Cognitive behavioural methods of the sort discussed in the previous section are often used (National Institute on Drug Abuse, 2006). A major problem in treatment at all stages and of all types has been the high rates of drop-out, especially among those with chaotic lifestyles (McSweeney & Hough, 2006; Harper & Chitty, 2005). Because of this and the high rates of offending associated with drug-taking, elements of coercion or compulsion have been introduced to motivate offenders' entry into, participation in, and completion of sustained courses of drug treatment (Seddon, 2007; National Institute on Drug Abuse, 2006). These have been found in some studies to be able to produce better retention in treatment and likely drops in drug-taking and in crime, though findings across the board are neither consistent nor unequivocal (Seddon, 2007). The underlying theory is that at each stage, the benefits of participation in treatment and behaviour in accord with it outweigh the costs in terms of the forgone benefits from the drugs and from acquiescence to temptations that follow from the groups to which criminal drug users typically belong (Frisher & Beckett, 2006).[2]

Enforcement

The criminal justice system in general and the police in particular are widely seen to be responsible for crime prevention. It is often assumed that detection and punishment are the keys to prevention. Although, as I hope is clear by now, a lot else can be done to prevent crimes, there is indeed much that the police and criminal justice system can also do, sometimes in collaboration with third parties. There are good theoretical grounds, backed by some persuasive evidence, for specific ways of doing policing and targeting criminal justice resources in the interests of crime prevention. Incapacitation and deterrence are two major crime prevention mechanisms which can be activated through criminal justice systems, although this does not exhaust the possibilities.

Incapacitation

Incapacitation is the most obvious way in which some penalties for crime can prevent further offending by those subject to it. Imprisonment stops those incarcerated from committing direct-contact predatory crimes outside the prison. I use the qualifier 'direct-contact predatory' to indicate that those incarcerated may still be able to organise or facilitate crimes outside the prison walls. I use the qualifier 'outside' to indicate that inmates can still (and indeed often do) commit crimes within prison. Most prisons are crime hotspots, where crime prevention measures are needed (Wortley, 2002).

Killing those convicted clearly stops them from committing further crimes. Likewise, chemical and surgical interventions as punishments may also incapacitate some offences, as with cutting off the hands of pickpockets or castrating sex offenders. There are lots of obvious objections to these that apply regardless of their preventive efficacy, which I don't go into here.

Deterrence

Deterrence is the second main mechanism through which the agencies of the criminal justice system are widely understood to prevent crime. Deterrence may be general or specific. General deterrence relates to primary prevention. The punishment of offenders deters us all from committing crime. We see the negative consequences for those committing crimes, and we decide therefore that we will not offend. Specific deterrence relates to tertiary prevention (prevention of continued criminal activity by those already involved in criminal careers). Known prolific offenders are punished so that they 'learn their lessons.' They realise what will befall them if they persist in offending and therefore cease criminal activity. Secondary preventive deterrence falls somewhere between the general and specific. It is targeted at those on the brink of criminal careers and is intended to divert them away from it. 'Scared straight' projects (which take youngsters on the fringes of criminal behaviour to prisons where they are confronted with the reality of the experiences they risk if they follow criminal careers) are an example. However, experimental studies have found these to have been ineffective or to have backfired (Petrosino, Turpin-Petrosino, & Buehler, 2002[3]).

There is a vast specialist literature on the theory, practice, and outcomes of activities of criminal justice systems and how they may deter crime, fail to do so, or perversely foster rather than prevent crime. Interested readers could usefully begin with a collection edited by Nagin Cullen, and Jonson (2018).

The main underlying theory of deterrence is rational choice. The potential utility of a crime is more than counterbalanced by the risk of incurring a negative penalty. If the offender's utility (or expected utility) is outweighed by the penalty (or expected penalty), they will not commit the crime. If the probability of being caught and convicted multiplied by the size of the penalty exceeds the value of the expected reward from committing the crime, the crime will not be committed. Either increasing the penalty itself or increasing the chances of conviction or both in conjunction with one another can help deter the commission of further crimes by decreasing the value of crime to the potential offender. This way of thinking lies behind calls to increase penalties or to put pressure on the police (and other agencies of the criminal justice system) to detect more offenders and convict them in court. This rational-choice theory goes for both general and specific deterrence. The theory has been refined by reference to temporal discounting. Future costs and benefits are weighted less than immediate ones. Hence, 'celerity' (swiftness) of punishment enters into the calculation of costs and benefits. The immediate (relatively certain) benefits from committing a crime may thus be 'over-weighted' and future (relatively uncertain) penalties 'under-weighted' in utility calculations by the potential offender.

In practice, as with rational choice as an underpinning theory of situational crime prevention, the simplifying assumptions of rational choice when applied in deterrence are unlikely to capture the complexity of offender decision-making. Perceptions are often mistaken; rational choice involves its own costs; values and emotions play a part alongside rational choice in offender decision-making; offending decisions are often made under peer group or other 'significant other' pressure; many offences are committed when those involved are less well placed to make rational choice because they are under the influence of alcohol or drugs or where emotions are heightened, and so on. Moreover, the consequences of conviction may include not only the punishment but also social disapproval, loss of non-criminal social associates, labelling, and increased difficulty in going straight where being a known offender makes following lawful lifestyles more difficult and following offending ones easier. The criminogenic side effects of successive criminal convictions and associated punishments may increase, while their preventive effects diminish once the law-abiding identity is spoilt. Conviction for a crime comprises one turning point.

Notwithstanding its common-sense appeal, there are clearly weaknesses in any simple-minded assumption that deterrence will follow from punishment and that crime will fall with increases in the severity of punishment. None of this is to say that there's no mileage in deterrence through the workings of the criminal justice system. 'Focused deterrence' and some forms of 'hotspot policing' provide examples.

The Boston gun project and the New South Wales drink-driving initiative mentioned earlier and outlined in Chapter 2 are cases in point. Hotspot policing is another, where randomly applied, short and intensive police patrols have led to temporary falls in crime (Braga, Papachristos, & Hureau, 2014). Common threads running through these include focused interventions that are orientated to deterrence, high levels of publicity for penalties, and offender inability to calculate risks and hence credible threats to offenders' sense that they will be able to control or eliminate risks of detection and conviction.

Recent developments in the empirical research literature on deterrence appear to be moving away from testing the hypothesis that penalties deter crime regardless of place, offender, or crime type, to ask more nuanced and realistic questions. These ask what types of deterrence can be activated in what ways against which sorts of offenders and which types of crime most effectively to prevent crimes (see, e.g. Loughran, Paternoster, & Piquero, 2018).

Disruption

While deterrence has mainly to do with reducing *individuals'* decisions to commit crimes, disruption is concerned with offending *groups and organisations*. Disruption may include some deterrence, but the main aim is to make it more difficult for groups to continue criminal lifestyles and activities (see Tilley, 2016b).

Disruption involves understanding specific criminal organisations and targeting any of a wide range of enforcement activities (available to diverse enforcement bodies) to undermine the criminal organisation's capacity to maintain its collective criminal endeavour, however formal or informal that criminal organisation might be. Examples of criminal organisations include youth gangs, sex trafficking circles, criminal families, mafia groups, drug trafficking networks, modern slavery, terrorist groups, groups perpetrating major frauds, networks of offenders committing armed robberies, political and other corruption, motorbike gangs, corporate crime such as price-fixing agreements, and so on. In some cases, groups may be relatively structured with clear members and a discernible hierarchy. In other cases, networks are relatively loose with no stable hierarchy and a fluid membership. It is often difficult to disable high crime, high-harm criminal organisations by focusing only on the most easily convicted individual members.

'Intelligence-led policing' involves the careful mapping of organised crime groups, their members and the relationship between them, their criminal activities, and their methods. The profile of an organised crime group is used to work out where interventions can practically be made by enforcement bodies most readily to frustrate their criminal activities. Possibilities include seeding disinformation and mistrust within criminal groups, focusing on key aspects of their criminal lifestyles that are most open to enforcement, and targeting enforcement activities on key members, even if they are hard to convict for their most serious crime as was famously the case with Al Capone. 'Offender self-selection,' to which I turn now, facilitates the disruption of serious organised crime.

Offender self-selection

Offender self-selection refers to the finding that people who commit serious crimes routinely also commit many more minor ones (Roach, 2019, 2023; Chenery, Henshaw, & Pease, 1999). Al Capone's tax fiddles are a case in point. Whereas bringing serious offenders to book for their most serious crimes may be tricky – perhaps because they can intimidate witnesses, bribe officials, obfuscate proceedings with corrupt lawyers, or because of the care they take to operate through third parties in their criminal endeavours and thereby avoid direct involvement – their habitual criminality is liable to leave scope for enforcement activities that undermine their criminal lifestyles. Moreover, for those concerned primarily with offender incapacitation and deterrence, focusing attention on minor crimes may produce preventive outcomes by focusing police attention on casually committed (and often readily detectable) minor crimes that tend routinely to be committed by serious, prolific offenders as part of their general lifestyle.

Other theory

This chapter has referred to theory that is orientated to crime prevention. There is an enormous amount of theory that can be drawn on in crime prevention but which is not specifically framed around crime prevention. Some of this focuses on understanding crime and criminals, and some is much more general and speaks to any kind of human behaviour, including crime. It would be beyond any book to do justice to all this theory, but in the pragmatic business of crime prevention, you should know that it is there and available for plundering. Here are just a couple of examples.

Examples of potentially useful theories relating to crime

We have mentioned some of these in passing already.

'Differential association,' formulated by Sutherland (1955), refers to the notion that in our everyday lives, some of us routinely come across others involved in crime from whom we pick up values, techniques, and incentives to commit crime which normalises it and inducts us into criminal behaviours. Others do not have these routine encounters. The former are more likely than the latter to become involved in criminal careers. The hypothesis about the role of joy riding, car theft, and later criminality outlined earlier accords well with Sutherland's theory. Its potential for crime prevention is clear: try to avoid situations where those not involved in crime at critical points in their lives spend time with those already heavily involved in it when the latter can influence the former. The backfire effects in the Cambridge-Somerville project associated with summer camps, as outlined in Chapter 2, may be a function of the failure to appreciate this.

'Techniques of neutralisation' were outlined by Sykes and Matza (1957). As noted earlier, they relate to ways in which offenders routinely try to justify their criminal behaviour. Call-in meetings that were held as part of the Boston Gun project included respected community members to challenge and undermine ways in which offenders tried to excuse their violent behaviour.

Sykes and Matza developed their ideas in disagreement with Sutherland. They argued that the use of techniques of neutralisation reflects offenders' adherence to conventional, mainstream values, which they do not abandon through their association with offenders. For our purposes – making pragmatic use of theories in the interests of crime prevention – we do not have to choose between them. Indeed, we can accept that both contain ideas that we can draw on for preventive purposes.

'Procedural justice' in policing and its potential effect on citizen compliance have been emphasised in much recent research (for pioneering work, see, e.g. Tyler, 2006, and Sunshine & Tyler, 2003). Enforcement bodies in general and the police more particularly routinely apply enforcement measures. The police are bestowed widespread powers in the interest of enforcement. They can stop people, search people, arrest people, and detain them. All these actions can provoke those affected. They may feel unfairly treated and therefore be reluctant to comply when asked or told to do things they would prefer not to do. Procedural justice has to do with the ways in which these enforcement powers are delivered. The idea is that if they are delivered in a procedurally just way, that is courteously, lawfully, equitably, and with full explanation of the grounds for the enforcement activity, they are less likely to antagonise and provoke violent responses and more likely to lead to compliance.

Examples of potentially useful general theories

'Reference groups' comprise those with whom we identify or compare ourselves. We use them as a source of values (normative reference groups) or as a basis for comparing how well we are doing in relation to others (comparative reference groups) (Merton, 1968). Potential offender reference groups (those youngsters in some areas, who are looked up to and admired) include rich local drug dealers. Measures to discredit such reference groups may undermine their capacity to encourage others to try and emulate them.

I remember going to an area in Birmingham to visit the police. They were concerned about intimidation by the local 'Green box gang' (named after the normal colour of street furniture containing telephone cables and connections). The response was to repaint these green boxes in the unmistakable colours of Mr Blobby (light pink with yellow spots), a well-known and ridiculous fictional TV cartoon character. The idea was to poke fun at and undermine the credibility of the Green box gang. The police believed that their strategy had been effective: no one was afraid of or wanted to join a Mr Blobby gang!

'Pluralistic ignorance' (Prentice & Miller, 1996) describes conditions where our beliefs about what others think lead us to act in ways we would otherwise not choose to, but where our beliefs about their beliefs are mistaken. Figure 4.4 shows how pluralistic ignorance can lead to shoplifting that none involved wants. Authoritative corrections to those misapprehensions should dissolve them and prevent the behavioural corollaries. Collective bullying, bravado, promiscuous sexual behaviours, vandalism, drunkenness, and illicit drug-taking may all plausibly be inflated as a result of pluralistic ignorance.

For further useful discussions of theory with potential for further application, see Wortley (forthcoming) and Roach (2023).

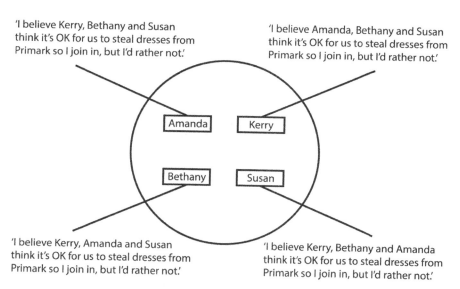

'I believe Kerry, Bethany and Susan think it's OK for us to steal dresses from Primark so I join in, but I'd rather not.'

'I believe Amanda, Bethany and Susan think it's OK for us to steal dresses from Primark so I join in, but I'd rather not.'

Amanda   Kerry

Bethany   Susan

'I believe Kerry, Amanda and Susan think it's OK for us to steal dresses from Primark so I join in, but I'd rather not.'

'I believe Kerry, Bethany and Amanda think it's OK for us to steal dresses from Primark so I join in, but I'd rather not.'

Figure 4.4 Pluralistic ignorance and criminal activity.

Conclusion

There is a mass of theory that can be helpful in informing crime prevention by suggesting possible preventive mechanisms and ways to activate them. The theories referred to in this chapter suggest mechanisms and interventions that might activate them in the interest of crime prevention, but they have less to say about the contextual conditions necessary for the mechanisms to produce positive preventive outcomes. At the start of this chapter, basic, better, and best theory were distinguished. In those terms, the theories that are outlined here are, thus, much 'better' than basic theories (hypotheses) that doing X will always produce crime prevention outcome Y, but they are not sufficient for identifying conducive conditions for the conjectured mechanisms to be activated or deactivated. They thus largely fall short of being 'best' for practical purposes.

Finally, note that crime and its prevention are marked by complexity, sources of which are touched on already in this chapter. Emergent developments, many not orientated to crime, comprise one source of complexity. These can alter crime opportunities or change offender availability. COVID-19 is one example, which changed offender supply as well as target accessibility. The invention of new technologies providing new crime targets or new tools for crime is another source. Mobile phones have been both emergent targets and emergent tools. Furthermore, offenders and preventers interact in ways that produce inherent instability. Mutual adaptation creates arms races that destabilise the effectiveness of specific situational measures; the history of safes and methods of breaking into them is an example. Offenders taking advantages of opportunities and drawing others into crime are another sources of complexity, where opportunity provides for the induction into criminality. Likewise, easy opportunities create temptations to which some succumb, rewarding them and thereby reinforcing their offending. We will touch on these issues in later chapters.

Exercise: Take a mass media report of any crime event and apply some theory explaining the event and developing a promising preventive intervention.

Notes

1 The Dawes Centre within the Jill Dando Institute at UCL focuses on future crime and its pre-emption (Johnson et al., 2019; Pease, 1997).
2 Frisher and Beckett (2006) suggest that the natural desistance in drug-taking widely found in the general population is not so much found in criminal, problematic drug-taking populations, where dependency has set in and where external persuasion is therefore needed to alter the balance of rewards in favour of treatment and desistance in drug-taking.
3 Chapter 7 discusses studies of the kind used in Petrosino et al.'s review and highlights some of their shortcomings.

References

Audit Commission. (2002). *Changing habits: The commissioning and management of community drug treatment services for adults*. London: Audit Commission.

Bichler, G., & Malm, A. (2015). *Disrupting criminal networks: Network analysis in crime prevention*. Boulder, CO: Lynne Rienner Publishers.

Braga, A. A., Papachristos, A. V., & Hureau, D. M. (2014). The effects of hot spots policing on crime: An updated systematic review and meta-analysis. *Justice Quarterly, 31*(4), 633–663. doi:10.1080/07418825.2012.673632

Brantingham, P. L., & Brantingham, P. J. (1981). Notes on the geometry of crime. In P. J. Brantingham & P. L. Brantingham (Eds.), *Environmental criminology* (pp. 7–26). Beverley Hills, CA: SAGE.

Brantingham, P. L., & Brantingham, P. J. (1984). *Patterns in crime*. New York: Macmillan.

Brantingham, P. L., & Brantingham, P. J. (1995). Criminality of place: Crime generators and crime attractors. *European Journal on Criminal Policy and Research, 3*, 5–26. doi:10.1007/BF02242925

Brody, S. (1976). *The effectiveness of sentencing – a review of the literature* (Home Office Research Study 35). London: HMSO.

Bullock, K., Clarke, R., & Tilley, N. (Eds.), (2010). *Situational prevention of organised crimes*. Cullompton: Devon Willan Publishing.

Chenery, S., Henshaw, C., & Pease, K. (1999). *Illegal parking in disabled bays: A means of offender targeting, policing and reducing crime* (Briefing Note 1/99). London: Home Office.

Civilotti, C., Sciascia, C., Zaccagnino, M., Varetto, A., & Acquadro Maran, D. (2020). States of mind with respect to adult attachment and reflective functioning in a sample of men detained for stalking: Evaluation and clinical implications. *SAGE Open, 10*(4). doi:10.1177/2158244020962820

Clarke, R. (1992). Introduction. In R. Clarke (Ed.), *Situational crime prevention: Successful case studies* (pp. 3–36). New York: Harrow and Heston.

Clarke, R. (1995). Situational crime prevention. In M. Tonry & D. Farrington (Eds.), *Building a safer society. Crime and justice* (Vol. 19). Chicago, IL: University of Chicago Press.

Clarke, R., & Bowers, K. (2017). Seven misconceptions of situational crime prevention. In N. Tilley & A. Sidebottom (Eds.), *Handbook of crime prevention and community safety* (pp. 109–142). London: Routledge.

Clarke, R., Chetty, K., & Natarajan, M. (2013). Eyes on the forest: CCTV and ecotourism in Indian tiger reserves. In A. Lemieux (Ed.), *Situational prevention of poaching* (pp.177–199). London: Routledge.

Clarke, R., & Mayhew, P. (1988). The British gas suicide story and its criminological implications. *Crime and Justice, 10*, 79–116.

Clarke, R., & Newman, G. (2005). Modifying criminogenic products: What role for government? In R. Clarke & G. Newman (Eds.), *Designing out crime from products and systems. Crime prevention studies* (Vol. 18, pp. 7–83). Monsey, NY: Criminal Justice Press.

Clarke, R., & Weisburd, D. (1994). Diffusion of crime control benefits: Observations on the reverse of displacement. In R. Clarke (Ed.), *Crime prevention studies 2* (pp. 165–184). Monsey, NY: Willow Tree Press.

Cohen, L., & Felson, M. (1979). Social change and crime rate trends: A routine activity approach. *American Sociological Review, 44*, 588–608. doi:10.2307/2094589

Cornish, D. (1994). The procedural analysis of offending and its relevance for situational prevention. In R. Clarke (Ed.), *Crime prevention studies 3* (pp. 151–196). Monsey, NY: Criminal Justice Press.

Cornish, D. B., & Clarke, R. V. (2003). Opportunities, precipitators and criminal decisions: A reply to Wortley's critique of situational crime prevention. In M. Smith & D. Cornish (Eds.), *Theory for practice in situational crime prevention: Crime prevention studies 16* (pp. 111–124). Monsey, NY: Criminal Justice Press.

Cromwell, P., Alexander, G., & Dotson, P. (2008). Crime and incivilities in libraries: Situational crime prevention strategies for Thwarting Biblio-Bandits and problem patrons. *Security Journal, 21*, 147–158.

Dannon, P. (2003). Topiramate for the treatment of kleptomania: A case series and review of the literature. *Clinical Neuropharmacology, 26*(1), 1–4. doi:10.1097/00002826-200301000-00001

Demetriou, C. and Silke, A. (2003). A criminological internet 'sting'. Experimental evidence of illegal and deviant visits to a website trap. *British Journal of Criminology, 43*(1), 213–222.

De Souza, E. and Miller, J. (2012). 'Homicide in the Brazilian Favela.' *British Journal of Criminology, 52*, 782–807.

Durkheim, E. (1933). *The division of labor in society*. New York: Free Press.

Eck, J. (2015). Who should prevent crime at places? The advantages of regulating place managers and challenges to police services. *Policing: A Journal of Policy and Practice, 9*(3), 223–233. doi:10.1093/Police/Pav020

Eck, J., & Spelman, W. (1987). *Problem-solving: Problem-oriented policing in Newport news*. Washington, DC: Police Executive Research Forum.

Ekblom, P. (1988). *Getting the best out of crime analysis* (Crime Prevention Unit Paper 10). London: Home Office.

Ekblom, P. (1997). Gearing up against crime: A dynamic framework to help designers keep up with the adaptive criminal in a changing world. *International Journal of Risk Security and Crime Prevention, 2*(4), 249–266.

Ekblom, P. (2011). *Crime prevention, security and community safety using the 5Is framework*. Basingstoke: Palgrave Macmillan.

Ekblom, P., & Tilley, N. (2000). Going equipped: Criminology, situational crime prevention and the resourceful offender. *British Journal of Criminology, 40*(3), 376–398. doi:10.1093/Bjc/40.3.376

Farrell, G., & Tilley, N. (2021). *Tap and pin': Preventing crime and criminal careers from increased contactless payments* (UCL JDI Special Series on COVID-19, No. 18). London: UCL Jill Dando Institute.

Farrell, G., & Tilley, N. (2022). Elegant security: Concept, evidence and implications. *European Journal of Criminology, 19*(5), 932–953. doi:10.1177/1477370820932107

Farrell, G., Chenery, S., & Pease, K. (1998). *Consolidating police crackdowns: Findings from an anti-burglary project* (Police Research Series, Paper 113). London: Home Office.

Farrell, G., Laycock, G., & Tilley, N. (2015). Debuts and legacies: The crime drop and the role of adolescence-limited and persistent offending. *Crime Science, 4*, 16. doi:10.1186/S40163-015-0028-3

Farrington, D. (1996). The explanation and prevention of youthful offending. In J. Hawkins (Ed.), *Delinquency and crime*. Cambridge: Cambridge University Press.

Farrington, D. (2007). Childhood risk factors and risk-focused prevention. In M. Maguire, R. Morgan, & R. Reiner (Eds.), *The Oxford handbook of criminology*. Oxford: Oxford University Press.

Felson, M. (1986). Linking criminal choices: Routine activities, informal control, and criminal outcomes. In D. Cornish & R. Clarke (Eds.), *The reasoning criminal* (pp. 119–128). New York: Springer-Verlag.

Fisher, H., Gardner, F., & Montgomery, P. (2008). Cognitive-behavioural interventions for preventing youth gang involvement for children and young people (7–16). *Cochrane Database of Systematic Reviews*, (2), CD007008. doi:10.1002/14651858. CD007008.Pub2

Flood-Page, C., Campbell, C., Harrington, V., & Miller, J. (2000). *Youth crime: Findings from the 1998/99 youth lifestyles survey* (Home Office Research Study 209). London: Home Office.

Friendship, C., & Debidin, M. (2006). Probation and prison interventions. In A. Perry, C. McDougall, & D. Farrington (Eds.), *Reducing crime: The effectiveness of criminal justice interventions*. Chichester: Wiley.

Frisher, M., & Beckett, H. (2006). Drug use desistance. *Criminology and Criminal Justice*, 6(1), 127–145. doi:10.1177/1748895806060670

Goldstein, G. (1990). *Problem-oriented policing*. New York: McGraw-Hill.

Goldstein, H. (1979). Improving policing: A problem-oriented approach. *Crime & Delinquency*, 25(2), 236–258. doi:10.1177/001112877902500207

Graham, K. (2009). They fight because we let them! Applying a situational crime prevention model to barroom violence. *Drug and Alcohol Review*, 28(2), 103–109.

Graycar, A., & Sidebottom, A. (2012). Corruption and control: A corruption reduction approach. *Journal of Financial Crime*, 19(4), 384–399

Guerette, R. (2004). Toward safer borders: Extending the Scope of situational crime prevention. *American Society of Criminology, Annual Meeting*, Nashville, 2004.

Guerette, R., & Bowers, K. (2009). Assessing the extent of crime displacement and diffusion of benefits: A review of situational crime prevention evaluations. *Criminology*, 47(4), 1331–1368. doi:10.1111/J.1745-9125.2009.00177.X

Halford, E., Dixon, A., Farrell, G., Malleson, N., & Tilley, N. (2020). Crime and coronavirus: Social distancing, lockdown, and the mobility elasticity of crime. *Crime Science*, 9, 11. doi:10.1186/S40163-020-00121-W

Hanmer, J. (2003). Mainstreaming solutions to major crime problems: Reducing repeat domestic violence. In K. Bullock & N. Tilley (Eds.), *Crime reduction and problem-oriented policing*. Cullompton: Willan.

Harper, C., & Chitty, C. (2005). *The impact of corrections on reoffending: A review of 'what works'* (Home Office Research Study 291, 3rd ed.). London: Home Office.

Hodgkinson, S., & Tilley, N. (2007). Travel-to-crime: Homing in on the victim. *International Review of Victimology*, 14(3), 281–298. doi:10.1177/026975800701400301

Hollin, C., Palmer, E., McGuire, J., Hounsome, J., Hatcher, R., Bilby, C., & Clark, C. (2004). *Pathfinder programmes in the probation service: A retrospective analysis* (Home Office Online Report 66/04). London: Home Office.

Homel, R. (2013). Developmental crime prevention. In N. Tilley (Ed.), *Hand book of crime prevention and community safety* (pp. 97–132). Cullompton: Willan.

Homel, R., Hauritz, M., Wortley, R., McIlwain, G., & Carvolth, R. (1997). Preventing alcohol-related crime through community action: The surfers paradise safety action project. In R. Homel (Ed.), *Policing for prevention: Reducing crime, public intoxication and injury. Crime prevention studies 7* (pp. 35–90). Monsey, NY: Criminal Justice Press.

Jacobs, J. (1961). *The death and life of great American cities*. New York: Random House.

Jeffery, C. R. (1971). *Crime prevention through environmental design*. Beverley Hills, CA: SAGE.

Johnson, S., Ekblom, P., Laycock, G., Frith, M., Sombatruang, N., & Rosas Valdez, E. (2019). Future crime. In R. Wortley, A. Sidebottom, N. Tilley, & G. Laycock (Eds.), *Routledge handbook of crime science* (pp. 428–446). London: Routledge.

Johnson, S., Guerette, R., & Bowers, K. (2014). Crime displacement: What we know, what we don't know, and what it means for crime reduction. *Journal of Experimental Criminology, 10*(4), 549–571. doi:10.1007/S11292-014-9209-4

Kahneman, D. (2011). *Thinking fast and slow*. London: Allen Lane.

Kelling, G., & Coles, C. (1997). *Fixing broken windows*. New York: Free Press.

Kim, J. H., Clarke, R. V., & Miller, J. (2013). Poaching and tiger populations in Indian reserves. In A. Lemieux (Ed.), *Situational prevention of poaching* (pp. 154–176). London: Routledge.

Laub, J., & Sampson, R. (2003). *Shared beginnings, divergent lives: Delinquent boys to age 70*. Cambridge, MA: Harvard University Press.

Laycock, G. (1992). Operation identification or the power of publicity? In R. Clarke (Ed.), *Crime prevention: Successful case studies*. New York: Harrow and Heston.

Lemieux, A., & Clarke, R. (2009). The international ban on ivory sales and its effects on elephant poaching in Africa. *British Journal of Criminology, 49*(4), 451–471.

Lester, D. (2009). *Preventing suicide: Closing the exits revisited*. Hauppauge, NY: Nova Science.

Lipton, D., Martinson, R., & Wilks, J. (1975). *The effectiveness of correctional treatment: A survey of treatment evaluation studies*. Springfield, MA: Praeger.

Loughran, T. A., Paternoster, R., & Piquero, A. R. (2018). Individual difference and deterrence. In D. Nagin, F. Cullen, & C. Jonson (Eds.), *Deterrence, choice, and crime* (pp. 211–236). London: Routledge.

Madensen, T. and Knutsson, J. (Eds.) (2011). '*Preventing crowd violence.*' *Crime Prevention Studies 26*. Boulder, CO: Lynne Rienner Publishers.

Maguire, M., Nettleton, H., Rix, A., & Raybould, S. (2003). *Reducing alcohol-related violence and disorder: An evaluation of the 'TASC' project* (Home Office Research Study 265). London: Home Office.

Makkai, T., & Payne, J. (2003). *Key issues from the drug use careers of offenders (DUCO) study* (Trends and Issues no. 267). Canberra: Australian Institute of Criminology.

Marsden, J., & Farrell, M. (2002). Research on what works to reduce illegal drug misuse. Appendix five. In *Changing habits: The commissioning and management of community drug treatment services for adults*. London: Audit Commission.

Martinson, R. (1974). What works? Questions and answers about prison reform. *The Public Interest, 35*, 22–54.

Mayhew, P., Clarke, R., Sturman, A., & Hough, M. (1976). *Crime as opportunity* (Home Office Research Study 34). London: HMSO.

McCord, J. (2003). Cures that harm: Unanticipated outcomes of crime prevention programs. *Annals of the American Association of Political and Social Science (AAPSS)*, 587, 16–30. doi:10.1177/0002716202250781

McCord, W., & McCord, J. (1969). *Origins of crime: A new evaluation of the Cambridge-Somerville youth study*. Montclair, NJ: Patterson Smith (Original work published 1959 by Columbia University Press).

McNally, M., & Newman, G. R. (Eds.), (2008). *Perspectives on identity theft* (Crime Prevention Studies, Vol. 23). Monsey, NY: Criminal Justice Press.

McSweeney, T., & Hough, M. (2006). Supporting offenders with multiple needs: Lessons for the 'mixed economy' model of service provision. *Criminology & Criminal Justice*, 6(1), 107–125.

Merton, R. (1968). *Social theory and social structure*. New York: Free Press.

Moffitt, T. (1993). Adolescence-limited and life-course-persistent antisocial behavior: A developmental taxonomy. *Psychological Review*, 100(4), 674–701. doi: 10.1037/0033-295X.100.4.674

Moffitt, T. (2005). The new look of behavioral genetics in developmental psychopathology: Gene-environment interplay in antisocial behaviors. *Psychological Bulletin*, 131(4), 533–554. doi:10.1037/0033-2909.131.4.533

Moreto, W. D., & Lemieux, A. (2015). Poaching in Uganda: Perspectives from law enforcement rangers. *Deviant Behavior*. Online First. doi:10.1080/01639625.2014.977184

Nagin, D., Cullen, F., & Jonson, C. (Eds.), (2018). *Deterrence, choice, and crime*. London: Routledge.

Natarajan, M. (2014). Differences between intentional and non-intentional burn injuries in India: Implications for prevention. *Burns*, 40, 1033–1039.

National Institute on Drug Abuse (NIDA). (2006). *Principles of drug abuse treatment for criminal justice populations: A research-based guide*. Washington, DC: National Institutes of Health, US Department of Health and Human Services.

Newman, G. R., & Clarke, R. (2003). *Superhighway robbery: Preventing E-commerce crime*. Cullompton: Willan Publishing.

Newman, O. (1972). *Defensible space*. New York: Macmillan.

Nivette, A., Zahnow, R., Aguilar, R., Ahven, A., Amran, S., Ariel, B., . . . Eisner, M. (2021). A global analysis of the impact of COVID-19 stay-at-home restrictions on crime. *Nature Human Behaviour*, 5(7), 868–877. doi:10.1038/S41562-021-01139-Z

Office of National Drug Control Policy (ONDCP). (2000). *Drug-related crime*. Washington, DC: Office of National Drug Control Policy.

Owen, N., & Cooper, C. (2013). *The start of a criminal career: Does the type of debut offence predict future offending?* London: Home Office.

Pawson, R., & Tilley, N. (1997). *Realistic evaluation*. London: SAGE.

Pease, K. (1997). Predicting the future: The roles of routine activity and rational choice theory. In G. Newman, R. Clarke, & S. Shoham (Eds.), *Rational choice and situational crime prevention*. Aldershot: Dartmouth.

Pease, K., & Laycock, G. (2012). Ron and the Schiphol fly. In N. Tilley & G. Farrell (Eds.), *The reasoning criminologist: Essays in honour of Ronald V. Clarke* (pp. 172–183). London: Routledge.

Petrosino, A., Turpin-Petrosino, C., & Buehler, J. (2002). Scared straight' and other Juvenile Awareness Programs for preventing juvenile delinquency. In *The Campbell collaboration reviews of intervention and policy evaluations (C2-RIPE).* Philadelphia, PA: Campbell Collaboration.

Petrossian, G., & Clarke, R. (2014). Explaining and controlling illegal commercial fishing: An application of the CRAVED theft model. *British Journal of Criminology, 54,* 73–90.

Petrossian, G., Weis, J., & Pires, S. (2015). Factors affecting crab and lobster species subject to IUU fishing. *Ocean and Coastal Management, 106,* 29–34.

Pires, S., & Clarke, R. (2010). Sequential foraging, itinerant fences and parrot poaching in Bolivia. *British Journal of Criminology, 51,* 314–335.

Pires, S., & Clarke, R. (2012). Are parrots CRAVED? An analysis of parrot poaching in Mexico. *Journal of Research in Crime and Delinquency, 49*(1), 122–146.

Pires, S. F., Guerette, R., & Stubbert, C. (2014). The crime triangle of kidnapping for ransom incidents in Colombia, South America: A "Litmus" test for situational crime prevention. *British Journal of Criminology, 54,* 784–808.

Popper, K. (1967). La Rationalité Et La Statut Du Principe De Rationalité. In E. Classen (Ed.), *Les Fondements Philosophiques Des Systèmes Economiques* (pp. 142–50). Paris: Payot.

Prentice, D., & Miller, D. (1996). Pluralistic ignorance and the perpetuation of social norms by unwitting actors. *Advances in Experimental Social Psychology, 28,* 161–209. doi:10.1016/S0065-2601(08)60238-5

Prichard, J., Scanlon, J., Krone, T., Spiranovic, C., Watters, P., & Wortley, R. (2022). Warning messages to prevent illegal sharing of sexual images: Results of a randomised controlled experiment. In *Trends and issues in crime and criminal justice no 647.* Canberra: Australian Institute of Criminology.

Reppetto, T. A. (1976). Crime prevention and the displacement phenomenon. *Crime & delinquency, 22*(2), 166–177.

Reynald, D., & Leclerc, B. (2018). *The future of rational choice for crime prevention.* London: Routledge.

Roach, J. (2019). Those who do big bad things still do little bad things: Re-stating the case for self-selection policing. In R. Wortley, A. Sidebottom, N. Tilley, & G. Laycock (Eds.), *Routledge handbook of crime science* (pp. 320–333). London: Routledge.

Roach, J. (2023). *Practical psychology for policing.* Bristol: Policy Press.

Ross, L., & Nisbett, R. (2011). *The person and the situation: Perspectives of social psychology.* London: Pinter and Martin.

Sampson, R., Raudenbush, S., & Earls, F. (1997). Neighborhoods and violent crime: A multilevel study of collective efficacy, *Science, 277,* 918–924.

Seddon, T. (2007). Coerced drug treatment in the criminal justice system: Conceptual, criminological and ethical issues. *Criminology and Criminal Justice, 7*(3), 269–286. doi:10.1177/1748895807078867

Shaefer, L., Cullen, F., & Eck, J. (2016). *Environmental corrections: A new paradigm for supervising offenders in the community.* Los Angeles, CA: SAGE.

Shane, J., & Magnuson, S. (2014). Successful and unsuccessful pirate attacks worldwide: A situational analysis. *Justice Quarterly,* 1–26. doi:10.1080/074 18825.2014.958187

Sidebottom, A. (2012). 'On the application of CRAVED to livestock theft in Malawi.' *International Journal of Comparative and Applied Criminal Justice, 37*(3), 195–212.

Simon, H. (1955). A behavioral model of rational choice. *Quarterly Journal of Economics, 69*(1), 99–118. doi:10.2307/1884852

Simon, H. (2000). Bounded rationality in social science: Today and tomorrow. *Mind & Society*, *1*(1), 25–39. doi:10.1007/Bf02512227

Sunshine, J., & Tyler T. R. (2003). The role of procedural justice and legitimacy in shaping public support for policing. *Law and Society Review*, *37*(3), 513–548. doi:10.1111/1540-5893.3703002

Sutherland, E. (1955). *Principles of criminology*. Chicago, IL: Lippincott.

Svensson, R. (2002). Strategic offences in the criminal career context. *British Journal of Criminology*, *42*(2), 395–411. doi:10.1093/Bjc/42.2.395

Sykes, G., & Matza, D. (1957). Techniques of neutralization: A theory of delinquency. *American Sociological Review*, *22*(6), 664–670. doi:10.2307/2089195

Terry, K., & Ackerman. A. (2008). Child sexual abuse in the Catholic Church: How situational crime prevention strategies can help create safe environments. *Criminal Justice and Behavior*, *35*(5), 643–657.

Tilley, N. (2004a). Karl Popper: A philosopher for Ronald Clarke's situational crime prevention. In S. Shoham & P. Knepper (Eds.), *Israel studies in criminology 8* (pp. 39–56). Willowdale: De Sitter.

Tilley, N. (2004b). Using crackdowns constructively. In R. Burke-Hopkins (Ed.), *Hard cop soft cop*. Cullompton: Willan.

Tilley, N. (2012). Crime reduction: Responsibility, regulation and research. *Criminology and Public Policy*, *11*(2), 361–378.

Tilley, N. (2016a). Middle range radical realism for crime prevention. In R. Matthews (Ed.), *What is to be done about crime and punishment towards a "public criminology"* (pp. 89–122). London: Palgrave Macmillan.

Tilley, N. (2016b). Intelligence-led policing and disruption of organized crime: Motifs, methods, and morals. In T. Delpeuch & J. Ross (Eds.), *Comparing the democratic governance of police intelligence* (pp. 153–179). Cheltenham: Edward Elgar.

Tyler, T. (2006). *Why people obey the law*. Princeton, NJ: Princeton University Press.

Verma, A. (2009). Situational prevention and elections in India. *International Journal of Criminal Justice Sciences*, *4*(2), 83–97.

Vollard, B. (2015). Temporal displacement of environmental crime: Evidence from marine oil pollution. *Center Discussion Paper No. 2015-037*. Available at SSRN: http://ssrn.com/abstract=2633964 or http://dx.doi.org/10.2139/ssrn.2633964

Weber, M. (1949). *The methodology of the social sciences* (E. Shils & H. Finch, Trans.). New York: Free Press.

Weber, M. (1964). *The theory of social and economic organization* (A. Henderson & T. Parsons, Trans.) New York: Free Press.

Wilkins, L. (1967). *Social policy, action and research*. London: Tavistock.

Wilson, J., & Kelling, G. (1982). Broken windows. *Atlantic Monthly*, *249*(3), 29–38.

Wortley, R. (2002). *Situational prison control: Crime prevention in correctional institutions*. Cambridge: Cambridge University Press.

Wortley, R. (forthcoming). *Psychological criminology* (2nd ed.). London: Routledge.

Wortley, R., & Smallbone, S. (2006). Applying situational principles to sexual offences against children. In R. Wortley & S. Smallbone (Eds.), *Situational prevention of child sexual abuse. Crime Prevention Studies* (vol. 19, pp.7–35). Monsey, NY: Criminal Justice Press.

Wortley, R., & Tilley, N. (2017). Does situational crime prevention require a rational offender? In D. Reynald & B. Leclerc (Eds.), *The future of rational choice for crime prevention*. London: Routledge.

5   Principled crime prevention?

The following is a (fictional) discussion of crime prevention in a government department. It is intended to show how those who begin with contrasting views on the ethics of crime prevention argue through their positions, often reflecting their differing vested interests, ideological positions, or academic backgrounds. Look out for some rather unexpected convergences in view. Emma Bluestocking has convened an *ad hoc* meeting to discuss the principles that should guide crime prevention policy and practice. She welcomes her minister's interest in the issue – a change from the usual crisis management as one set of headlines follows another suggesting that there is a crime wave (guns, knives, romance scams, domestic violence, shop theft, rural crime, fly-tipping, violence against women and girls, cybercrime, ransomware and extortion, child pornography, shop theft, etc.) and that 'The government should do something about it'!

Interested readers will see that two of the protagonists at the meeting, Emma Bluestocking and Frank Candour, were involved in an earlier discussion of smoking cessation, as reported in Pawson and Tilley (1997), although both have moved on from their previous roles. Discussions in which the others have participated have not previously been reported in print. I admit I have awarded Baroness Elizabeth Blue a peerage that has not been awarded to her on the grounds that it should have been! She was a pioneering, progressive police officer who has gone on to make major contributions to public life. I have not met Prudence Pennyfeather in person. What I have her say is based on reading both her work and that of her admirers, on reports of her by friends and colleagues, and on assumptions that she is reasonable in debate. Sir Algernon Appetite is someone met in the course of university and Home Office meetings, as well as at social events. I have known Emma Bluestocking and Frank Candour for a long time as friends, colleagues, and sparring partners whose written work I also know well. I hope it is clear that I have a healthy respect for all those taking part in the following discussion.

DOI: 10.4324/9780429356155-5

I hope, dear reader, that you will find some or all of these characters as irritating and endearing, as well as admirable, as I do. I also hope that you will want to argue with them. There are quite a lot of loose ends. At the end of their discussion, reported here verbatim, I attach a list of sources that those at the meeting provided for Emma Bluestocking. These elaborate the points they were able to make only briefly.

The action takes place in a meeting room at the government department where Emma Bluestocking works.

The dialogue

Emma Bluestocking (E.B.):	Thanks for coming. I have recently assumed departmental responsibility for crime prevention, having moved over from the Department of Health where I was in charge of health promotion. Frying pans and fires spring to mind. Anyway, I've asked you to come here for us to discuss the ethics of crime prevention. I've deliberately invited you because you are bright, articulate, and have diverse views and interests. So please feel free to say what you think. This meeting is being held under Chatham House Rules – nothing said will be attributable to anyone! I don't believe you know each other so let's begin with introductions. Prudence, why don't you begin?
Dr Prudence Pennyfeather (P.P.):	I'm Prue Pennyfeather, and I'm a senior research fellow at St Barnabus College, Harbridge. My background is in law. I have a special interest in public policy, especially as it relates to crime.
Professor Frank Candour (F.C.):	My name is Frank Candour. I've known Emma for many years and was involved in a previous discussion of smoking cessation, when she was at Health and I was Professor of Evaluation Studies at Haleford. I'm still at Haleford, but my interests have now shifted to policy studies.
Baroness Elizabeth Blue (B.B.):	Hello, I'm Betty Blue. I sit as a crossbencher in the House of Lords and was, I think, awarded my peerage for my

Sir Algernon Appetite (A.A.):

E.B.:

P.P.:

B.B.:

charitable work on behalf of victims of crime, in particular women and girls. However, in an earlier life I was Chief Constable of New Yorkshire.

Hi, and I'm Algie Appetite, now based in Chicago. I run an international security company: Keepsafefolk Incorporated.

Thanks. Prue, I gather you've raised some concerns about what you call 'securitisation.' Please, provide us with a brief summary of your main worries.

OK, here goes! Basically, I think that concerns about crime are overstated; that these concerns create undue anxiety and have adverse effects on quality of life where people limit what they do for fear that they will be victims in a dangerous world; that the security industry as well as government has traded on the anxiety about crime to warrant infringements on civil liberties to make money, make political capital, and protect the rich; that what is defined as crime largely reflects dominant social interests; and that the criminal justice system is both ineffective as a means of controlling most crime and regulates the poor rather than the rich and the harms they do. Perhaps I should stop there for now!

I'm not sure I agree with all you say, Prue, but I would add that much crime prevention is guilty of victim-blaming. The classic example is of women who are attacked by men at night and it is suggested that they wear less revealing clothes, that they drink less, that they travel in pairs, and that they do not accept lifts home by men. It needs to be crystal clear that it is the men who are guilty of any physical or sexual attacks they make on women, and no-one else, whatever the women are wearing, wherever they are, whatever they have been drinking, and at whatever time of day. We should never lose sight of that. Less extreme, but equally wrong are suggestions that those who leave their windows open are partly to blame if they suffer burglary and that those whose cars are stolen should make sure that they leave their vehicles in well-lit places and that when at home they hide their keys or cards to make sure that the burglar cannot easily find them to steal the car. For the most part, criminals alone are guilty of crimes and the police need to focus their attention on catching and convicting them, then treating them or putting them away so that they cannot commit further crimes. Punishments should be meted out to deter others who might be tempted to offend, to make them think twice before committing further crimes. That's what we tried in New Yorkshire.

A.A.: Hang on. I disagree with most of what Prue says. I'd like to put in a word for business and the security industry. Businesses are often victims of crime. They also create wealth. My company provides security services to shops, for example some of which suffer huge rates of shop theft that jeopardise their economic viability. Without security measures they would go bust. In practice, detection rates for many crimes are very low, so much so that victims get fed up with reporting them. In an ideal world, people would be kind to one another or the police would always catch people who commit crimes, but that's not the world we live in. We need a dose of realism. The notion that the police are enough to control crime, or that crime prevention can be dispensed with is naïve. The police can do their bit, but others will also choose to use measures to protect themselves from the real crime risks they face, and the security industry has a major part to play in helping them.

E.B.:   Thanks Prue, Betty, and Algie. I can already see that there are conflicting views and that arguments could become heated. Perhaps Frank could help us sort the real bones of contention so that we can explore these coolly.

F.C.:   Thanks Emma; hmph, I'll do my best! OK. Can I start with Prue's interesting and challenging, but wide-ranging critical comments on the whole crime prevention enterprise?

P.P.:   Actually, I was only just beginning.

F.C.:   I get that, but let's start with what we have so far. Take your argument that concerns with crime prevention are overstated. At what level would crime need to be for current crime prevention concerns, policies, and practices to be warranted? Should we be mounting campaigns of reassurance that people are unduly concerned about crime and should therefore abandon their efforts to prevent crime against themselves and others?

P.P.:   Well no, that would be absurd on two grounds. First, a simple thought experiment suggests that advocating the abandonment of crime prevention would be ridiculous. Think of a world where no precautions against crime were taken. Doors were left open. There were no locks. No one took care of their possessions. No one looked out for risks of attack from strangers. We don't have to imagine a state of nature where there is a war of all against all to appreciate that absent any crime prevention activity, crime levels (or rather interpersonal harms now widely defined as crimes) would increase enormously. Indeed, arguably, some are insufficiently worried about crime and some circumstances for crime, for example students going off to university and inadvertently putting themselves at risk. Moreover,

F.C.:

P.P.:

patterns of repeat victimisation, whereby the experience of one crime leads to an increased risk of another, do suggest that those who have suffered crime need greater crime prevention attention.

Given these concessions, in what way are concerns with crime prevention overstated?

My point is that a generalised preoccupation with crime risk, whipped up by businesses profiting from providing crime prevention services, by journalists running scare stories about a lack of control over crime, by police leaders trying to justify their resources, or by politicians trying to ride (or create) a wave of crime and order populism, creates a mood where citizens' quality of life is adversely affected. At worst, a harmful environment of mutual suspicion is created, impeding tolerance and social solidarity. There is a risk that all those involved in the crime prevention enterprise, inadvertently or otherwise, get caught up in inflating concerns with crime to the detriment of the public good. We have entered a surveillance society, where concerns about crime prevention are being used as a warrant for infringing cherished civil liberties.

B.B. and A.A. shake their heads in disbelief.

E.B.:

F.C.:

Betty and Algie, hold your horses, we'll come back to you.

Thanks. Prue, can we now turn to your suggestion that crime prevention is all about serving the interests of dominant groups in society and regulating the poor? How about the regulatory regimes in place relating to workplace safety, disposal of toxic waste, minimum wages, slavery, and protection of workers' rights? The regulations are there to protect the relatively weak, and efforts to prevent the relatively strong from breaching those regulations comprise attempts to protect the weak. Moreover, surely efforts to prevent inter-personal violence, theft, and burglary all serve the interests of subordinate groups as well as superordinate ones show that crime prevention is even-handed.

P.P.:   (Laughing) Whoa. Again, you are right to a point. The definition of some behaviours that are harmful to disadvantaged groups as crimes and efforts then to prevent those crimes does, of course, bring them ben-efits. However, most of those gains were hard won. Moreover, the penalties tend to be low for unlawful behaviours that bene-fit business. A recent crime harm index for England and Wales, for example, made illegal waste disposal among the seventh lowest of 684 crime types, based on sen-tencing of offenders. This says something about the circularity of the harm index itself. Sentencing reflects assumptions about harms, and these assumptions then inform the harm index, reflecting dominant interests. There is no independ-ent measure of harm, so neglected and understated high-harm crime has its low status confirmed. It is reminiscent of Erin Brockovich and her advocacy on behalf of those numerous citizens suffering serious long-term health problems as a result of failures to dispose of toxic waste lawfully. The company involved paid a heavy price in terms of compensation to the victims but without criminal prosecutions. In any case, in the England and Wales harm index, what they did would be accounted as among the lowest harm offences. In addition to this, of course, a minimum level of social order is a precondition for commercial activity, and steps to prevent criminal behaviour are an important part of this. The benefits to individual poten-tial victims are a happy by-product.

E.B.:

Thanks. Again, this is helpful. Let's leave the history of law making and the interests that may or may not be served by it to one side. It is an important issue in its own right of course, but I'd like to maintain our focus on crime prevention activities rather than the definitions of what comprise crimes. What I found especially interesting was the implication that preventive resources may not be devoted to the most harmful crimes experienced by the most vulnerable sections of the community.

P.P.:

Yes, there are risks that preventive resources (assuming that prevention is a good idea!) tend to go towards the less vulnerable (or least disadvantaged generally) at the expense of the more vulnerable (and the most disadvantaged generally). Those less advantaged are shorter of capital, social and otherwise, to devote to reducing their crime risks. This includes both physical crime prevention measures, such as sophisticated locks, alarms, and CCTV, and social ones, such as Neighbourhood Watch. Clearly better-quality security measures cost more than cheaper ones, and organising Neighbourhood Watch and attracting police involvement in it is especially difficult in fractured, high crime neighbourhoods.

E.B.:

Yes, I remember the waste of resources on the rich and worried well from my days working in health! I can see that there may be parallels.

A.A.:

Hang on a moment! We live in a market society and enjoy the benefits of doing so. The free market has stimulated innovations in products people want and improvements in efficiency that make those products affordable to more and more people. We are all carrying cell phones as is now the case among large sections of the population across the globe. None of this would have happened without the operation of market forces. I acknowledge that a side effect of our successes in producing high-quality, portable goods such as those that are craved by most people has made them attractive to thieves. Crime has followed, but so too have innovations in crime prevention that reduce the risk to possible victims. Take the electronic immobiliser. It played a large part in reversing the apparently inexorable rise in car theft. Of course, it made money for those developing and refining the technology and (alongside other changes in car design brought in to thwart the car thief) was initially installed in high-end cars that were affordable only by the relatively rich. However, security devices soon trickled down and nowadays help reduce the crime risks to all. Another example is the kill switch to your mobile phones, which make them less attractive to thieves.

F.C.:   Algie, is this the whole story? Hasn't the market often been led by or stimulated by governmental actions? Or by pressure groups? Should we think of crime prevention as a public good, requiring governmental or organised citizen action to overcome shortcomings in the free market? In the interests of redressing the inequity in the distribution of crime and to protect the most vulnerable, there are schemes to subsidise the costs of upgrading the security of households. In order to make sure that drivers of less expensive cars are protected by the most effective crime prevention technology, minimum standards may be required for electronic immobilisers. Preventive police patrols are directed disproportionately to areas with high rates of crime in the interests of deterring crime in those locations and so on. Crime prevention is, thus, not

necessarily allocated only on market principles. Moreover, citizen groups have been
active in promoting preventive attention
towards those in high need whose vulnerability would not be addressed were the
market alone to determine its allocation.

E.B.:

Betty, apart from your passionate comments on culpability, you have been quiet
so far. I'd be interested now, both in your
capacity as a sometime senior police officer
and as a current champion of victims, to
hear your views on the ethics of crime prevention and on how you would respond to
Algie's and Prue's remarks so far?

B.B.:

Let me begin by donning my ex-police
officer's helmet! Policing is tricky and
faced by competing demands. There are
perennial temptations to cut ethical cor-
ners, and there are genuine ethical dilemmas that go to the heart of police crime
prevention efforts. It is easier to remain
pure-at-heart from the academic or minis-
terial ivory tower than it is to do so in the
complex world of attempting to deliver
defensible crime prevention in real life.
As Prue recognised, we have to fight for
resources, we have to remain independent of politicians but be responsive to
their priorities, we have to deal with news
reporters who typically combine profound
ignorance and profound confidence in the
alarmist impressions of crime they convey
in the interests of flogging their papers.
I also had to deal with corrupt police officers, especially those working in organised
crime, who could be tempted with bribes
by those they were supposed to police.
I therefore had an internal problem of
crime prevention to address but had also to
reassure the public that they could depend
on the police for fair treatment. The temptation is to bend police priorities to please
politicians (themselves often beholden to

party ideologues), to overclaim both achievements and crime risks in the interests of securing greater resources (or to avoid losses in periods of austerity), and to follow media moral panics rather than to deliver services that meet those most in need. I would certainly sign up to a harm-minimising agenda and would want to recognise that this puts crime prevention centre stage but that the role of the police in this can be quite limited. As Algie said, we arrest few now but cannot realistically make substantial improvements in this, given the number of crimes committed and the difficulty detecting many of them. Our resources for patrol are limited although we now realise that these can be used in ways that maximise their potential for producing a preventive effect. Moreover, for the most part we have no control over the social and physical conditions that are conducive to criminal behaviour. That requires others to take action and accept responsibility. In hindsight, I'd be inclined to concede that the police alone can do rather little (although not nothing) to prevent crime and that we should neither claim credit for crime drops nor incur blame for crime increases. These result from causal forces over which we have little or no direct leverage, although we can sometimes help persuade those who are in a position to prevent crime to take action.

E.B.:   Thanks Betty. What you have to say for policing and its compromises comes as no surprise. Parallel compromises happen as government departments jockey for resources. Strong principles play second fiddle to political and personal pragmatics. I imagine this is the case in universities too, Frank and Prue?

P.P. and F.C.:   (looking sheepish and in unison): Fraid so!

E.B.:

B.B.:

Back to you Betty.

I'll now put on my baronial headgear and talk about ethical crime prevention. I'll return to the prevention of sexual crimes against women and girls in particular. Can we arrest our way out of this problem? The answer is almost certainly no, as is the case for most crimes. In terms of prosecution, a cardinal principle is that individuals who are accused are innocent until proven guilty beyond reasonable doubt. For many sexual assaults against adult victims, this clearly comprises a problem. And it's not a question (at least not always) of disbelieving the victim's account. It is also that of the harm done to the victim and the person charged with the crime, if indeed he is innocent. As I said earlier, the perpetrator is guilty, and he alone is guilty of the crime he has perpetrated, and in clashes over what was said or done behind closed doors with both parties having a strong interest in their own accounts, the innocent-till-proven-guilty principle stacks the argument against the woman and in favour of the man. This is not a reason not to prosecute men: it is an argument that doing so routinely will almost inevitably lead to failed convictions in many cases and the hurt experienced on all sides as a consequence. A different preventive approach is needed. I do not believe that advising women and girls to act in ways that reduce their risk implies victim responsibility among those who ignore the advice, any more that it would diminish the offenders' responsibility for most other crimes. It is simply prudent. Of course, in many cases, the advice is pretty redundant: most women and girls already adopt a range of precautionary measures to reduce their risk. There is much to be said for preventive approaches focused on men and those who are well placed to influence both their assumptions about their rights and women's consent and to persuade men that they should control one another's behaviour in situations when sexual assaults are most likely, perhaps in fraternity houses.

F.C.:   Are there any situations, Betty, when blaming the victim is justifiable in the interests of crime prevention?

B.B.:   I need to put my police helmet back on to answer this! There are some circumstances when being a victim produces predictable external costs to third parties. In these circumstances, I think victims do have a duty to reduce their own vulnerability. Shop theft comprises a significant example. A classic study of a store in London's famous Oxford Street, one of the world's most famous places to go shopping, brings my point home. It was a music shop, then selling vinyl records and tapes. They wanted a high turnover so did not remove the disks or cassettes from their packaging. They used a lot of store detectives to catch the thieves. They then called for the police to arrest and charge them. The merchant resisted advice that they run their retail outfit in ways that made them less vulnerable to theft. The number of arrestees produced a highly disproportionate burden on the local police. In my view, the store was blameworthy. The costs to the general public were unacceptable. The store was attracting and tempting shop thieves. The rest of us were paying a high price.[1]

A.A.:   Can I butt in, here? I've been quiet for quite a long time. I know some of my business customers would take a pretty dim view of Betty's comments on their responsibilities. They pay their taxes and expect that in return the state will discharge their responsibilities and protect them from crime. Being blamed for crime they suffer is a bit rich, just as it is for women. In relation to shop theft, stores do their bit in trying to catch criminals. It is for the state to deal with them. Having said that, for commercial reasons it makes a lot of sense for businesses to invest in crime prevention. At worst case, losses from crime can jeopardise a business's economic viability. In these circumstances, the decision to incur crime prevention costs is made for commercial rather than ethical reasons. I know of one chain of shoe shops that displayed shoes in pairs and went bankrupt because of the level of thefts. Displaying only one means more storage space and more staff to fetch the stored shoe. . . . We don't try to sell security devices because customers have a duty to buy them. We supply them because there is a market, and we have to try to innovate and improve devices to make them ever more affordable; otherwise, we will lose out to our competitors. Spending on crime prevention and security is undertaken grudgingly. It yields no direct utility to the individual consumer and falls on the negative side of the balance sheet for companies. We are forced to be smart! If the government wants to discharge its responsibilities to control crime by upping the security levels in high crime businesses, perhaps governments should pay for that security rather than passing the burden of crime control on to businesses!

F.C.: Thanks Algie, but would you accept that businesses have crime prevention responsibilities to third parties whose vulnerability to crime increases as a consequence of commercial activities, from which they profit? For example car park proprietors who show drivers' payments using time-printed tickets to be left on windscreens, who allow open access to their car parks, and who do not staff exits, heighten the risk of car theft for users of the car park; bar owners who continue to serve alcohol to aggressive customers who then go on to commit assaults; and manufactures of mobile phones that are easily stolen and hard to trace. In these cases, the issue is not that of businesses being potential victims but crimes being suffered by others whose criminality is being enabled or provoked by business practices.

A.A.: OK, I do accept that businesses need to be persuaded that they should consider the effects they have on third parties in relation to crime, as for example they have to in relation to toxic waste disposal or health and safety to our employees. But I worry about excessive regulation, which often requires businesses to incur costs where they are unnecessary or to put in place more costly measures than are needed. For example setting minimum security standards for every car park would clearly be unreasonable and unrealistic. Many car parks would suffer crimes only very infrequently, and the costs of the measures would reduce the private sector supply of parking facilities, which are much needed. Business folk are hard-headed and have to be if they are to survive but for the most part are open to appeals to their sense of responsibility. However, we do welcome effective, industry-wide regulation where the costs incurred by responsible businesses put them at a competitive disadvantage in comparison with businesses that prosper because they choose not to discharge their responsibilities. So, we are not altogether opposed to regulation.

E.B.:

P.P.:

Can we come back to Prue now? Prue, I don't think you'd finished your critique of crime prevention. Please, pick up now where you left off.

Thanks, Emma. I want to add three further points. First, crime prevention can often distort public services. Schools are for nurturing and teaching children to think and to understand the world they live in. Schools are not vehicles for crime prevention, to mould children into law-abiding citizens. Social services are for protecting vulnerable children and helping them to thrive, not for controlling them. Improving the life chances of the disadvantaged is important in the interests of social justice, not as a way of diverting young people from crime. Reductions in crime may be a happy side effect of some of these actions, but they are not the reason for them. The kicker is that should it be found that any of these measures taken to increase social justice were to increase crime that would be no reason not to apply them! Economic improvements in the years following the Second World War, the advent of the welfare state, the beginnings of the emancipation of women as they joined the labour market in growing numbers, and the new-found freedom of youth all seem to have produced crime as an unintended side effect. I don't think anyone would want to reverse them because doing so might reduce crime! Second, some forms of situational crime prevention are both ugly and exclusionary. City centres with shutters, gated communities, and shopping malls that make 'undesirables' unwelcome are all cases in point. Here, even if the crime prevention is effective, its social and physical form makes it unacceptable. Third, in more general terms, focusing on crime prevention is socially divisive, giving rise to mutual suspicion, intolerance towards anyone looking different, and, as we noted earlier, ever growing surveillance that undermines civil liberties, in particular privacy.

F.C.: So, what would you do, Prue? Ban crime prevention? Make it entirely a private matter, where the state takes no interest? Confine concern with crime to the criminal justice system, ensuring those suspected are given a fair trial and are penalised accordingly, aiming for just deserts rather than any effect on future criminal behaviour?

P.P.: I'm mainly a critic. It is for others to make suggestions that are not open to the valid objections I make to crime prevention. I conceded earlier that abandoning crime prevention would be absurd. Indeed, it would almost be unnatural. Other members of the animal kingdom routinely act in ways that reduce their risks from potential predators. Their spikes, colours, smells, cries, hiding places, and so on are there because of their advantages for survival from potential predators and hence advantage in procreation. Although the social world humans inhabit is rather different from the ecological niches occupied by other animals (and for that matter plants), there is something fundamental about our efforts to reduce our vulnerability to risks from others' behaviours that we now widely define as crimes. So, in this sense, crime prevention is here to stay. I certainly try to reduce my own vulnerability. You've been to my house, Frank. You will know that I have locks, bars, an alarm, and CCTV to try to make my place as impenetrable as I can. And I do think the main responsibility of the state in relation to crime is to secure justice in relation to those properly found to be guilty of crime. I would be inclined to regulate forms of crime prevention that threaten social justice, for example by excluding people or otherwise infringing their civil liberties.

A.A.: I'm rather surprised but also pleased to find myself agreeing with much that Prue says. I favour a libertarian position with minimal state interference. Things go awry when the state steps in. Deleterious unintended consequences frequently follow. Leave crime prevention as much as possible as a private matter. Let people pay for their own protection as they think they need it or as they prioritise it in use of their resources. The market will provide for the supply of citizens' desires for crime prevention. I'm confident that there will be enough demand that I can make money from supplying security. However, I fear that some of you might not like this approach because it does nothing to reduce the variations in crime impact across different sections of the community, where the costs of effective crime prevention make a small dent in the income of the well-to-do but a large one for the poor who are most vulnerable to many types of crime.

B.B.: I have to say that the direction the discussion is taking, though interesting, worries me a lot. I worry about the harms done to victims. I remember that Sir Robert Peel put prevention at the centre of policing. Modern approaches to policing stress the need to respond in a preventive way to troubles the public expect the police to deal with. Moreover, as I intimated earlier, the police recognise that they are not able to put in place many measures needed to deal with the crime problems the public bring to them. Third parties have to be brought in. They must be 'responsibilised' if effective measures are going to be put in place. The anarchy of the market where 'anything goes' is in my view a recipe for disaster. It leaves many unprotected, and it leaves the market for crime prevention open to charlatans selling the crime prevention equivalent of snake oil. Treating victims justly involves taking their concerns seriously and doing our best to reduce risks to them. The vulnerable women and girls in whose interests my charity now works need informed and sensitive preventive help. It seems to me that they have a right to expect that. The quite proper concern that justice be done for alleged perpetrators does not mean that public servants either cannot or ought not to be concerned with their practical protection.

E.B.: (Interrupting) We need to begin winding up now. I have another meeting focused on counterterrorist strategies in 15 minutes and I need to prepare for that.

A.A.: But I have more to say . . .

P.P.: And so do I.

E.B.: Sorry, as I say I have to leave very soon, and I'd like to ask Frank, who has for most part been listening to what the rest of you have been saying, to try to draw the threads together, and help me feed into advice to ministers on a crime prevention policy. Frank . . .

F.C.: It is clear that this discussion could go on and on. We have certainly not followed up on all the points made. There is no doubt that although at first sight crime prevention looks a common-sense activity performed by well-meaning people for the general good, behind the surface it raises some knotty ethical issues. That said, I do detect some convergence in views. First, crime prevention in one form or another is here to stay, at least for the foreseeable future. Second, there is some role for the state in supplying and/or regulating crime prevention activities. Third, issues of distributive justice cannot be sidestepped in relation both to crime harms and crime harm prevention. Fourth, the police alone cannot realistically assume full responsibility for preventing crime. This implies some sharing of responsibility among those competent to prevent crime. Fifth, it follows that even if criminal responsibility rests ultimately with the offender, this does not mean that no one else has any crime harm prevention responsibilities. Sixth, it again follows that the key ethical question is not whether or not crime prevention is a good thing but rather what comprises good crime prevention. The practical issue for Emma is that of advising ministers about what comprises good crime prevention and how it might best be supplied.

E.B.: (laughing) I'm not sure that everyone would agree with all this, Frank. I detect something of your own spin . . .

A.A., B.B., and P.P. join in laughter and nod.

E.B.: So, have you any advice, Frank, on ways forward? At the level of abstraction you use in your summary, the supposed convergence in views is not very useful. How should we urge whom to do what in relation to crime prevention? How could we characterise good crime prevention?

F.C.: Ouch! Let me try. As you know, the classic means used by the state to encourage people to do what they would otherwise choose not to do fall into three broad categories: sticks, carrots, and sermons. There are practical as well as ethical issues at stake in choosing between them. Sermons are cheap, appealing to the moral sense of those addressed, but they are easily ignored by those not wanting to change the behaviour from which they benefit. Carrots are expensive but effective in appealing to the self-interest of those provided with them: they can also be criminogenic in attracting fraudulent claims. Sticks are intrusive, inflexible, often backfire, and can lead to resentful and minimal compliance. Different forms of encouragement will be needed for different people in relation to different actions. Some are responsive some of the time to some exhortations relating to some behaviours. The same goes for carrots and sticks. The choice has to be context sensitive. We need to produce and test 'context-mechanism-outcome pattern configurations' for sticks, carrots, and sermons, as espoused by realist evaluators, focusing on unintended as well as intended outcomes, just as we do in relation to crime prevention measures. Sorry, I'm back to my earlier evaluation obsessions.

E.B.:

Get off your hobbyhorse, Frank! We get the message. Move on to how we might characterise good crime prevention in light of today's discussion.

F.C.:

Point taken! I *would* argue, however, that we should be empirical when we can be in selecting both methods of eliciting compliance to advice and in the crime prevention activity we encourage, as well as making sure that what we do and what we advocate is principled. Indeed, encouraging crime prevention in ineffective ways or encouraging ineffective crime prevention would seem to me itself to be unethical! I suspect that we'd all agree that one of the desiderata of any crime prevention measure that is put in place is that it is effective or rather that it produces net benefits in terms of outcomes and that teasing these out empirically is therefore important.

I guess we'd also agree that other things being equal, crime prevention measures, be they physical or social, that are aesthetically neutral or attractive, convenient to use, do not jeopardise civil liberties, are socially inclusive and are costly in terms of neither money nor effort, are preferable to those that are ugly, inconvenient, intrusive of civil liberties, socially divisive, or costly in terms of money or effort. I doubt whether any of us would quarrel with pursuing an agenda where the direction is from the latter set of qualities towards the former. The problem is that at any given point in time, there may have to be trade-offs between reductions in crime risk and achieving other requirements of crime prevention policies, practices and designs. . . . If the problem is serious enough and the risk of experiencing it high enough, my guess is that most would accept that measures that would otherwise be objectionable become tolerable.

E.B.: I'm not sure you would all agree with Frank's summing up. I suspect he heard what he wanted to hear and used it to prop up his own prejudices! I'd like to thank you all for coming. I'm sorry we can't go on. It falls to me now to feed this discussion as best I can into yet another new crime prevention strategy being prepared by the government. If there are readings that help spell out your positions more fully, please send them to me. Be aware, however, that the strategy will almost inevitably be more populist than principled and more attentive to political hacks and influential tweeters than thoughtful and knowledgeable folk like yourselves and the literature I'm hoping you'll refer me to. What ministers will likely want is a new slogan. Again, if you have any thoughts do let me know: no more than ten words, memorable, and motherhood and apple pie in its sentiments – the slogan doesn't have to mean much in practice! Finally, don't forget to hand your passes in as you leave. You will see that we take great care to minimise the risks of terrorist attacks from those entering the building. We take for granted that the small inconvenience warrants the reduction in risk!

Later in the day . . .

Emma returns home. She is greeted by her partner, Chris.

Chris: How was your day?

Emma: As ever interesting. I'd like to help ministers develop an effective and ethical crime prevention strategy. Today, I met with a variety of clever people with different perspectives to discuss principles for crime prevention.

Chris: Was it useful?

Emma: Yes and no. Yes, there is more common ground than I expected. Yes, it's refreshing to be asked to consider ethical issues in crime prevention strategy development. But no, the remaining differences are significant, and I doubt they can easily be reconciled. Moreover, it's hard realistically to get ministers, poor dears, to look beyond short-term personal and political self-interest. But, as a public servant, I'll do my best!

Exercise: Draft a two-page note from Emma to her minister, summarising the meeting and the implications of what was said.

Note

1 See Chapter 6 which discusses this example and shop-theft prevention more generally.

References sent to Emma

Ayres, I., & Braithwaite, J. (1992). *Responsive regulation*. Oxford: Oxford University Press.

Clarke, R., & Bowers, K. (2017). Seven misconceptions of situational crime prevention. In N. Tilley & A. Sidebottom (Eds.), *Handbook of crime prevention and community safety* (2nd ed., pp. 109–142). London: Routledge.

Ekblom, P. (1986). *The prevention of shop theft: An approach through crime analysis* (p. 5). London: Home Office.

Ekblom, P. (2010). *Crime prevention, security and community safety using the 5IS framework*. Houndsmill, Basingstoke: Macmillan.

Ekblom, P. (2017). Crime prevention through product design. In N. Tilley & A. Sidebottom (Eds.), *Handbook of crime prevention and community safety* (2nd ed., pp. 207–233). London: Routledge.

Engstad, P., & Evans, J. (1980). Responsibility, competence and police effectiveness in crime control. In R. Clarke & M. Hough (Eds.), *The effectiveness of policing* (pp. 139–162). Farnborough: Gower.

Farrell, G., & Tilley, N. (2020). Elegant security: Concept, evidence and implications. *European Journal of Criminology*, 19(5), 932–953. doi:10.1177/1477370820932107

Felson, M., & Clarke, R. (1997). The ethics of situational crime prevention. In G. Newman, R. V. Clarke, & S. G. Shoham (Eds.), *Rational choice and situational crime prevention*. Aldershot: Ashgate.

Garland, D. (2012). *The culture of control: Crime and social order in contemporary society*. Oxford: Oxford University Press.

Goold, B., Loader, I., & Thumala, A. (2010). Consuming security? Tools for a sociology of security consumption. *Theoretical Criminology*, 14(1), 3–30.

Hardie, J., & Hobbs, B. (2005). Partners against crime: The role of the corporate sector in tackling crime. In R. Clarke & G. Newman (Eds.), *Designing out crime from products and systems: Crime prevention studies 18* (pp. 85–140). Monsey, NY: Criminal Justice Press.

Hazelbaker, K. (1997). Insurance industry analyses and the prevention of motor vehicle theft. In M. Felson & R. Clarke (Eds.), *Business and crime prevention* (pp. 283–293). Monsey, NY: Criminal Justice Press.

Laycock, G. (2004). The UK car theft index: An example of government leverage. In M. Maxfield & R. Clarke (Eds.), *Understanding and preventing car theft: Crime prevention studies 17* (pp. 25–44). Monsey, NY: Criminal Justice Press.

Matthews, R. (Ed.). (2016). *What is to be done about crime and punishment towards a "public criminology"* (pp. 89–122). London: Palgrave Macmillan.

Neocleous, M. (2007). Security, commodity, fetishism. *Critique*, 35(3), 339–355. doi:10.1080/03017600701676738

Reiner, R. (2016). *Crime*. Cambridge: Polity Press.

Scott, M. (2005). Shifting and sharing responsibility to address public safety problems. In N. Tilley (Ed.), *Handbook of crime prevention and community safety* (pp. 385–409). Cullompton: Willan.

Shearing, C., & Stenning, P. (1992). From the Panoptican to Disney World: The development of discipline. In R. Clarke (Ed.), *Situational crime prevention: Successful case studies* (pp. 249–255). New York: Harrow and Heston.

Squires, P. (2017). Community safety and crime prevention: A critical reassessment. In N. Tilley & A. Sidebottom (Eds.), *Handbook of crime prevention and community safety* (2nd ed., pp. 32–53). London: Routledge.

Thumala, A., Goold, B., & Loader, I. (2011). A tainted trade? Moral ambivalence and legitimation work in the private security industry. *The British Journal of Sociology*, 62(2), 283–303. doi:10.1111/j.1468-4446.2011.01365.x

Tilley, N. (2012a). Community, security and distributive justice. In V. Ceccato (Ed.), *The urban fabric of crime and fear* (pp. 267–282). Cham, Switzerland: Springer.

Tilley, N. (2012b). Crime reduction: Responsibility, regulation, and research. *Criminology and Public Policy*, 11(2), 361–378. doi:10.1111/j.1745-9133.2012.00814.x

Tilley, N. (2018). Privatising crime control. *Annals of the American Academy of Political and Social Science*, 679(1), 55–71. doi:10.1177/0002716218775045

Tonry, M. (2004). *Punishment and politics: Evidence and emulation in the making of English crime control policy*. London: Routledge.

Von Hirsch, A., Garland, D., & Wakefield, A. (Eds.), (2000). *Ethical and social perspectives on situational crime prevention*. Oxford: Hart Publishing. doi:10.5040/9781472562258

Zedner, L. (2003). Too much security? *International Journal of the Sociology of Law*, 31, 155–184. doi:10.1016/j.ijsl.2003.09.002

6 Doing crime prevention

Pretty much everyone does crime prevention. It is perfectly natural. We referred in Chapter 1 to predation prevention measures in nature. Birds, insects, reptiles, mammals, and even plants do it. Patterns of survival turn on predation prevention strategies. If the strategies are too weak, extinction follows. This is the acid test where the effectiveness of predation prevention strategies is at issue.

In this chapter, we begin with doing crime prevention in the private sector for the private sector, illustrating what is involved with the example of shoplifting prevention where a retailer's survival may be at stake. We then turn to 'public' crime prevention by which I mean prevention that involves the state and its public sector organisations, most notably the police. As will become clear, both involve similar processes of problem-solving where what is done needs to be adapted to the particular conditions within which preventive interventions are called for.

Private sector crime prevention: shoplifting

Retail organisations can thrive or fail for lots of reasons. One source of failure is crime. Too much loss through crime will lead a business to fail. Short of failure, businesses lose potential profits through crime. But there is a dilemma. Preventive measures generally cost money. If costs exceed the benefits from reduced losses, it will not be worth devoting resources to prevention. Retailers therefore need to work out what preventive measures will lead to net benefits for them.

On a Home Office advisory group, I heard the representative of a large retailers' organisation argue strongly that it was the responsibility of the police and the criminal justice system to prevent retail thefts by arresting shoplifters, prosecuting them, getting them convicted, and then punishing them. The shop would try to identify offenders and detain suspects and expected the police then to arrive quickly to take the offenders away and charge them. Shop theft is, it was supposed, committed by bad people in

DOI: 10.4324/9780429356155-6

need of punishment. They would be deterred by the prospect of that punishment. The retailers' preferred preventive strategy was to pass on most of the costs to the public purse – after all they pay taxes. This position embraced the fundamental attribution error which, as we saw in Chapter 4, involves treating crime exclusively as a product of offender attributes while ignoring the attributes of situations conducive to crime.

An alternative view is that shops can be run in ways that proffer greater or fewer opportunities for shop theft. Although shoplifting has a very long history (Bamfield, 2012), self-service shops in particular furnished fresh temptations and opportunities, where customers can handle goods rather than having to look at them one at a time, asking a shop assistant to retrieve them from a locked cabinet or back storage space (see Tilley, 2010). Self-service is cheap and attractive to customers. Customers and retailers both see the benefits. But self-service is criminogenic. To reduce shop theft, preventive measures are needed.

The weaknesses and costs of the arrest strategy for preventing retail theft were brought out in a study by Ekblom (1986). Ekblom focused on a music store in London's Oxford Street. The preventive strategy was to employ store detectives to catch shoplifters. The detectives then called the police who were expected to take over. This was quite expensive but not very effective in preventing shop thefts. It also put huge pressure on the police – some 40% of calls to the police for shop theft in the police district covering Oxford Street came from this one store. The problem, as Ekblom saw it, was that the retailer put the entire product (records and cassettes) on display in the shop rather than just the cover. This saved the costs incurred by storing whole products behind the counter and then finding and retrieving them for customers. Ekblom argued, however, that there were better ways of reducing shop theft in the store than arrest. Changes in the store layout and management could be introduced to reduce opportunities in relation to the types of product that were most often stolen.

The strength of Ekblom's analysis was brought home to me when a local cut-price shoe shop went bust. A large contributary factor was shop theft. The low prices were achieved by displaying pairs of shoes rather than single ones, which meant that the shop assistant did not have to retrieve pairs from the store room at the back of the shop. Here, the balance between a widely used but expensive preventive strategy and the losses from shop theft seemed to favour acceptance of the costs of prevention.

What will be effective and economically worthwhile for retailers attempting to reduce shop theft is not obvious. There are various strategies. I've mentioned detection, arrest, and deterrence as those that do not seem to have a good track record. Here are some others (see also Clarke & Petrossian, 2013; Tilley, 2010).

- Keep goods behind the counter: this is generally used by retailers of small high-value goods or for high-value goods sold by general retailers. Think jewellers and retailers of CRAVED items such as cameras, expensive cosmetics, cigarettes, mobile phones, and classy handbags (see Chapter 4 for an explanation of CRAVED).
- Keep CRAVED items close to the till where they can be seen by shop assistants (often used for small computer peripherals).
- Maximise natural surveillance within stores, with mirrors, wide aisles, clear lines of sight, and training for store staff to look out for likely shop thieves to make clear to them that they are a focus of attention.
- De-anonymise customers by welcoming them as they enter the store and hence reminding them that they have been noticed.
- Install CCTV so that shop thieves can more easily be detected and detained and/or to give customers a sense that they are at increased risk of being detected if they steal from the shop.
- Introduce signage of various kinds to remind customers that shop theft is a crime and that they will be prosecuted if they are found committing it.
- Cooperate with fellow retailers in a given area so that shoplifting suspects' details can be circulated in real time thereby enabling others to be on their guard should the suspect enter their shop.
- Restrict the number of shoppers allowed into the shop to improve the chances of watching each of them (and making them aware they are being watched). This is often done with children in small sweetshops.
- Attach security tags to goods that are removed or deactivated only when the goods are paid for. These tags may increase risk to the shoplifter if they trigger an alarm as the thief leaves the store or may reduce the value of the stolen item as an indelible dye is released when the tag is forcibly removed from the stolen item.

Shopkeepers will often be unaware of the extent and nature of their shop-theft problem. An observational study, systematically watching a random sample of those entering a store, found that shop theft is quite common (Buckle and Farrington, 1984 report that 1.8% of the 503 shoppers tracked for an average of 6.9 minutes in a store in Peterborough were seen shoplifting). Self-report survey studies examining crimes people say they have committed also find shop theft to be widespread (Tilley, 2010) but with substantial variations across studies. For example Kivivuori (2007) found that across Nordic and Scandinavian capitals – Copenhagen, Helsinki, Oslo, and Stockholm – between 25% and 32% of males and between 19% and 25% of females aged 13–16 years said they had already shoplifted. Tilley (2010, pp. 54–55) summarises findings from 11 British self-report studies between 1963 and 2008. One in 1967 found that 70% of

London males aged 13–16 years said that they had shoplifted. Another in 1983 found that just 2.4% of males and 1.3% of females aged 14–15 years across England and Wales said they had shoplifted at least once where they had stolen goods worth at least £1. Yet another study in 2006 reported 11.8% of males and 16.1% of females aged 14–15 years in Peterborough had shoplifted in the past year, with an average of 3 offences for boys and 2.6 for girls.

Victimisation surveys and recorded crime depend on traders identifying shop thefts, shop recording and reporting practices, and police crime-recording decisions, all of which are liable to change and to vary from place to place.[1] Routinely, however, individual retailers will generally have a hazy idea of sources of stock 'shrinkage.' These may include delivery shortfalls, wastage, damaged goods, free gifts, spoilt goods, and staff theft, for example, as well as shop theft. Retailers may also not know which preventive strategies are most effective in general or which will serve their own preventive needs most effectively. Research in this area is sparse,[2] and the needs of individual retailers are liable to vary by shop location, the range of goods sold, customer base, transport links to and from the shop, and other nearby retailers. Moreover, shoplifters are themselves adaptable.

The efficacy of a preventive measure at one time may not be found at another as techniques to overcome preventive interventions are devised and disseminated (see Sidebottom & Tilley, 2018). For example some widely used types of security tag can be overcome, and guidance on how to do so is available on the Internet. Shop staff are also adaptable. For example there is some evidence that where security technologies are put in place, staff vigilance can go down as it is no longer deemed necessary (Beck & Willis, 1999). Moreover, technologies change as the 'same' intervention may change over time. CCTV cameras have become cheaper and images of offenders clearer. Security tags have evolved in efforts to improve them as offenders learn to overcome earlier versions.

Hunter, Garius, Hamilton, and Wahidin (2018) report a study where they interviewed 32 prolific shoplifters in an English city, the vast majority of whom indicated that the offences for which they had been convicted represented only a tiny proportion of all their shop thefts. Hunter et al. found that these 'expert' offenders were sensitive to security measures and adapted their behaviour accordingly. Their choice of when to steal, for example, was attuned to their knowledge of the times when security guards would not be on duty or when staffing levels were low. They could circumvent some CCTV systems by being attentive to the direction in which the cameras were pointing. They would observe the responses (or lack of responses) to alarms set off when customers left the store and steal when they saw low levels of vigilance (there are many false activations, and this leads staff to reduce attention to them, not least because of hostile customer reactions). Prolific shoplifters were well-aware of means to circumvent security tags. Moreover, they shared their expertise with one another.

What we do not know is the proportion of shop thefts that can be attributed to prolific shoplifters and the proportion that can be attributed to occasional shoplifters. Measures that are ineffective among experts may be effective among occasional or one-off shoplifters who lack the skills or confidence to ignore or circumvent security measures. Some shoplifters may simply be seduced by the ready availability of tempting goods to steal and the apparent ease with which they can be taken. Moreover, among prolific shoplifters we do not know what proportion are stealing from shops to raise funds for illicit drugs, nor the numbers whose drug-taking is fuelled by the ease with which funds to buy illicit drugs can be obtained through shop theft.

Decisions about what crime prevention measures to use have to take account of the major aim of retailers – to make money. Some security measures occupy staff time that could be spent on other activities to increase sales and thereby contribute to the profitability of the business. Tags again furnish a useful example. It takes time to fit them and to remove them. Moreover, in busy times, shop assistants may forget to remove them much to the annoyance of their customers, risking goodwill, reputation, and future sales. In a recent study focused on tags as a way of reducing shop theft, we heard of retailers suspending their use at busy times, such as during sales, on the grounds that at these periods the bottom line was better served by tolerating avoidable shop-theft losses in the interests of greater sales and the profits thereby produced.

Let us suppose now that we are a retailer concerned about the effect of shop theft on our bottom line. We want to reduce losses from shop theft in a cost-effective way. We may also be a retailer with a social conscience, concerned that by making shop theft easy we may inadvertently be facilitating illicit drug-taking and the harms that this may produce. We realise we may also be facilitating 'debut crimes' that propel some into more serious criminal careers. How do we go about preventing shop theft in an informed way? The answer lies in problem-solving and action research.

Ekblom (1988) lays out a basic model that applies to all crime problems, as shown in Figure 6.1. This action research approach is described also in Clarke (2002) and lies at the heart of problem-oriented policing as initially advocated by Herman Goldstein (1979, 1990) and operationalised as the SARA model by Eck and Spelman (1987). It is also the model exemplified in the Kirkholt Burglary Prevention Project, as discussed in Chapter 2.

Some small retailers will be confident that they know what they are losing through shop theft. Many others will not. They may be able to estimate shrinkage, but sources of shrinkage will often be unclear. Moreover, even when the proportion of shrinkage that can be attributed to shop theft is evident, that will not provide the detail needed for targeted and cost-effective

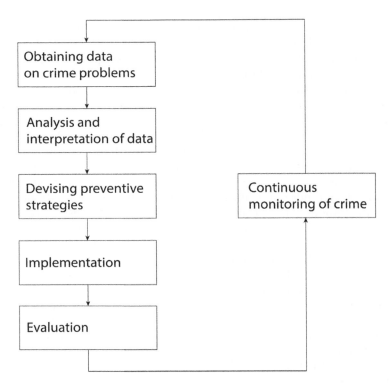

Figure 6.1 Ekblom's preventive process.

preventive interventions. The starting point for shop-theft prevention is, therefore, to develop a clear, detailed, and quantified description of the problem. This involves looking at crime concentrations of the sort discussed in Chapter 3. Questions under the following headings need to be asked:

Data on the crime problem

- What proportion of shrinkage can be attributed to shop theft?
- What losses are incurred through shop theft?
- What is being stolen?
- Where are the thefts taking place (stores, locations in stores)?
- When are thefts taking place (although this will generally be tricky to gauge)?
- Who is committing the shop thefts that are occurring (organised groups, occasional impulsive shop thieves, prolific shop thieves, employees)?

- What are the trends over time?
- Are there seasonal patterns?

Analysis and interpretation

Having mapped out the extent of the problem and how it is concentrated, the next stage is to work out what is producing the observed patterns.

- What makes the commonly stolen products attractive to thieves (e.g. what CRAVED attributes they have)?
- What makes the locations of the thefts attractive to thieves (multiple entrances and exits, blind spots, staff indifference or collusion, convenience for likely shoplifters, goods sold, etc.)?
- What explains the times when goods are stolen (lack of staff on duty, busy staff unable to provide surveillance, when likely shop thieves are about, etc.)?
- What attracts which types of shop thief stealing from the store (for example what's stolen; what's done with the goods taken; methods of access to and escape from the shop; attributes of the surrounding area/community facilitating the supply of likely shoplifters)?

It will never be possible to find out everything about a shop-theft problem. Dodgy records of offences and offender characteristics, the churn of offender populations, emerging adaptive offender techniques, changing products, the expense of primary research focused on offenders, the time needed to check and recheck findings, the urgency of putting interventions in place, and so on all mean that scanning and analysis will always be partial and provisional. A sensible 'stopping point' for practical problem-solving purposes will be when it is believed that enough is known with sufficient confidence to develop a preventive strategy that warrants the costs and risks of trialling it. What amounts to enough will depend on the extent of the problem and the resources available to the retailer.

Developing a preventive strategy

A strong analysis should inform decisions over which preventive interventions to abandon and which to add.

- What measures, if any, are currently in place to reduce shop theft and how well are they working (security guards, CCTV, mirrors, etc.)?
- How might conditions attracting, tempting, or enabling the types of shoplifters taking from the store be changed to make shop theft (seem) too risky, too difficult, or insufficiently rewarding (e.g. CCTV, shop layout,

mirrors, and size and distribution of display units providing for clear lines of sight)?

- How might payment for goods be facilitated and avoidance of payment made more difficult for shoplifters (e.g. staff to hand, tills, automatic scanning of goods leaving the store)?
- How might the specific goods being targeted be protected effectively and economically by making their theft seem too risky, insufficiently rewarding, and/or too difficult for the types of shoplifter stealing from the store (e.g. tags, locked display cabinets, goods kept behind the counter)?
- What might be done to reduce shop theft at times when it tends to take place, by making it too difficult, too risky, or insufficiently rewarding (e.g. collaborative early-warning systems for gangs of shoplifters, adjusting staffing patterns – such as arranging staff breaks so that the shop floor is not left without sufficient supervision at peak shop-theft times, and controlling access to the shop when groups of thieves may provide cover for one another as they steal)?
- What relevant evidence is there to draw on in relation to the potential effectiveness of particular measures that might be introduced in relation to the shop's specific circumstances?

Evaluation

An informed shop-theft prevention strategy is no guarantee that it will be successful or that it cannot be improved. Moreover, checking on unwanted side effects may avoid using measures that are causing unnecessary damage to the business. Hence, putting in place provisions for evaluation is important.

- Are the interventions (individually or jointly) producing a fall in the shop-theft problem, in the short-, medium-, and longer term?
- Are shop thieves successfully adapting to the interventions that have been put in place?
- If focused on specific products that are being stolen, are other unprotected items being stolen instead?
- If focused on thefts from specific locations, are others being targeted instead?
- Are the interventions being cost-effective in their preventive impact?
- Are staff members being less attentive to shop theft because they assume that preventive measures have dealt with the problem?
- How are customers responding to the preventive measures (e.g. by resenting being treated as suspicious, being reassured by CCTV systems, being annoyed by alarms ringing, etc.)?

Continuous monitoring

Shop theft problems change, for example with the development of new hot products and through adaptations by shoplifters. Hence, final solutions to most shop-theft problems are unlikely. Monitoring is therefore needed.

- How are shop-theft patterns changing (goods being stolen, population of shop thieves, locations of thefts, times of thefts, etc.)?
- Are the intervention measures put in place still relevant and effective (technology, staff behaviours, thief behaviours)?
- Are adjustments needed in view of changes that are occurring?
- Can effective shop theft be delivered at a lower cost?

Applying the problem-solving approach

There is a substantial literature on shop theft and its prevention that those trying to address their problem can draw on. Some of this reflects carefully designed experiments, where intervention and control groups are compared, at best using random allocation, which try to assess the effectiveness of measures that are being trialled (see Farrington et al., 1993 and Hayes and Downes, 2011 for excellent examples). However, acknowledged implementation difficulties for such experiments are endemic. Moreover, in the interest of controlling for external factors impinging on theft patterns, very specific conditions facilitating accurate measurement are required which may reduce the relevance of findings beyond the particulars of the experimental conditions (Pawson & Tilley, 1997). Such experiments can enjoy high levels of internal validity (we can be pretty sure that they tell us whether an intervention had the effects that are measured). This means we can infer that the intervention can produce those effects. However, external validity (the degree to which the findings hold elsewhere with other populations and at other times) is much more questionable (see more on this in Chapter 7). In the case of retail theft, products, places, times, offender mixes, and so on vary widely meaning that what held for some specific experimental conditions might not hold elsewhere. Judgement is needed by those drawing on experimental findings as when drawing on other types of research.

What this means is that the retailer adopting a problem-solving approach has to take a pragmatic approach, often working with informed hunches about answers to the questions listed earlier, checking those hunches in proportion to their importance for decision-making and the ease with which relevant data can be acquired.

Drawing on a wide range of research and case studies of shop-theft reduction, including (but not restricted to) carefully designed experiments, Clarke and Petrossian catalogue what findings for different responses suggest in terms of how they work, the conditions for them to work best, possible side effects, and additional considerations in deciding whether to adopt them. Table 6.1 is a very brief summary of their own table, which tries to capture what they discuss in their text. The significance of the approach adopted by Clarke and Petrossian (which is used also in sister guides focused on a wide range of other targets for crime prevention – see ASU Centre for Problem-Oriented Policing, 2022a) is that it does not assume that crime prevention interventions work unconditionally in all circumstances. Rather, they depend on conducive contexts. Interventions may also produce unintended negative effects and in addition may be inadvisable on grounds other than their crime prevention efficacy. Clarke and Petrossion's table thus reflects 'best' theory as we described it in Chapter 4. Given uncertainties over all interventions in the unique conditions of any specific intervention and the processes of adaptation by offenders, staff, and paying customers, it is important to monitor what is being achieved, to adjust as necessary, and to try to take lessons for future practice and policy.

Figure 6.2 shows a logic model specifically for security tags used to try to reduce shop theft (Sidebottom & Tilley, 2018, p. 392). It summarises the detailed considerations needed in relation to their adoption as an intervention to help reduce shop theft. It lists mechanisms that may prevent shop theft, as intended (mechanisms A). It also shows mechanisms that may operate unintentionally to produce unwanted effects (mechanisms B). It highlights that any particular use of tags will take place in particular contextual conditions that will be crucial for the activation of mechanisms producing their own outcome patterns.

Bigger retailers can conduct more systematic shop theft problem-solving exercises than small shops. For small shops, shopkeepers will often know in detail what is happening by way of shop theft patterns and losses, although they may sometimes be at a loss as to what they alone can do about them, and many will want to pass responsibility for shop theft prevention onto the police.

When conducting our review of research relating to the effectiveness of tags in reducing shop theft, we spoke to some large-scale retailers. We found that at least some tried to adopt a problem-solving approach. This included identifying the products that tended to be sold that also led to high losses, the locations in the shops from which items were most often stolen, the time taken and consequential costs of applying and removing security tags, and the practicalities of displaying goods with security tags attached to them. These retailers also monitored the patterns of theft before and after the introduction of the tags.

The crime prevention experts working in these stores spoke of the tensions between those with marketing or sales responsibilities and those with loss prevention responsibilities. Apparently, the former were not much

Intervention	Mechanism(s)	Conducive context	Side effects/considerations
1. Modify shop layout	Facilitate surveillance, increase perceived risk	Trained and motivated staff	Cheapish but sometimes hard to implement in practice
2. Tighten stock controls	Facilitates the detection of rares and patterns of shop theft	Managers incentivised to reduce shop theft	Source tagging will improve stock control
3. Warning notices attached to products	Alerts potential shoplifters to attention paid to them, increase perceived risk	Most effective if attached to hot products	Low cost, might alarm some shoppers
4. More sales staff	Harder for shoplifters to operate	Staff increases at high-risk times	Liable to be expensive
5. Security guards	Increase perceived risk	Trained security staff with active visible presence	Poor guards have no effect
6. Civil recovery	Recoups some costs from shop theft; deterrence of those caught	Clear and simple admit procedures	Not an option for small retailers lacking time and resources for it
7. Informal police sanctions	May deter but saves time for retailer, police, and Criminal Justice system	Linked to efforts to change attitudes to shop theft	Normally applied only to juvenile/first-time offenders
8. CCTV	Focused on hot products, identifies offenders and provides evidence for charges	Cameras close to key areas; high-quality kit	Employee training in use of kit; staff soon become fatigued from watching monitors
9. Electronic article surveillance (EAS – tags)	Detects offenders leaving with stolen goods	Tags hard to remove without damaging goods	Expensive; staff may become complacent about other antitheft policies
10. Ink tags	Removes rewards from stolen goods	If combined with EAS	Can be circumvented; customer irritation of tags not removed
11. Early-warning system (of active shoplifters), often in partnership with other retailers	Allows for pre-emptive action to remove the element of surprise for organised shoplifting groups	Relevant to stores where organised shoplifters operate	Low-cost sensible precaution for stores vulnerable to organised shoplifters
12. Store detectives	Deters casual shoplifters	Large stores (otherwise store detectives recognised)	Store detectives identified by organised shoplifters
13. Arrest and prosecute shoplifters	Specific and general deterrence	Perceived chances of detection high	Generally low risk of being caught shoplifting
14. Shame first-time offenders	First-time offenders learn not to repeat	Sanction is combined with some other informal sanction	Uncertain effective, most promising with young offenders
15. Ban known shoplifters	Denies opportunities to offend	Publicity for names of those convicted	Possible legal challenge of shoplifters not convicted in court.
16. Public information campaign	Encourages reporting; increases the understanding of penalties	Used to advertise new anti-shoplifting measures	Little evidence that these campaigns reduce shop theft

Source: Summarised from a selection taken from Clarke and Petrossian (2013) and available through ASU Centre for Problem-Oriented Policing (2022a).

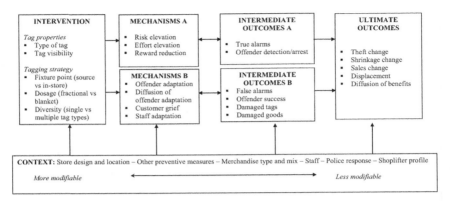

Figure 6.2 A logic model for product tagging as an intervention to reduce shop theft.
Source: From Sidebottom and Tilley (2018, p. 392).

concerned with the ways in which sales practices might tempt and facilitate theft. The latter were not much concerned with ways in which security measures might slow sales. The compromise in one store chain seemed to be to change focus according to which was deemed most likely best to maximise profitability: focus on loss (and hence theft) prevention in quieter sales times when sales losses would be minimised; and focus more on sales in busier places and periods when the time and attention required from preventive interventions would significantly impede sales. In another chain, a preventive intervention they trialled for small frequently stolen CRAVED products – bulky locked and tagged containers – was found effective in reducing thefts but too awkward for display and for removal at point of sale for their general adoption.

Although the problem-solving model for addressing shop theft makes sense as an ideal, it would be naïve to present it as the way in which crime prevention decisions are or could routinely be made. Given the shortage of systematic research on the effectiveness of most security measures, the contextual specificity of their application, and the dynamic changes in shop theft problems that restrict the temporal generalisability of findings, shopkeepers have to use informed discretion in their decision-making over crime prevention measures. They need habitually to be sceptical over the patter of those marketing pat solutions: *caveat emptor*!

For retailers, as with private citizens and other organisational bodies, taking measures to prevent a crime involves costs that they would prefer to devote to their main interests, be that making profits (businesses), enjoying consumer goods (private citizens), educating young people (schools and universities), or curing the sick (hospitals). Other things being equal, all have an interest in prevention being effectively provided by the state, as noted earlier. The next section therefore moves on to the role of the state in doing crime prevention. In relation to expenditure on security measures to reduce the risk of victimisation, research suggests that it is incurred reluctantly and grudgingly (Loader, Goold, & Thumala, 2015).

Private sector crime generation

The private sector doesn't only suffer crime, as in the shop theft example discussed here. It also generates crime. Some of this has already been alluded to in the case of retail, where some methods of retailing are shown to be criminogenic. However, inadvertent crime generation within the private sector goes much wider. Products and services which we mostly welcome, and which are provided by businesses in the interests of revenue and profit, can sometimes unintentionally also provoke or facilitate crime. This can present substantial challenges for those in the public sector with crime prevention responsibilities.

Public sector crime prevention

Crime prevention roles, responsibilities, and competencies

As noted in Chapter 1, according to Hobbes (1651), life in a state of nature would be 'solitary, poor, nasty, brutish and short.' The deal individuals accept in sacrificing their freedom to do just as they please is the sovereign's provision of conditions where life would differ from that in a state of nature, and we could go about our business securely without having to fight one another. In this sense, a fundamental responsibility for crime prevention lies with the state. A given government can try to discharge that responsibility in different ways, but ultimately the buck stops with them.[3]

Setting rules prohibiting specified forms of predation and making provision for their enforcement are pretty generic but also pretty crude. Advocates for the minimal state would not want to do much more and would only prohibit the most egregious forms of violent and acquisitive behaviour and do so only by threatening severe punishment to deter or disable. It would otherwise be up to the citizen to protect themselves, as in nature. Advocates of the welfare state would criminalise a wide range of deliberate behaviours that adversely affect the well-being of citizens and with a wide range of interventions to prevent those behaviours.

In the case of the minimal state, what counts as 'egregious' may not extend to all the most harmful behaviours (such as marital rape) and may go beyond harms to include outrages to standards of public decency as construed at the time (such as homosexual behaviours or abortion). In the case of the welfare state, the range of interpersonally harmful behaviours for criminalisation is open to endless disputation, and the range of possible means to prevent those behaviours is also almost infinite. As noted in Chapter 1, most contemporary crime prevention has focused on the intersection between harmful behaviours and rules prohibiting them.

There are lots of positions between the minimal state and the maximal welfare state, and there are many possible means to prevent crime, with their own competing, passionate advocates. New harms emerge (or are recognised) and new laws passed relating to them. Societies change and crime problems mutate. This makes crime a 'wicked' problem, but ultimately governments bear responsibility for the prevention of criminalised harmful behaviours, however these are defined.

Beyond generic rule setting and enforcement, governments lack crime prevention competency in the sense that those in power know little about how to prevent crime and also that they are not in a position directly to activate many of the crime prevention mechanisms discussed in Chapter 4. They may also be hamstrung in the exercise of those capabilities they do have by ideology, obligation to please the public (or to pander to uninformed news organs), noisy pressure groups, and obligations to their own financial supporters. Chapter 8 has more to say about this.

What governments can do is to create or pass on responsibilities to competent third parties. This responsibilisation has a long history. Garland (2001) writes about recent processes of responsibilisation to deliver non-enforcement forms of crime prevention. However, even when enforcement was the primary or only form of state-sponsored crime prevention, there were processes of responsibilisation in view of the limited competence of central government itself directly to deliver what was needed.

In the Middle Ages in England and Wales, local Manorial Courts, often with their own officials, alongside Hue and Cry[4] responsibilities assigned to community members, comprised the institutions responding to what was then considered crime. The courts raised money through the imposition of fines both for the Hue and Cry itself (imposed on the offender in addition to the fine for the crime itself) and for those making the Hue and Cry if it was determined that there had been no grounds for it in terms of a crime committed. Müller (2005) presents case studies relating to two, 14th-century villages. Unsurprisingly, she finds that these operated in favour of the powerful, a suggestion still made in relation to the current criminal justice system (see Reiner, 2016).

Over the past 200 years, the professional police have emerged as the specialist organisation to which the state allocates responsibility for crime control. The main tools entrusted to the police have related to enforcement. The police have been expected to discharge their crime-controlling enforcement responsibilities alongside the wider criminal justice system, including the courts and corrections services providing punishment, treatment, and supervision.

Governments and the public continue to expect the police to take major responsibility for the control of crime. However, as indicated in Chapter 4, there is much that can be done to prevent crime that lies beyond the direct reach of the police or wider criminal justice system. In particular, the police cannot deliver most situational measures; they are unable to reduce risk factors within the home, school, or community; they cannot intervene at turning points; and their ability to intervene directly before a crime has been committed is confined to patrol. Police competence to prevent crime is therefore limited (albeit that this can be increased by using more effective strategies, as we saw in Chapter 2 with focused deterrence). For much crime prevention, others need also to be involved. Recognising this, governments have responsibilised various actors to play their part in crime prevention, both independently and alongside the police. Moreover, the police themselves in discharging their crime prevention responsibilities have drawn third parties (e.g. businesses) into the prevention of crime; in some cases even when those third parties have been reluctant to play their part (Mazerolle & Ransley, 2005).

Governments can use 'sticks,' 'carrots,' and 'sermons' to persuade non-police third parties to play a part in crime prevention (Bemelmans-Videc, Rist, & Vedung, 1998). Carrots, sticks, and sermons each have particular advantages and disadvantages. Police services can use similar methods to persuade others to play ball in crime prevention.

Sermons

Sermons comprise the least coercive means used to try to persuade others to act differently. They involve exhortation of some kind. Sermons might include information on the problem (say the number of car thefts in a given car park over a given period), advice (say on methods of making the car park less vulnerable to car thefts), formal or informal requests (asking the owner of the car park to improve the security of the car park), moral pressure (e.g. arguing that the car park owner has some responsibility to operate their car park so that those using it are at reduced risk of having their cars stolen), suggestions that the changes may be in the interests of the targeted person or organisation (e.g. arguing that a more secure car park will attract more customers), or public shaming (e.g. publicly naming the car park as one where those using it are at especially high risk of having their car stolen).

The advantage of sermons is that they are relatively cheap and do not require any legislative mandate. The disadvantage is that the audience for the sermon is free to ignore it. Moreover, simple sermonising in favour of changed behaviours, where it will lead to heightened cost, inconvenience, or risk with little or no compensating benefit to the target of the sermon, may receive a rather dusty or evasive response. Many private sector businesses may be reluctant (or even unable) to incur the costs of changes that bring them no benefits even if they provide greater protection to customers or the general public.

In England and Wales, a series of government circulars (HO 8/84; 44/90) promoted local crime prevention partnerships involving statutory, voluntary, and private sector bodies, prior to legislation in 1998 (Crime and Disorder Act), which required that such partnerships, under the joint leadership of the police and local authorities, be established in all areas.

Carrots

Carrots comprise rewards for making changes, most commonly in the form of economic incentives. Some patterns of crime prevention activity are largely a function of the supply of carrots. The very large number of closed-circuit television cameras in public places in Britain is largely a function of the series of programmes in which successive governments have provided funding, one of which was £150 million as part of the 1999–2002 Crime Reduction Programme. Additional money was provided for the remainder of the programme to incentivise other police and partnership crime reduction efforts (Homel, Nutley, Webb, & Tilley, 2004). In the United States, the 1994 Crime Bill provided resources for 100,000 additional or redeployed community police officers over five years. Other financial carrots include performance-bonuses that are provided for individuals whose behaviour and achievements accord with stated crime prevention priorities.

The advantage of economic incentives is that they are stronger than sermons and tend therefore to be more effective. The disadvantages, of course, are their cost; the fact that for those measures that call for revenue expenditure, the effect lasts only so long as the funds are provided; that they are open to artful exploitation by those aiming to make use of funding but not necessarily for the purposes intended; and that they pay for activities that would have occurred even without provision of the extra resource. Moreover, most importantly ill-directed incentives may lead to activity that is ineffective or addresses relatively minor problems simply because the funding or rewards are made available for it. This is almost certainly the case with the monies made available for installing CCTV in public places.

Non-economic incentives such as prizes or kite marks represent alternative carrots. The Goldstein and Tilley Awards, respectively in the United States and United Kingdom, are designed to recognise and encourage strong problem-solving activities by police and partnerships (see ASU Center for Problem-Oriented Policing (2022b) where entries can be downloaded). The principal benefit for the winner in both cases is recognition rather than the relatively small material rewards. In relation to car crime in the UK, the Safer Car Parks scheme provides a kite mark for car parks that meet required security standards (Safer Parking Scheme, 2023).

The literature on carrots also refers to negative incentives: the withholding of benefits or the provision of negative recognition where crime prevention behaviour fails to accord with that which is wanted. Funding may be kept back if and where preventive standards are inadequate. League tables provide both positive and negative incentives. Those at the top are rewarded through the recognition of their achievements, and those at the bottom may be shamed into attempting improvements. The Car Theft Index comprises a powerful example of a league table that seems to have incentivised improvements in the security of vehicles (Laycock, 2004). Makes and models have been listed in order of their theft rate. In this case, being at the top was a sign of failure. Publication of the first car theft index in 1992 (Houghton, 1992) was followed by a rapid improvement in the levels of security built into new cars and has been associated with a steady decline in the rate of car theft since. Moreover, repeated publication of the car theft index helped maintain attention to vehicle security (Laycock, 2004). The Car Theft Index was technically quite difficult to produce but has been an inexpensive way of leveraging attention to theft risks by manufacturers, who were most competent to reduce car theft but had hitherto not been held responsible.

Sticks

It might seem that the discussion has strayed into 'sticks' in referring to negative incentives. The term 'sticks,' however, is reserved for compulsion by way of statute. It refers to legal requirements that individuals, agencies, or organisations act in particular ways. The European requirement that new cars be fitted with immobilisers from 1998 (mandate by EU directive 95/56/EU in 1995) is a case in point (see Brown, 2004). Legislative requirements in Germany that steering wheel locks be fitted to all cars from 1963 and in Britain that they be fitted to all new cars from 1971 are earlier examples of sticks used on vehicle manufacturers obliging them to incorporate that security measure into vehicles. The Crime and Disorder Act (1998, as amended by s97 and s98 of the Police Reform Act 2002 and s1, Clean Neighbourhoods and Environment Act, 2005) imposes statutory duties in England and Wales on police, police authorities, local authorities, fire and rescue authorities, local health boards, and primary care trusts to address local crime and disorder issues in partnership.

Some sticks bestowing crime prevention responsibilities are clearly more effective than others. Section 17 (S17) of the Crime and Disorder Act (1998) imposes responsibilities on a range of authorities to take account of crime in their decision-making and activities. It describes an effort to mobilise routine attention to the potential crime consequences of policies and practices that ostensibly are unrelated to crime and hence addresses the ways in which crime may be generated unintentionally (Bullock, Moss, & Smith, 2000). It is, though, quite a loose requirement that has in practice lacked teeth and of course relates only to a limited range of bodies that might be competent to reduce or pre-empt crime. While often referred to there are few examples of S17's application.

Local partnerships have sometimes made imaginative use of sticks at their disposal to put pressure on organisations that are competent to act to reduce crime but may otherwise be reluctant to do so. One case in point in Salford was to draw on the Health and Safety at Work Act (1974). This assigns a duty on employers to ensure the health, safety, and welfare at work of all employees, including attention to the risk of violence. The Act also bestows powers of entry to premises, used by local authority Environmental Health Officers, to check that responsibilities are adhered to. The legislation is being used to persuade those running businesses, where there is a high risk of commercial robbery as revealed by local crime statistics, to operate their businesses and install security measures aimed at reducing the chances that staff will become victims or, in the case of premises already victimised, repeat victims of what is a violent offence.

The clear advantage of sticks is that they provide a means of coercing action from those who would otherwise be inclined to refuse to take it. The downside is that it can take a great deal of time and effort to pass legislation, that drafting is difficult and the final product can often lack effective teeth, that pursuing prosecutions is generally costly, and that it can elicit resistance and resentment from those who believe that unreasonable burdens are being placed on them.

Of course, as illustrated in the first part of this chapter with shop theft, individuals, families, and private sector organisations do much crime prevention independently of government or the public sector. It is in their own interests to do so, just as in the animal kingdom, anti-predation strategies are used to try to control risk. In this case, the role of the public sector may be to ensure that the crime prevention measures are not themselves harmful to third parties. In many countries, this lies behind gun control measures.

Let us turn now to how to decide what to do to prevent crimes effectively and ethically, alongside who needs to be involved in particular cases.

Doing effective and ethical crime prevention

'Problem-oriented policing' (POP) originates in the work of Herman Goldstein (1977, 1979, 1990). It is sometimes now referred to as 'problem-oriented policing and partnership' (POPP) and has emerged as the main framework for delivering crime prevention involving the public sector.

POP's remit is wider than crime prevention and relates to all those issues the police are expected to address. POP was developed as a way of defining the police role in free societies, where the police are awarded awesome powers over citizens, which need to be used as little as possible in addressing the kinds of problems (including, of course, crime) to which the police respond (Goldstein, 1977). In this section, the focus is on POP and POPP, specifically in relation to crime prevention.

SARA (scanning, analysis, response, assessment) has emerged as the most widely used framework for delivering POP/POPP. It was devised by Eck and Spelman (1987) to have a simple logic. First, identify the problem as precisely as possible (scanning) to give the problem-solving focus. Then, work out what is producing the problem, in particular, the aspects of its production that are open to practical intervention. Next, develop one or more interventions that remove or reduce causal conditions producing the problem. Finally, assess the effectiveness of the intervention or interventions put in place. These processes resemble those outlined by Ekblom (1986, 1988) and illustrated earlier in this chapter in relation to private sector crime prevention.

The SARA model has been subjected to a variety of criticisms and revisions (see Borrion et al., 2020), but the basic approach remains in part because it is simple and accords with common sense (Sidebottom & Tilley, 2011). What has changed, however, is that it is now recognised that the process is seldom, if ever, a simple, linear one. Definitions of problems may need to be refined if the initial specification does not lend itself to the identification of preventive interventions. The analysis may likewise need to be revisited if the initial conditions identified for the problem do not seem to be open to practicable interventions. The interventions initially chosen may need to be modified in the light of difficulties in their implementation. For especially challenging problems, discovering, understanding, and implementing effective measures that reduce the problem may be complex, difficult, and time-consuming. Moreover, problems are apt to mutate over time with adaptive offenders, adaptive victims, emergent targets, and emergent tools for committing crime.

In view of the recognition that the processes of crime prevention problem-solving can be complex, with feedback between stages, the SARA process tends now to be represented as a recursive one, as shown in Figure 6.3.

Scanning

The acronym CHEERS is sometimes used to describe what counts as a problem for POP (Clarke & Eck, 2003). 'CHEERS' requires that problems

1. Affect the **community.**
2. Produce **harm**.
3. Fit with public **expectations** of the police, and
4. Relate to **events** that are **recurrent,** and **similar.**

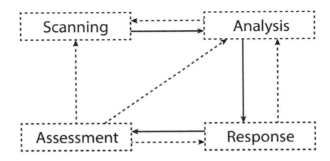

Figure 6.3 The SARA process.[5]

'Scanning' involves defining a problem as precisely as possible to provide for analysis, which will help identify potential practical 'pinch-points' that may be closed by interventions which will reduce or remove key conditions that produce the problem or allow it to persist. In practice, an initial pre-senting problem is often very broad (say theft). Scanning involves using any data that are available to identify and home in on a more closely specified patterned problem (say theft from curtain-sided trucks parked overnight at service stations).

The general findings on the patterns of crime concentration described in Chapter 3 provide a steer for specifying significant crime problems that could be open to intervention: offence types, locations, times, targets, victims, and offenders may all comprise concentrations of crime to focus on in preventive problem-solving.

Analysis

Analysis is orientated to working out how patterns of crime events are produced and what might therefore be done to prevent them from recurring. As with the case of shop theft already discussed, for practical problem-solving a stop-ping point arises when practical interventions drop out of the analysis. In pure research, complete and comprehensive understanding is also never possible. There are stopping points there also, but they are rather different (see Pawson, forthcoming). In problem-solving, stopping points in analysis are pragmatic – to do with when enough is known to devise and trial a promising response.

Individual crime events have complex causes and conditions. Jim (age 22) was high when he shot Donna (age 20) and killed her on Friday just before midnight in the room which they shared with Donna's two-year-old child, Freda. Neighbours called the police when they heard screaming, a shot, and then silence. The police arrived rapidly, arrested Jim, and took Freda into care. Jim and Donna's room was part of a housing project in a high crime and predominantly black neighbourhood in Chicago where levels of trust between citizens and the police are low. Jim and Donna had a history of fighting each other, and the police had been called previously to deal with disturbances involving them. Both Jim and Donna were in care as children because of parental neglect. Both had extensive criminal records, Jim latterly as a member of a 'gang.' Neither was in paid work. Both were drug dependent. Jim is not Freda's father. She was born from a previous relationship in which Donna was involved.

What caused Donna's homicide? Lots of possible causes spring to mind. Lots of things might have been different in ways that could have prevented Donna's tragic loss of life. Jim might not have been high; he might not have had a gun; he might not have had ammunition. Effective drug treatment or drug control could have been stronger. Gun control could have been tighter. The police and police referral agencies could have intervened in earlier incidents in ways that led to improvements in the relationship between Jim and Donna or to their separation (maybe with Donna moving into a refuge) or to deterrents (or treatment) inhibiting Jim's violence. Housing provision could have improved, taking Jim, Donna, and Freda from the single room they occupied to more spacious accommodation where they could each have their own space and live in a less stressed way. Jim's and Donna's neighbours and the wider neighbourhood they lived in could have offered more control over the criminal behaviour of residents, including Jim's murder of Donna. Jim and Donna could both have had less disrupted and more caring childhoods, reducing their vulnerability to involvement in criminality as both victims and offenders. And so on. Readers will be able to think of other possibilities.

Donna's murder could have formed a case for inclusion in a wide range of repeat problems for preventive attention. It could have been included as an incident of violence, violence against women and girls, domestic violence, repeat domestic violence, shootings, homicides, high crime housing projects, high crime neighbourhoods, gang-related crime, crimes following adverse childhood experiences, drug-related crimes, and so on. Each is liable to lead to a different focus for aggregate analysis of incidents forming part of the relevant set within the defined problem. Donna's murder clearly fits within the CHEERS criteria for a problem, as do the differing aggregate problems within which it could fit.

The reason for sharpening definitions of problems is to find promising specific pinch-points that are relevant to the precise problem that is the focus of problem-solving preventive attention. If we take Donna's murder, it could form a class of repeat domestic violence offences culminating in the murder itself, building on the Killingbeck project outlined in Chapter 2. Analysis would test the hypothesis that those victimised (or reported victimised to the police or other agency) once were at greater risk of a second incident, that those twice victimised (or reported victimised twice) were more likely to be victimised a third time, and so on. It could look retrospectively to see whether women murdered (shot or otherwise) had had earlier incidents reported. This would not only narrow the problem definition but also point to the consideration of interventions of cumulative intensity (focused on both victim and perpetrator) that could interrupt the series by steering Donna away from her vulnerable position, mobilising protection for her from neighbours, as well, maybe, as deterring or disabling Jim. It would also offer a way to reduce the risks to women such as Donna in vulnerable positions in the short term, rather than waiting for longer-term (and maybe broader) effects that might be achieved by other potential interventions that speak to different, wider sets of offences into which Donna's murder could be put, with possible interventions that would prevent it or make it less likely.

Let us suppose that Donna's murder became a *cause célèbre* in the city where she lived. It was picked up by local media. Politicians demanded that something be done. The initial problem could be set very wide, say violence against women and girls or firearms crime. Problem-solving might begin with either of these, but analysis would likely soon conclude that this was too broad for the development of practical interventions that could bring quick benefits. Initial analysis might suggest that the problem needs to be broken down to manageable subsets open to practical intervention. This would return attention again to scanning where the problem could be broken down and reframed, including that of repeat domestic violence, but maybe others too out of which practical interventions would emerge.

The 'problem analysis triangle' (PAT) has been devised to analyse problems to help identify potential preventive pinch-points. It is rooted in the routine activities approach, as outlined in Chapter 4. Each side of the triangle refers to one of the essential conditions for a crime to take place. The idea is to understand these conditions and how they come about in relation to the specific problem defined during scanning. What made the targets suitable and available? What led to the presence of likely offenders to commit the crimes against the suitable targets? What made the suitable targets unprotected at the time/s and place/s of the crimes? What led likely offenders to believe that it was permissible to commit crimes against the targets at the times and places of the offences?

Take Donna's case. Jim lived with Donna so was available to assault her. Donna lived with Jim so was an available target for his wrath. Because they lived together with no one else there, she was largely unprotected by third parties at night-time. When high Jim had little self-control. Jim also carried a gun, so had the wherewithal to shoot her.

The utility of PAT for crime prevention problem-solving should be obvious. What might we be able to do to reduce the suitability or availability of the targets where and when they have been available to likely offenders? What might we do to reduce the availability, motivation, or capacity of the likely offenders against the targets where and when they are committing crime against them? What might be done to add protection to the targets where and when they are the focus of criminal activity? How might the offenders be made to feel that they should not commit the crimes where and when they might otherwise be tempted to do so?

In relation to cases like Donna's murder, Donna could have been empowered to move out and given the opportunity to relocate to a safe haven. Jim could have been warned not to persist in assaults on Donna and failing that sent away at the time of an incident or warned that he should not act violently or return to the accommodation he shared with Donna when high. He could have had his gun confiscated and been subjected to targeted stop and frisk to check that he did not carry a gun. He could have been subjected to a court order prohibiting him from going to the accommodation. He could have been mandated to attend an anger management course. Neighbours could have been asked to alert the police if they suspected that Jim and Donna were fighting. Both Jim and Donna could have had impressed on them that the menu of interventions of increasing intensity to protect Donna and control Jim, which would inexorably follow if the domestic violence continued. These interventions clearly speak to the place, victim, and offender, in accordance with the problem analysis triangle.

Crime scripts were introduced in Chapter 4. They lay out the steps that are involved in a crime, from its preparation to realisation of its benefits. For some complex crimes, such as large-scale frauds, trafficking in goods or people, and international waste dumping, there will be multiple steps involving multiple people. Mapping the scripts involved is a way in which points of greatest vulnerability to intervention might be found. Identifying empirically the specific crime scripts for specific complex crime problems thus offers a way of working out what makes for the most promising points of intervention, especially those that are least likely to be circumvented by those involved in the offence. Crime scripts are less relevant to spontaneous interpersonal crimes such as Jim's murder of Donna.

Response

Developing a response or set of responses involves drawing on the analysis to work out who could do what to close what seem to be the most promising potential pinch-points. Who can do what in relation to the weakest points in the crime script? Who can do what in relation to likely offender availability, motivation, or capacity to commit a crime? Who can do what in relation to the accessibility, availability, or suitability of the target? Who can do what

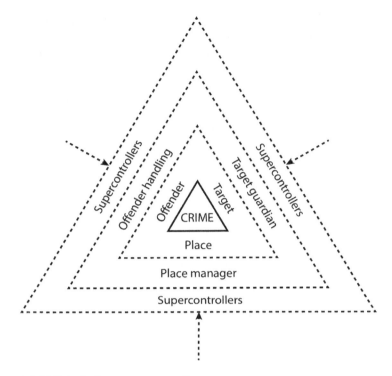

Figure 6.4 PAT, including super controllers.

in relation to the location where and when the offender is liable to offend against the target?

The 'Who can do . . . ?' part of the question about responses recognises that working out how to persuade those in a position to close the most promising potential pinch-point that they should do so forms part of the problem-solving process. An elaboration of the problem analysis triangle, shown in Figure 6.4, shows 'supercontrollers' acting on those who can directly affect the conditions for a given crime problem.

'Supercontrollers' comprise those able to exert influence over those who can act in ways that help close potential pinch-points. A range of regulatory bodies, for example local authorities and environmental, building, licencing, planning, public health, fire safety, road safety, transport, and educational bodies, may be able to function as supercontrollers. Part of determining responses to try out includes finding not only potential pinch-points creating or enabling the problem but also ways of persuading those who could close them to do so. And, of course in principle, supercontrollers are themselves open to external mobilisation. Figure 6.4 builds on earlier basic work developing and refining the problem analysis triangle (Sampson, Eck, & Dunham, 2010).

Goldstein and Scott (2011) list a hierarchy of levers that can be used to persuade competent third parties to act as guardians, handlers, or place managers[6]:

1. Inform them of the crime problem and ask them to take preventive action.
2. Reward them for acting differently to reduce the risk of the crime.
3. Tell them about crime harms to which they are contributing, and what they can do to reduce them, with a tacit threat that they may face adverse publicity if they fail to cooperate.
4. Warn them that a failure to cooperate in the interests of reducing the crime problem will be publicised to their detriment.
5. Take or threaten enforcement action if they fail to cooperate in preventive efforts.
6. Withdraw (or threaten to withdraw) services if they fail to cooperate by taking action.
7. Lobby for new rules requiring changed behaviour in ways that will reduce the crime.

Pressures on third parties grow from top to bottom, but so too does the effort required to use them, the time taken to put them in place, and the likelihood of resistance. The message is clear: the lower the level of leverage needed the better. If, for example a shop selling the types of knives that tend to be used in knife crimes decides to withdraw them on being told that known knife offenders have bought them from the store, no further action is needed. If the shop declines to take action, then levers can be ratcheted up by police and their partners.

'Logic models' are useful in working through potential responses to decide whether they are plausible as a way of addressing the problem and what might be their side effects. Figure 6.2 gave the example of security tags as responses to the problem of shop theft. Figure 6.5 presents another example: the use of focused deterrence to reduce gun crime, which was outlined in Chapter 2, a version of which appears in Sidebottom et al. (2021).

Figure 6.5 takes us through who is involved ('inputs and resources') in doing what ('activities') and what they deliver ('outputs'). It also specifies the 'potential mechanisms' through which the 'outputs' could generate a range of 'intended outcomes' and 'unintended outcomes.' Figure 6.5 also shows that the delivery of focused deterrence and the response to it depend on context. Those contemplating using focused deterrence to address their problem need to understand this in relation to their own conditions and the specific problem they are addressing. A logic model will help figure out whether a given

Focussed deterrence

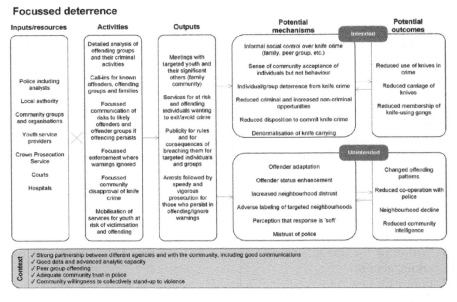

Figure 6.5 A logic model for focused deterrence (with thanks to Matt Ashby and Aiden Sidebottom for their contributions to this figure).

intervention could prevent the specific crime problem in their conditions and the risks of unwanted side effects.

Bespoke logic models for interventions are useful not only in considering what might make sense in addressing a specific problem in a specific place. They also provide a basis for assessments by identifying what needs to be tracked and measured as the interventions are delivered alongside their intended outcomes and possible negative side effects.

Even when decisions on responses have been made and third parties have agreed to play their part, implementation can be difficult (Laycock & Tilley, 1995). There are many examples where putting interventions in place has been surprisingly challenging. For example those offered security upgrades to their properties may be reluctant to accept them (Hunter & Tseloni, 2018); there may be legal/planning problems in installing some measures, for example alleygates or CCTV (Johnson & Loxley, 2001; Kantar, 2023); practitioners may resist requirements that they act in ways required by the intervention and thereby subvert it, as in follow-ups to Killingbeck (see Hanmer, 2006); funding rules may prevent sensible patterns of intervention delivery, as with the Crime Reduction Programme (Homel et al., 2004); agreements in one part of an organisation may not cohere with those in other parts of the organisation (ibid.); partnerships falter where different missions and cultures clash; and events may occur out of the blue upsetting plans, as with COVID-19 and the start of the British Safer Streets initiative (Kantar, 2023).

Problem-solving measures always require the adoption of something new and hence, implicitly if not explicitly, a critique of and move on from what went before. It is, perhaps, unsurprising that planned measures are often resisted by those with vested interests in the status quo. Crime prevention problem-solvers should not be surprised but focus on the nuts and bolts of implementation, attempting to anticipate and forestall obstacles.

Assessment

Assessment is about systematically learning from problem-solving efforts. The learning can be both for those who are trying to deal with the specific crime problem they are working on and for others who can benefit from their experience.

For those addressing the problem, knowing whether the problem remains or not or whether it has diminished is clearly important in deciding whether to continue to devote resources to dealing with it, whether a different tack is needed, or whether they can move on to address other problems.

Those involved may also benefit from finding out about the practicalities of implementing their strategy locally so that they can make improvements if necessary and so that any transferable lessons for their future work can be gleaned. It is often in practice tricky to apply planned interventions. This can be because third parties need to be persuaded to take particular actions or to assume responsibilities or because arrangements for delivery are complex.

Moreover, when assessments of problem-solving efforts fail to demonstrate effectiveness to learn practical lessons, it is useful to work out why. Rosenbaum (2002) usefully distinguishes between 'theory failure' (the basic idea turned out not to work as expected); 'measurement failure' (our methods of detecting effects were too insensitive to identify them); and 'implementation failure' (what was intended may have been effective, but what was in practice put in place did not match up to what was planned). Unless we understand why the results do not match up to expectations, we are liable to draw erroneous conclusions for the future.

Interventions often produce side effects. A strong assessment will be attentive to these, especially where the intervention has inadvertently caused harms. We saw in Chapter 2 that the well-meaning Cambridge-Somerville project, as it was in practice implemented, seems to have done more harm than good. If there is evidence that serious negative unintended side effects are being produced, this should clearly lead those delivering a response to change it or abandon it. If the assessment fails to look out for unintended negative side effects, there is a strong chance that they will be missed and consequently that the intervention is continued in spite of its harms.

An 'EMMIE' assessment captures what is needed for those hoping to learn from crime prevention case studies. It refers to 'Effects' (what positive and negative outcomes were produced by the specific interventions or overall strategy?); 'Mechanisms' (what was it about what was done that produced the outcomes that resulted?); 'Moderators' (what was learned about the conditions needed for the intervention to trigger the mechanisms producing the outcomes?); 'Implementation' (how were the interventions put in place by whom with what obstacles which were overcome in what ways?); and 'Economy' (what did the interventions or strategy cost, who bore the costs, what were the benefits, and who realised them?). Armed with answers to these evaluation questions, decision-makers will be well-informed about whether, why, where, and how to emulate a crime prevention effort. In practice, delivering on EMMIE is tricky, and most assessments are only partially successful in producing a robust EMMIE compliant assessment. EMMIE remains, however, an ideal standard against which assessments can be tested.

Chapters 7 and 8 will deal with issues of evidence and evaluation in crime prevention in more detail.

Conclusion

Some crime problems require quite complex problem-solving to develop acceptable, practicable, and effective responses. They will generally require partnerships to work out what to do and how to track and measure positive and negative outcomes. Other crime problems, however, are more straightforward to deal with once understood for problem-solving purposes. The following is a selection of specific problems for which effective and relatively uncontroversial preventive interventions were identified and implemented.

- Motor car theft: we referred to this in Chapter 2 and have returned to it repeatedly. Inconspicuous security built into cars and activated by default effected a massive and sustained fall in car theft.
- Vandalism: late-night repeated criminal damage at a local tourist attraction caused by stones being thrown to break windows was prevented by removing the loose rubble used as ammunition.
- Antisocial behaviour: repeated reports of incidents by elderly residents relating to antisocial behaviour by young people were stopped by moving the playground equipment, around which the young people congregated, beyond earshot of the complainants.
- Theft of white goods: thefts of white goods from newly built houses yet to be occupied were reduced by postponing the installation of those white goods until the properties were occupied (Clarke & Goldstein, 2003).
- Theft of catalytic converters: widespread thefts of catalytic converters were reduced by signs alerting drivers in hotspots to sights and sounds

indicating that the offence was taking place and encouraging citizens to report crimes in progress (see Sessions, 2022).

- Glassings (broken beer glasses with shards poked into adversary's face): a switch to different types of drinking vessels, which do not produce sharp shards when broken.

In relation to very specific problems, it is often easier to identify simple, straightforward, and effective responses that can command widespread support, even if their implementation may still be difficult. Box 6.1 summarises a recent example of the application of problem-solving to one specific example of computer-related crime (Halstead, 2022), which as we saw in Chapters 3 and 4 is burgeoning.

Box 6.1   Problem-solving PDQ fraud

Scanning

PDQ (Process Data Quickly) machines are widely used for card payments and refunds. The initial case related to an incident where a team of three offenders went to a hotel in North Wales late in the evening. Two distracted the night porter while the third went behind the registration desk to find the PDQ machine, where he entered the default security code and instructed refunds totalling £18,000, thereby attempting to defraud the hotel (in this case, the fraud was discovered quickly enough to stop the transactions going through). The police subsequently found that similar incidents had occurred in other hotels in the area using the same Modus Operandi. Looking further afield still, they found that using PDQ machines and default security codes was widespread, leading to substantial losses nationally (over £64 million in 2019). Detecting the crimes was tricky as the losses were often not immediately apparent and hence potential leads lost.

Analysis

The explanation for the problem lay in the provision of default codes and their routine use in businesses, especially where there were many staff members, and changing the code would be administratively tricky. This understanding of the problem was facilitated by the fact that one of the police officers involved had had experience working in the hotel industry.

Response

Some efforts were made to alert businesses to the risks they faced and the need to correct their lax security habits. However, a broader solution was found by engaging financial institutions in discussions over ways in which they could supply and use PDQ machines to reduce the risks of fraud against the businesses using them. For example instead of providing machines with standard passwords that the business was able to change, each machine was allocated an individual code which was supplied separately from the machine itself; limits were set on refunds; and unusually large refunds precipitated an alert to a suspicious transaction.

Assessment

Although there was some evidence that numbers of cases fell following the interventions put in place, for example no new instances occurred in North Wales and none was found in efforts to trace court proceedings relating to this form of fraud, the data available were not sufficient to be confident that the responses had been effective. What is clear from a follow-up survey of 24 independent hotels in North Wales is that the problem-solving interventions had led a) to changed service from PDQ providers and b) to the hotels adopting more secure procedures.

Exercise: Identify six ways of reducing homicide (or some specified subset of homicides) by reading relevant literature, thinking hard, or searching the Internet. Work out a logic model for at least one of your responses, along the lines shown in Figures 6.2 and 6.5. Then provide a persuasive critique of what you believe to be the three strongest responses you were able to formulate.

Notes

1 The Commercial Victimisation Survey of England and Wales has asked retailers about their experience of crime (see Home Office, 2022). The best shop theft estimates for 2020–2021 are the following. Prevalence of shop theft by sector: retail supermarkets, 77%; non-supermarket beverage and food retailers, 39%; clothes, 38%; electrical goods, 23%; household goods, 22%; and other retail, 20%. Across retailers, the figures for frequency of shop thefts are: once only, 14%; several times a year, 27%; roughly once a month, 16%; roughly once a week, 20%; roughly once a day, 11%; and several times a day, 12%. Food (39% of incidents); alcohol (25%), clothing (14%), and cosmetics (12%) were most frequently stolen. Shop

theft is a relatively common and frequent crime, even if losses per incident are generally modest.

2 Some larger retailers undertake internal trials to test the effectiveness of their preventive interventions, but many are reluctant to publish findings for fear of losing the competitive advantage they enjoy from the adoption of effective preventive strategies.

3 More optimistic (Rousseauian) accounts of human nature would predict that in a state of nature, absent interference, people would be able to rub along peacefully, without need for governmental interference, but crime prevention assumes that without some deliberate efforts to prevent crime, there would be much more of it. If we take the non-human natural world as indicative of the state of nature, there is certainly a lot of predation across species and violent competition within, as well as measures by potential victims to reduce the risk of it, as again touched on in Chapter 1. Notwithstanding this, there is some evidence of a biological basis to altruism, at least among some (see Reuter, Frenzel, Walter, Markett, & Montag, 2011), as well as an evolutionary biological base for interpersonal violence (Sell, 2019). Apparently, altruistic behaviours by an organism may also sometimes favour survival at the level of the gene and hence prospects for reproduction (Dawkins, 1976). Whatever the basic source of violence or other forms of predation, the Hobbesian case for state (and hence governmental) responsibility appears compelling.

4 'Hue and Cry' refers to the obligation of victims or witnesses of crime to raise the alarm and pursue offenders.

5 The solid arrows represent the logical sequence of SARA. The broken arrows represent feedback loops in the practical conduct of problem-solving, where processes of refinement occur in problem-specification, analysis, and the development of responses.

6 Goldstein and Scott refer to police use of levers. However, they can also be used by others with crime prevention responsibilities to engage third parties.

References

ASU Centre for Problem-Oriented Policing. (2022a). *POP guides.* Retrieved April 27, 2023, from https://popcenter.asu.edu/pop-guides

ASU Centre for Problem-Oriented Policing. (2022b). *POP project reports.* Retrieved from https://popcenter.asu.edu/content/pop-projects

Bamfield, J. (2012). *Shopping and crime.* Basingstoke: Palgrave Macmillan.

Beck, A., & Willis, A. (1999). Context-specific measures of CCTV effectiveness in the retail sector. In N. Tilley & K. Painter (Eds.), *Surveillance of public space: CCTV, street lighting and crime prevention: Crime prevention studies 10* (pp. 251–269). Monsey, NY: Criminal Justice Press.

Bemelmans-Videc, M., Rist, R., & Vedung, E. (1998). *Carrots, sticks and sermons: Policy instruments and they evaluation.* New Brunswick, NJ: Transaction.

Borrion, H., Ekblom, P., Alrajeh, D., Borrion, A. L., Keane, A., Koch, D., Mitchener-Nissen, T., & Toubaline, S. (2020). The problem with crime problem-solving: Towards a second generation POP? *The British Journal of Criminology,* 60(1), 219–240. doi:10.1093/bjc/azz029

Brown, R. (2004). The effectiveness of electronic immobilization: Changing patterns of temporary and permanent vehicle theft. In M. Maxfield & R. Clarke (Eds.), *Understanding and preventing car theft: Crime prevention studies 17.* Monsey, NY: Criminal Justice Press.

Buckle, A., & Farrington, D. (1984). An observational study of shoplifting. *British Journal of Criminology*, *34*(1), 63–73. doi:10.1093/oxfordjournals.bjc.a047425

Bullock, K., Moss, K., & Smith, J. (2000). *Anticipating the impact of section 17 of the crime and disorder act* (Briefing Note 11/00). London: Home Office.

Clarke, R. (2002). Introduction. In R. Clarke (Ed.), *Situational crime prevention: Successful case studies* (1st ed.). New York: Harrow and Heston.

Clarke, R., & Eck, J. (2003). *Become a problem-solving crime analyst in 55 small steps*. London: Jill Dando Institute of Crime Science, University College London. Retrieved from https://popcenter.asu.edu/sites/default/files/library/reading/PDFs/55stepsUK.pdf

Clarke, R., & Goldstein, H. (2003). *Reducing thefts at construction sites: Lessons from a problem-oriented project*. US Department of Justice, Office of Community Oriented Policing Services. Retrieved from https://popcenter.asu.edu/sites/default/files/library/reading/pdfs/constructiontheft.pdf

Clarke, R., & Petrossian, G. (2013). *Shoplifting* (Problem-Specific Guides Series 11). US Department of Justice, Office of Community Oriented Policing Services. Retrieved from https://popcenter.asu.edu/sites/default/files/shoplifting_2nd_ed.pdf

Crime and Disorder Act. (1998). *c.37*. Retrieved from www.legislation.gov.uk/ukpga/1998/37/contents

Dawkins, R. (1976). *The selfish gene*. Oxford: Oxford University Press.

Eck, J., & Spelman, W. (1987). *Problem-solving: Problem-oriented policing in Newport news*. Washington, DC: Police Executive Research Forum.

Ekblom, P. (1986). *The prevention of shop theft: An approach through crime analysis* (Crime Prevention Unit Paper 5). London: Home Office.

Ekblom, P. (1988). *Getting the best out of crime analysis* (Crime Prevention Unit Paper 10). London: Home Office.

Farrington, D., Bowen, S., Buckle, A., Burns-Howell, T., Burrows, J., & Speed, M. (1993). An experiment on the prevention of shoplifting. In R. V. Clarke (Ed.), *Crime prevention studies 1* (pp. 93–119). Monsey, NY: Criminal Justice Press.

Garland, D. (2001). *The culture of control*. Oxford: Oxford University Press.

Goldstein, H. (1977). *Policing a free society*. Cambridge, MA: Ballinger.

Goldstein, H. (1979). Improving policing: A problem-oriented approach. *Crime and Delinquency*, *25*, 236–258. doi:10.1177/001112877902500207

Goldstein, H. (1990). *Problem-oriented policing*. New York: McGraw-Hill.

Goldstein, H., & Scott, M. (2011). *Shifting and sharing responsibility for public safety problems*. US Department of Justice, Office of Community Oriented Policing Services. Retrieved from https://popcenter.asu.edu/sites/default/files/shifting_sharing_responsibility_for_public_safety_problems.pdf

Halstead, A. (2022). *Secure your PDQ* (Tilley Award Entry 2022). North Wales Police.

Hanmer, J. (2006). Maintaining solutions to major problems: Reducing repeat domestic violence. In K. Bullock & N. Tilley (Eds.), *Crime reduction and problem-oriented policing* (pp. 252–284). London: Routledge.

Hayes, R., & Downs, D. (2011). Controlling retail crime with CCTV domes, CCTV public view monitors, and protective containers: A randomised controlled experiment. *Security Journal*, *24*(3), 237–250. doi:10.1057/sj.2011.12

Hobbes, T. (1651). *Leviathan*. Many Editions.

Home Office. (2022). *Crime against businesses: Findings from the 2021 commercial victimisation survey*. London: Home Office. Retrieved November 28, 2022, from www.gov.uk/government/statistics/crime-against-businesses-findings-from-the-year-ending-march-2021-commercial-victimisation-survey/crime-against-businesses-findings-from-the-2021-commercial-victimisation-survey

Homel, P., Nutley, S., Webb, B., & Tilley, N. (2004). *Investing to deliver: Reviewing the implementation of the UK crime reduction programme* (Home Office Research Study 281). London: Home Office.

Houghton, G. (1992). *Car theft in England and Wales: The Home Office car theft index* (Crime Prevention Unit Paper 33). London: Home Office.

Hunter, J., Garius, L., Hamilton, P., & Wahidin, A. (2018). Who steals from shops, and why? A case study of prolific shop theft offenders. In V. Ceccato & R. Armitage (Eds.), *Retail crime* (pp. 71–97). Cham: Palgrave Macmillan.

Hunter, J., & Tseloni, A. (2018). An evaluation of a research-informed target hardening initiative. In A. Tseloni, R. Thompson, & N. Tilley (Eds.), *Reducing burglary* (pp. 165–193). Cham: Springer.

Johnson, S., & Loxley, C. (2001). *Installing Alley-Gates: Practical lessons from burglary prevention projects* (Briefing Note 2/01). London: Home Office. Retrieved July 30, 2023, from https://popcenter.asu.edu/sites/default/files/tools/implementing_responses/PDFs/Johnson.pdf

Kantar. (2023). *Evaluation of the safer streets fund round 1, year ending March 2021*. London: Home Office. Retrieved July 30, 2023, from www.gov.uk/government/organisations/home-office

Kivivuori, J. (2007). *Delinquent behaviour in Nordic Capital cities* (Scandinavian Research Council in Criminology). Helsinki: National Research Institute of Legal Policy.

Laycock, G. (2004). The UK car theft index: An example of government leverage. In M. Maxwell & R. Clarke (Eds.), *Understanding and preventing car theft* (pp. 25–44). New York: Criminal Justice Press.

Laycock, G., & Tilley, N. (1995). Implementing crime prevention. In M. Tonry & D. Farrington (Eds.), *Building a safer society: Crime and justice 19* (pp. 535–584). Chicago, IL: University of Chicago Press.

Loader, I., Goold, B., & Thumala, A. (2015). Grudge spending: The interplay between markets and culture in the purchase of security. *The Sociological Review, 63,* 858–875. doi:10.1111/1467-954X.12329

Mazerolle, L., & Ransley, J. (2005). *Third party policing*. Cambridge: Cambridge University Press.

Müller, M. (2005). Social control and the Hue and Cry in Two Fourteenth-Century Villages. *Journal of Medieval History, 31*(1), 29–53. doi:10.1016/j.jmedhist.2004.08.005

Pawson, R. (forthcoming) *How to think like a realist*. Cheltenham: Edward Elgar.

Pawson, R., & Tilley, N. (1997). *Realistic evaluation*. London: SAGE.

Reiner, R. (2016). *Crime*. Cambridge: Policy Press.

Reuter, M., Frenzel, C., Walter, N., Markett, S., & Montag, C. (2011). Investigating the genetic basis of altruism: The role of the COMT Val158Met polymorphism. *Social Cognitive and Affective Neuroscience, 6*(5), 662–668. doi:10.1093/scan/nsq083

Rosenbaum, D. (2002). Evaluating multi-agency anti-crime partnerships: Theory, design and measurement issues. In N. Tilley (Ed.), *Evaluation for crime prevention: Crime prevention studies 14* (pp. 171–225). Monsey, NY: Criminal Justice Press.

Safer Parking Scheme. (2023). *Park Mark®*. Retrieved from https://parkmark.co.uk/

Sampson, R., Eck, J. E., & Dunham, J. (2010). Super controllers and crime prevention: A routine activity explanation of crime prevention success and failure. *Security Journal, 23*, 37–51. doi:10.1057/sj.2009.17

Sell, A. (2019). Evolutional psychology. In R. Wortley, A. Sidebottom, N. Tilley, & G. Laycock (Eds.), *Routledge handbook of crime science* (pp. 33–42). London: Routledge.

Sessions, M. (2022). *Operation blink (and you'll miss it)*. Surrey Police. Tilley Award Entry.

Sidebottom, A., Brennan, I., Agar, I., Ashby, M., Bullock, K., Hales, G., & Tilley, N. (2021). *Knife crime: A problem-solving guide*. College of Policing.

Sidebottom, A., & Tilley, N. (2011). Improving problem-oriented policing: The need for a new model? *Crime Prevention and Community Safety, 13*, 79–101. doi:10.1057/cpcs.2010.21

Sidebottom, A., & Tilley, N. (2018). Towards a theory of tagging in retail environments. In V. Ceccato & R. Armitage (Eds.), *Retail crime* (pp. 379–402). Cham: Palgrave Macmillan.

Tilley, N. (2010). Shoplifting. In F. Brookman, M. Maguire, H. Pierpoint, & T. Bennett (Eds.), *Handbook of crime* (pp. 48–67). Cullompton: Willan.

7 Evidence-based crime prevention

Being realistic about evidence, evidence needs, and evidence use

It might seem obvious that strong evidence is crucial to delivering effective and well-targeted crime prevention, but public discussions of crime prevention suggest otherwise. Rishi Sunak, the British Prime Minister at the time of writing (2023), is reported saying, without reference to evidence warranting the policy,

> Well I want to reduce crime, right. And that means I want to make sure we can catch criminals. . . . The 'logical consequence' of that would be a spike in the numbers in jail. That's why we're building 10,000 more prison places over the next few years, to make sure we have prison capacity for that. . . . I want to make sure my kids and everyone else's can walk around safely.
>
> Asthana (2022)

Even when evidence is used as the basis for policy decisions, if it is inconvenient, it is liable to be repudiated or ignored, and if it accords with what political decision-makers want, it is invoked and celebrated. An especially blatant example is in the British Government's *Beating Crime Plan* of 2021 (UK Government, 2021). This report begins by presenting a graph showing recent violent crime patterns, estimated using data from the reliable Crime Survey of England and Wales (CSEW, see Figure 7.1). After noting the CSEW finding that both violent and property crime had been falling, the *Beating Crime Plan* comments that, '(T)his is not a reality that is recognised by the public and we share their determination to see a renewed fight against crime and anti-social behaviour.' The document then lays out the plan, citing evidence that accords with it, but none that relates specifically to crime prevention

DOI: 10.4324/9780429356155-7

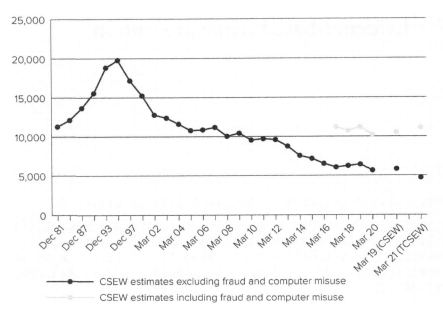

Figure 7.1 Beating Crime crime-trend graph.

Note: This figure is sloppy and misleading. Note the variation in times along the X axis. The first two numbers cover six years ('81–'87); the next two also cover six years ('87 –'93); the next two cover four years ('93–'97); the next two cover five years ('97 –'02); thereafter two years, before two dots that go backwards then forwards. This gives an erroneous impression of trend rates. It may reveal carelessness and ineptitude, rather than cynical misuse of data! There is an important lesson here for readers of research: don't trust the text, look critically at the numbers and graphs.

measures and their efficacy. Evidence is used to dress up rather than to inform plans.

This is not to say that government departments are indifferent to evidence, but they can be selective in its use. I spent ten years as an academic seconded to the British Home Office, which then had strong internal research units. I was (naively!) shocked to attend a meeting with a senior official, who told me of the minister's plans and asked me for any evidence that he could use to support them. The role of evidence here was not to inform policy but rather to justify it. Chapter 8 has much more to say about the politics of crime prevention, including research. Box 7.1 briefly attempts to correct some common myths about science, evidence, and evidence use in general.

Box 7.1   Some myths about science evidence and policy

Recognising the political and social realities surrounding evidence use in policy development, the American evaluator, Carol Weiss (1999), notes that research may enlighten over time and inform action when the time is ripe but not necessarily before that. This is a tendency not only for governments but also for other decision-making bodies with strong views or vested interests in particular crime prevention policies, practices, or devices to use evidence that supports what they want to do anyway, while neglecting evidence that suggests differently.

More generally, we all (and here I include academic researchers) tend to have cognitive biases in searching for, interpreting, and drawing on evidence. This goes even in the physical sciences where there is a long history of selectivity in evidence use. Stephen Jay Gould's book, *The Mismeasure of Man*, is a classic case study allegedly showing unconscious machinations in the conduct and use of research relating to the measurement of intelligence, in particular in Morton's work on skull capacity (Gould, 1981). However, even Gould himself in that book has been accused of unconscious bias in his interpretation of Morton's work (see Lewis et al., 2011)!

The history of science is littered with examples of scientists playing fast and loose with evidence in relation to their preferred theories (see, e.g. Broad & Wade, 1983). Among those cited are some who are credited with major discoveries (e.g. Gregor Mendel). This is not the place to go into the sociology of science, itself a much-contested field. Suffice it to say that the best explanation for the remarkable successes of science, despite the history of shenanigans in the production, interpretation, and use of evidence, lies in its social processes (Collins & Evans, 2017; Merton, 1973; Tilley, 1981, 1993a). There are institutional values covering truth-telling. Moreover, claims are criticised and checked. Out of the blue claims that seem to contradict established bodies of theory underpinning new scientific work will tend initially to be ignored or at best treated very sceptically.

The following discussion is normative in the sense that it speaks to what can be done with what types of evidence to come to warranted conclusions about promising ways of ethically preventing crimes. It is beamed at readers of research, newcomers to research, established researchers, those commissioning research, and those hoping to draw on research in practice and decision-making. It takes us through study design standards and hierarchies, reviews of evidence, evidence-based toolkits, evidence application, and the creation of evidence, before ending with a few precepts for those in the business of evidence production and use. The final two chapters (Chapters 8 and 9) of the book will have more to say about the realities of bringing good evidence to the improvement of policy and practice.

Reading evidence

The volume of available evidence in crime prevention is overwhelming and growing. Criminological research has proliferated in the past 50 years (Bowling & Ross, 2006). The first department specialising in the scientific study of crime in the UK was the Department of Criminal Science, established in Cambridge in 1941, which became the Institute of Criminology in 1959. By now, there are few universities in the UK which do not have departments of criminology or crime science.

The Home Office Research Unit was set up in 1957, which has been a major base for empirical policy-related criminological research including work on crime prevention. The Home Office has produced and continues to produce its own large output. The Home Office, as well as research councils, funds a large volume of contracted criminological research, which is normally published. The Office for National Statistics publishes crime statistics based both on police recorded crime and on a large victimisation survey, sweeps of which go back to 1981. The expansion in the UK's research capacity in relation to crime is mirrored in many other countries. Monographs, textbooks, edited collections as well as specialist and generalist national and international journals have proliferated. In addition to all this, there is a burgeoning grey research literature, only some of which is available through the Internet. In relation to problem-solving, for example annual entries to the Goldstein and Tilley awards are numbered in hundreds. Each entry requires attention to evidence, and some furnish excellent examples of evidence collection and use.

Navigating this evidence jungle to find that which is robust and relevant and then working out how best to draw on it are major challenges. No one could keep up with all of it. How is the busy policymaker or practitioner to find what they need and how are they to use it in decision-making?

Evidence hierarchies and gold standards

Consider evidence hierarchies as a basis for sifting research evidence. These put randomised controlled trial (RCT) studies as the gold standard, at the top of the pile for individual studies with other study types lower down as they depart further from the RCT ideal. Evidence hierarchies are used in health.

The Maryland Scale, shown in Box 7.2, was such a hierarchy developed specifically for crime prevention (Sherman et al., 1998).

Box 7.2   'Maryland Scale of Scientific Methods'

Level 1. Random assignment and analysis of comparable units to programme and comparison groups.

Level 2. Comparison between multiple units with and without the programme, controlling for other factors, or using comparison units that evidence only minor differences.

Level 3. A comparison between two or more comparable units of analysis, one with and one without the programme.

Level 4. Temporal sequence between the programme and the crime or risk outcome clearly observed or the presence of a comparison group without demonstrated comparability to the treatment group.

Level 5. Correlation between a crime prevention programme and a measure of crime or crime risk factors at a single point in time.

The Maryland Scale was produced as part of The Maryland Report, a landmark document which summarised 'what works,' 'what's promising,' and 'what doesn't' from evidence available up to 1998 from studies that passed minimum standards. 'What works' included programmes where at least two studies at level three or above with statistically significant results found the programme to have been effective in terms of reducing crime or risk factors. 'What doesn't' included programmes, where at least two studies at level three or above with statistically significant results found the programme to have had no positive effects in terms of reducing crime or risk factors. 'What's promising' included programmes 'for which the level of certainty from available evidence is too low to support generalisable conclusions' (Sherman et al., 1998, p. 6).

Systematic reviews, using meta-analyses of available studies that pass methodological muster, are undertaken to summarise what is known from studies that use RCTs (or that come close to them). They increase the power of the analysis by combining results from multiple studies and help users avoid the risk of being misled by individual studies with fluke results. Forest plots are typically used to represent findings of individual studies with the overall result from combining the studies shown as the best conclusion that can be drawn from the most rigorous studies. An example is shown in Figure 7.2 for 'alleygating,' a burglary prevention measure that limits access to alleys going to the back of houses by gating them.

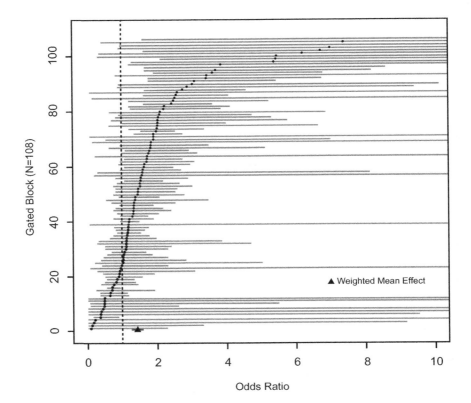

Figure 7.2 Forest plot of findings relating to burglary prevention outcomes of alley-gate installation.

Source: From Sidebottom et al. (2018).

The Cochrane Collaboration (2023) for health and The Campbell Collaboration (2023) for social policy, commission and warehouse systematic reviews, which are periodically updated as new studies are undertaken.

The stimulus for the Cochrane Collaboration was the widespread failure of health policymakers and practitioners to pay heed to what was known. These practitioners therefore delivered many interventions that were known to be ineffective or harmful (Cochrane, 1972). I have heard passionate advocates of RCTs being rightly concerned about the persistence of harmful standard practices. For example mothers had been routinely advised to place babies on their stomachs to help them sleep. It turns out, however, the net effect of this is that more babies die. The (untested) well-meaning advice was therefore harmful overall. On this basis, the RCT has a strong emotional pull: indeed, at a meeting I attended at which this example was presented, all those present

were asked one by one to promise that they would adopt RCTs as their preferred method and proselytise on behalf of them. (Luckily, the meeting broke
up before it came to my turn!).

The logic of RCTs is not complicated, although in practice their production is generally fraught with problems. The logic is this. We assess impact by
estimating a counterfactual (what would have happened without the intervention) by randomly allocating the pool of potential treatment recipients to
treatment or non-treatment (non-treatment may sometimes refer to standard
or some other treatment where relative effects are at issue). The outcomes for
each group can then be compared either through before and after measurements or by after only measurements when it can be assumed that there were
no initial differences between the groups in relation to the measured outcome
variable(s) (see Campbell, 1957 for a classic account of different experimental designs and when they should be used). The change in the untreated group
comprises the counterfactual against which changes in the treatment group
can be compared.

What RCTs and their next best alternatives focus on is removing 'threats to
internal validity.' These relate to ways in which we may be misled in attribut-
ing changes to the programme or intervention in question. RCTs promise an
unbiased estimate of effect sizes that speak to the programme or intervention,
and we have seen that such biases are widespread. There are many threats to
internal validity, as shown in Table 7.1. By creating equivalent treatment and
non-treatment ('control') groups and comparing changes in them, we automatically eliminate these threats. Any variation in change between the treatment and non-treatment groups can, so the logic goes, be attributed to the
intervention, within confidence limits set by the size of the sampled population. The forest plot shown in Figure 7.2 gives the confidence limits for the
studies included, with the combined result (with narrower confidence limits
due to the combined populations) at the bottom. Ideally, RCTs include 'blinding' or 'masking' of treatment providers, treatment targets, and analysts as to
which cases are in the treatment and which are in the control groups. This is
to reduce the risk that treatment providers, treatment recipients, and results
analysts are unconsciously affected by knowledge of group membership. In
clinical research, placebos are also often used in control groups to deal with the
risk that change in them may be due to the fact that (any) treatment is provided
rather than the suspected active element(s) within the treatment being trialled.

RCTs and systematic reviews that filter out designs that fall short of their
ideal have an obvious appeal for decision-makers. They promise clear-cut
answers to questions about the effects of a measure either in absolute terms
or in comparison to alternative interventions. RCTs and systematic reviews
of them save decision-makers having to wade through myriad studies of
dubious quality. Effect sizes estimated through RCTs can feed into economic
analysis where the costs of the intervention are measured and the benefits

Table 7.1 Threats to internal validity.

Threat to internal validity	Explanation
History	Something happens to create change that would have happened anyway, without any intervention
Maturation	Treatment subjects mature in the change direction anyway, regardless of intervention
Testing	The measurement creates the change not the intervention measure itself
Instrumentation	The measurement methods change and create the impression of real change while there is none
Statistical regression	Treatment targets begin at an extreme position and tend naturally to regress towards the mean without any need for intervention
Seasonality	Changes may be part of a regular set of rhythms unrelated to the measures put in place
Selection	Those selected for treatment are atypical and especially susceptible to influence
Mortality	Dropouts may be different from those staying the course
Interactions with selection	Selection biases may interact with other threats to internal validity, for example selection-maturation
Ambiguity about direction of causality	Apparent effects may be associated with treatments, but it may be the effect causing the treatment
Diffusion or imitation of treatments	Those not treated or those areas not treated (for comparison purposes) may adopt the intervention measure themselves
Compensatory equalisation of treatments	Those not treated (and used for comparison purposes) may be given additional services to compensate for missing out on the treatment given to the target group
Compensatory rivalry by respondents receiving less desirable treatments	Those not treated (and used for comparison purposes) may work especially hard to equal or outperform the treatment group or area
Resentful demoralisation of respondents receiving less desirable treatments	Those not receiving treatments (and used for comparison purposes) may underperform because they feel neglected and resentful

quantified in some objective way, so that the allocation of limited resources to maximise overall utilities can be better informed.

In view of the promise of RCTs (and their nearest equivalents) to yield robust effect size estimates that could be fed into policy decisions on the allocation of resources, in 2013 the British Government prompted the establishment of 'What Works' centres going across the policy waterfront. One of these centres focused on crime reduction, which continues to belong to a network comprising, at the time of writing (2022), ten centres.

The What Works Centre for Crime Reduction (based in the College of Policing) commissioned and funded, alongside the British Economic and Social Research Council, a 'University Consortium for Evidence-Based Crime Reduction.' I was part of the bid that was contracted to do this work. Indeed, I was deputy director and played a major part in writing the bid. What those commissioning the work wanted was a search for existing systematic reviews of what works in crime prevention and the conduct of new reviews to fill gaps in the supply of reviews relating to interventions of interest. The findings were to populate a 'what works crime reduction' toolkit to be updated as new reviews become available. What resulted can be found on the College of Policing (2023) website. The toolkit promised a go-to source of reliable research findings curated by competent academics searching and sifting a mountain of findings to find those that can be distilled into overall results that can be depended on by busy policy and practice decision-makers. It also set an agenda for future research to fill gaps in what was known about what works.

Despite their obvious appeal and popularity, there are lots of shortcomings with RCTs and their syntheses and the notion that they comprise a 'gold standard' method for generating findings that can confidently be drawn on by decision-makers. For extended discussions of their limitations see, for example Sidebottom and Tilley (2020) and Deaton and Cartwright (2018). Here are some of the problems.

1. RCTs measure net effects. Interventions generally produce a mixture of positive, negative, and nil effects across the space and time-specific population from which random assignment takes place. The net effects reflect the balance of positive and negative outcomes that are measured for that population. Decision-makers need, however, to know which parts of the population experience positive, which experience negative, and which experience nil effects. Even an intervention with net negative effects in the population for a given trial may produce positive effects in another population.
2. The results of RCTs hold for the population from which the random allocation takes place. We have to guess (or know more that we can gauge from RCTs) about their wider applicability. This is the problem of external validity and generalisability. Replications are the conventional route to attempts at generalisation. Points 5 and 7, of this list, highlight difficulties in them.
3. RCTs try to control out variability in conditions for the intervention and in the population in which the treatment is applied. This eliminates the normal variability in potential treatment target populations, which is of interest to the policy and practice decision-maker.

4. The controls which are introduced in some RCTs to provide a test in principle of the efficacy of programmes or intervention aim to make sure that the intervention is implemented exactly as designed in relation to the population for which it is designed in conditions which maximise the chances that any potential net intended outcome is achieved. In medical trials, this means carefully identifying potential beneficiaries for random allocation to treatment, no treatment or standard treatment, the application of treatments to those in the treatment group exactly as intended, and the minimisation of dropouts. Field trials try to measure effects in real-world conditions, where there are liable to be departures from the ideal treatment, in terms of who is treated, how the treatment is applied by the clinician, and the behaviours of those to be treated and those around them. The problem here is that of knowing what the ideal conditions are and what departures are tolerable for the trial still to count as a measure of the effectiveness of the treatment.

5. RCTs are generally flawed in their own terms in one way or another. Random allocation is imperfect. Those involved in allocation sometimes cheat. Some participants break blind, where they can detect if they belong to the treatment or control group. Few studies track long-term effects, partly due to the expense and partly because of the multitude of additional factors liable to kick in as time unfolds from the initial intervention. The Cambridge-Somerville example discussion in Chapter 2 is a rare exception.

    Where designs involve comparison groups where there is or can be no random allocation, equivalence is a matter of guesswork. Those in treatment conditions know they are involved and may modify behaviour accordingly in terms, for example, of interventions introduced and reporting and record keeping. Those in non-treatment conditions may likewise know it and adapt their behaviour accordingly. The all-round blinding techniques used in RCTs to reduce bias are missing. In crime prevention trials, area-matching may be in terms of correlates of the crime variable of interest rather than the crime variable itself. Crime levels fluctuate widely over short periods in local areas, meaning that it is all too easy to be misled by comparing changes in treatment and non-treatment areas.

6. Regarding replications and systematic reviews of studies that meet RCT or quasi-experimental standards, what counts and does not count as a real replication of the programme or intervention of interest is fluid and uncertain. Many programmes include multiple components, and decisions as to which are crucial are endlessly debatable (see Tilley, 1996 and later in the chapter for a discussion of this in relation to supposed replications of the Kirkholt project discussed in Chapter 2). With simple interventions, for example the use of physical measures such as CCTV, locks, safes, and alarms, the technologies evolve over time meaning that what nominally looks similar may change radically. Moreover, there are

processes of adaptation by offenders and crime prevention workers meaning that what was found then and there may no longer hold for here and
now. Furthermore, the systematic review that merges all these findings is
apt to disregard these developments and variations (see Piza, Welsh, Farrington, & Thomas, 2019 for a systematic review of the effects of CCTV
on crime).

7. Systematic reviews of RCTs and quasi-experimental studies jettison most
research relating to programmes and interventions, which is of potential
use to the decision-maker. At worst, such reviews find no research studies
that pass muster in relation to the fairly stringent standards set. Figure 7.3
gives an example in which I was involved, where we found no studies
that passed muster from a total of 7,922 papers that were found in an initial search of the published and unpublished literature (Perkins, Beecher,
Aberg, Edwards, & Tilley, 2017). This would suggest that there is no basis
in evidence to inform decisions about the use (on non-use) of personal
alarms as a preventive measure for healthcare workers.

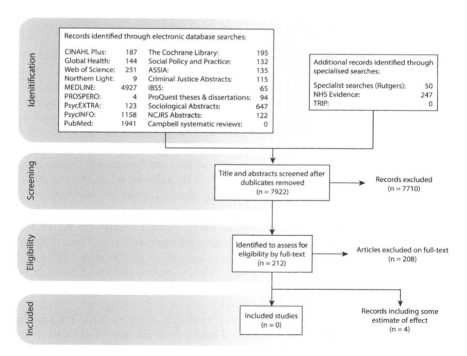

Figure 7.3 Flow of studies relating to personal alarms as devices for preventing violence against healthcare staff.

Source: Perkins et al. (2017).

8. Most studies involve dropouts: those allocated to treatment who do not receive it or fail to complete it for one reason or another. If they are excluded, there is a risk that they are atypical thereby distorting measurements of net effects (e.g. those completing the treatment might have improved without treatment anyway). If they are included, they dilute the effect that may only be achieved among those who experience the full treatment – enthusiasm to change may be a condition for treatments to be effective among those who would otherwise not change. The standard response to the dilemmas produced by dropouts is to focus on the 'intention to treat.' The treatment group for analytic purposes is taken to include all those for whom treatment was allocated regardless of whether they received any.

9. RCTs or designs that try to come close to them are impractical and unethical for measures aiming to prevent rare high-harm crimes such as terrorist attacks (Laycock, 2012). Think about randomly allocating security measures to protect those within buildings from perishing in the event of a terrorist attack. The sample of buildings would have to be very high for a trial, since the events are rare. Also, would anyone want to, and would it be morally defensible, to postpone installing measures such as bollards to targets attractive to terrorists, pending findings?

As I'll argue later, there is masses of evidence for use by decision-makers to inform what they do that does not come from RCTs and quasi-experimental studies that mimic the logic of the RCT design. Within the health community, diverse types of research methods using different types of evidence aiming to understand and inform the complex processes involved in treatment and its outcomes are employed. These can and need to be drawn to improve practice, as is now formally recognised in Medical Research Council guidelines on the development and evaluation of complex interventions (Skivington et al., 2021). Those in other fields that fail to acknowledge the contribution of and necessity for diverse research methods appear increasingly to be behind the curve.

What practical conclusions can be drawn from well-conducted RCTs and studies akin to them about the effectiveness of interventions? First, if positive effects are found, they show that the intervention *can* have the measured effect among some. Second, if no or negative net effects are found, they show that the intervention *may be* ineffective or may produce negative outcomes for some in relation to what is measured.

RCTs may be especially useful where entrenched treatments, backed by tradition or by celebrated but occasional improvements, have followed treatments supported by enthusiastic (often self-interested and dogmatic) proponents of them. In medicine, there are classic cases of this: laying babies to rest on their stomachs, radical surgery in responses to some cases of breast cancer, hygiene practices in maternity wards, and the use of thalidomide to reduce morning sickness among pregnant women. In some cases (including thalidomide and hand hygiene), initial alerts came from non-RCT studies. In other cases of unintended adverse effects, notably the carcinogenic consequences of smoking, other research designs prevailed. But the concern with unintended backfire effects is important, and well-run RCTs and their like have an important role in showing how unintended net negative outcomes can sometimes be produced. The Cambridge-Somerville study outlined in Chapter 2 is a case in point in relation to crime prevention.

RCTs may also be useful in crime prevention settings where default measures are at issue, either because responses need to be made by those without the time or know-how to use discretion wisely or because general measures that are costly are at issue in which knowing their net effects is important for informing decisions. In health, vaccination provides an example. In crime prevention, police arrest of the perpetrator as a response to calls relating to domestic violence may be a case in point (see Sherman, 1992). RCTs promise robust net effects measurements in these general situations, but they are not the only methods that can be used. Two of the examples from Chapter 2 show this. The evidence on the effects of security improvements to cars on vehicle theft were shown using crime survey data. For victims of car theft, respondents were asked about vehicle security measures at the time of the theft. The analyses found that detailed patterns of change in theft accorded well with what would be expected if security measures were responsible for overall falls. Likewise, the falls in repeat domestic violence observed in Killingbeck also accorded with the specific theoretically expected outcome pattern.

The College of Policing Toolkit

The College of Policing Toolkit was designed and initially populated through the research support programme for the What Works Centre for Crime Reduction, mentioned earlier. The original idea was a) to systematically search for systematic reviews of crime prevention interventions whose impact had been assessed using studies reaching levels 3–5 of the Maryland Scale and b) to conduct new reviews of the same kind where no systematic review of an intervention had yet been undertaken. The findings were to be made available for policy and practice decision-makers through the College of Policing. In other words, the plan was to draw together findings that met the standards outlined (and critically assessed) above, to distil what is known with reasonable confidence about what does and doesn't work to prevent crime.

In the event, the research support team argued that the toolkit should focus on decision-maker needs (not necessarily wants) and that these needs were not adequately met simply by summarising the net effects that emerge through systematic reviews of studies that met minimum standards of the kind shown in the Maryland Scale. 'EMMIE' (which is drawn on in examples in Chapter 6) is the acronym developed to capture the evidence needs of those working in crime reduction (see Johnson, Tilley, & Bowers, 2015).

- The initial 'E' of EMMIE refers to positive and negative effects, the net outcome of which is the focus of RCTs and other studies meeting minimum Maryland Scale standards. Policymakers and practitioners clearly need to come to a judgement about the expected effects of the courses of action they are contemplating. The past track record of policies and practices is therefore of interest.
- The first 'M' refers to mechanisms – how the policy or practice is expected to bring about positive and negative outcomes. Without attention to mechanisms (how things work), interventions fly blind and could in principle include anything! Established mechanisms are routinely invoked and drawn on in medicine and engineering in developing promising interventions, and their inclusion as part of EMMIE simply reflects their revealed importance in other successful applied fields. Changes are brought about by the activation (or deactivation) of causal mechanisms by the introduction of interventions.
- The second 'M' refers to 'moderators' – the conditions shaping the mechanisms that are activated to produce patterns of effect. Understanding mechanisms and moderators provides a basis for determining what results are liable to be produced by an intervention being put in place in the specific conditions facing the policy or practice decision-maker.Laycock and Tilley (1995) discuss the example of Neighbourhood Watch and the varying community contexts for them to produce crime reduction outcomes.
- The 'I' refers to implementation. Funding, securing agreement for, installing, applying, operating, and maintaining crime prevention interventions are often complex and challenging. Decision-makers need to know about these realities in choosing any intervention. The Cambridge-Somerville study mentioned in Chapter 2 shows how far implementation conditions (in that case some of which were entirely unpredictable) can undermine the activities needed to activate the mechanisms postulated for the intervention.
- The second 'E' refers to 'economics.' Resources are always limited and can always be put to alternative uses. Hence, knowing about expected costs and expected benefits from policies and practices is crucial to rational decision-making. Knowing about them in relation to crime prevention interventions is, therefore, important.

The systematic reviews populating the College of Policing database include all that met the specified methodological criteria, which means that they did not include studies with different designs which might have spoken to mechanisms and implementation. This selection reflected the priority attached to impact, the original brief, and the original aspirations for the toolkit.

Figure 7.4 shows that, beginning with almost 14,000 records identified from systematically searching databases of journal articles and the grey literature, eventually through screening processes, only 70 eligible systematic reviews were found up to 2015, covering 44 topics. Fifty-one of the 70 reviews related to offender-focused interventions, ten to place-based ones, and nine to a mix of place and offender.

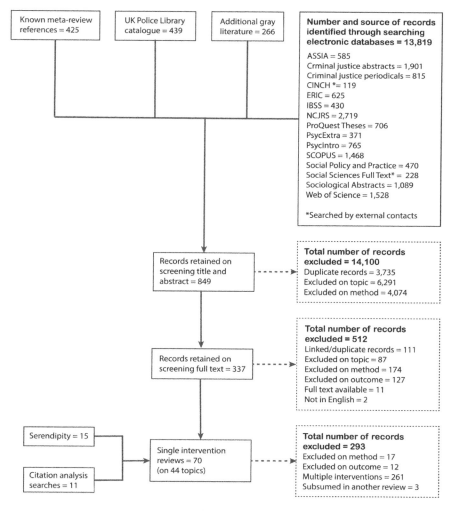

Figure 7.4 The search for systematic reviews meeting inclusion criteria for the College of Policing Toolkit.

Table 7.2 The quality of evidence in systematic reviews.

Q-score	Effect	Mechanism	Moderator	Implementation	Economics
0	4	9	10	11	64
1	13	36	21	30	5
2	14	15	29	16	1
3	25	8	5	12	0
4	14	2	5	1	0
Total	70	70	70	70	70

The quality of the evidence in the 70 reviews was assessed for all EMMIE variables. Table 7.2 shows the results (going from 4 where the evidence was exemplary to 0 where there was none, Tompson et al., 2020). Suffice it to say that the findings do not indicate that there is a plethora of useful evidence for decision-makers from the kinds of studies included in systematic reviews, most notably for interventions focused on place! The College of Policing Toolkit provides a user-friendly way of accessing what is known about 'What works' from the kinds of studies included which were, when the What Works Centres were established, taken to provide the most robust evidence.

The need for the synthesis of diverse sources of evidence

The study of reviews of personal alarms as an intervention to prevent violence against staff in healthcare settings brings out the general shortcomings of RCTs and kindred studies for informing decisions about whether or not to supply alarms to staff. As Figure 7.3 shows, no such studies were found. But this does not mean that we know nothing that is helpful. There are, studies including evidence about alarms in other settings, for example in relation to domestic burglaries, commercial burglaries, shop theft, mobile phone theft, bank robberies, theft of and from cars, and domestic violence. We also know that there are many different types of personal alarms, for example those attached to mobile phones, those requiring button pressing, those designed to be available in a pocket or handbag, those that are automatically sounded in given circumstances, and those actively or passively activated by the victim. There are, furthermore, many contexts in which personal alarms are used, for example as standalone devices or as part of a security system including dedicated staff on hand to respond when the alarm is passively activated or intentionally triggered. We know enough to build a plausible theory of alarms for healthcare workers as a violence prevention measure which is informed by evidence and which decision-makers can productively draw on to work out whether they make sense in their conditions.

Let us look in a little more detail at the available evidence to do with personal alarms for preventing violence against healthcare workers. First, there are research findings on the rates, distribution, and costs of violent incidents impacting healthcare workers, including the following.

- Internationally, a third of nurses have been assaulted and injured, and two-thirds have experienced non-physical violence (Spector, Zhou, & Che, 2014).
- In England and Wales, 5% to 8% of frontline NHS staff have been physically assaulted (Ipsos MORI, 2010).
- Nurses are four times more likely to experience assaults than any other NHS worker, with student nurses and those in psychiatric and learning disability areas at the highest risk of victimisation (Wells & Bowers, 2002).
- A quarter of reported assaults occur in acute wards (Wells & Bowers, 2002).
- Seven in ten reported incidents of violence against healthcare workers involve those with mental health problems and learning disability (Spector et al., 2014).
- Violence is commonest in geriatric wards (45.9%), emergency departments (49.5%), and psychiatric departments (55%) (Spector et al., 2014).
- Assaults are predominantly committed by patients (64%) and patient family members and friends (30%), the remainder by nurses, doctors, or staff (11%) (Spector et al., 2014).
- The prevalence rate of violence against health and social care workers (at 6.2% in a year) is more than four times that for all adults of working age (1.3%) (Health and Safety Executive, 2017).
- The Home Office had estimated the total average cost of each common assault at £540, which includes the physical and emotional impact, victim services, lost output, and the police court and prison costs (the average for more serious incidents of violence against the person, excluding homicide, rising to £19,000) (Brand & Price, 2000).
- Causal factors identified in analyses of violent incidents impacting healthcare workers include patient mental health, alcohol, and drugs; waiting times/delays; anxiety about practical issues (such as transport); and failed expectations about service (Ipsos MORI, 2010; Rew & Ferns, 2005).

Second, there is a research literature on the uses of alarms for other crime prevention purposes alongside a more general research literature relating to crime prevention mechanisms and their activation. Let us see how this research, alongside findings relating to violence against healthcare workers, might help the decision-maker concerned with the problem. Let us also think again about what kind of research agenda is most likely to be useful in informing future decisions. Table 7.3 cross-tabulates points of concentration

Table 7.3 Violence concentrations, alarms, and possible crime-related mechanisms.

Mechanism

	Summons help	Disables attacker	Deters attacker	Reminds rules	Improves confidence	Renders complacent	Stimulates attack
Violent departments							
Geriatrics	✓				✓	✓	
Psychiatric	✓				✓	✓	✓
Emergency	✓		✓	✓		✓	
Vulnerable victims							
New staff	✓				✓		
Lone workers	✓	✓				✓	
Violent people							
Patients (mentally ill, drugged up, drunk)	✓	✓		✓			✓
Family	✓		✓	✓			
Bystanders	✓		✓	✓			

Note: This relates specifically to healthcare workers as they discharge their professional duties. More would be needed to cater for panic alarms more generally and in other settings.

in violence against healthcare workers and crime-related mechanisms, which may be activated by alarms to produce intended or unintended outcomes.

The potential mechanisms will vary, for example, by type of alarm (e.g. silent or noisy, including the volume); by complementary local conditions (e.g. availability of security staff, signage/publicity); by the reliability of the alarm system (too many false alarms may desensitise potential interveners); by other measures changing the environment (such as physical layout, lighting, treatment procedures, escape routes, CCTV, proximity of security staff); by longer-term adaptations by health workers (such as decisions whether to carry alarms and make sure they work); and by adaptations of potentially violent people (who may learn that alarms do or don't in practice increase risk to them).

In these circumstances and against the background of the available evidence, searching for a single summary effect size looks unhelpful for the crime prevention decision-maker. They want to work out whether using alarms is a promising strategy in their circumstances, and, if so, how to get the most (cost) effective outcomes. For this, they have quite a lot of research resources to draw on, but RCTs and their related counterparts focusing on finding one effect size through an experiment do not look especially useful. It was tempting to conclude from our systematic review, which found no studies meeting minimum standards, that such studies were badly needed. However, we conceded this would have been a mistake (Perkins et al., 2017).

Violence is too heterogeneous, alarms are too different from one another, contexts are too variable, and the human actions necessary as a corollary of the technology are too complex for RCTs to add much value for the decision-maker in his or her specific situation. Decision-makers need to cobble together a theory of how alarms might reduce the violence with which they are concerned in their settings, drawing on the research literature to try to anticipate how a reduction in violence would likely follow and what other side effects might inadvertently be produced. This will provide a template with which to track what in the event follows and subsequently to adjust accordingly.

Where else might the decision-maker look for useful evidence?

Case studies

In crime prevention, case studies are much more widespread than RCTs and their like. Case studies have also been important in changing crime prevention practice. One risk is that the rhetoric surrounding weak case studies may lead to the wider adoption of poor work. Another risk is that strong case studies may be neglected in the absence of persuasive advocacy. Moreover, the practical lessons to be learned from strong case studies reporting success are often unclear. Here, I want to explain the value of case studies in crime prevention and suggest how, used properly, they can play an important role in advancing effective crime prevention.

Case studies in the physical and biological world can have a massive impact by showing what is possible. These achievements can later be built on in programmes of improvement. The Wright brothers' demonstration in 1903 that fixed-wing human flight was possible put paid to the gainsayers, plausibly drawing on centuries of failure, that no such thing was possible. The rest is history: what followed was a programme of research and experimentation that goes on to this day, refining human flight and making it cheaper, quieter, safer, and less polluting. Christiaan Barnard's demonstration in 1967 that successful human-to-human heart transplant was possible likewise led to a programme of research and experimentation that has made heart transplants safer with increasing survival rates for recipients.

Crime prevention is replete with case studies purporting to demonstrate the effectiveness of the interventions put in place. Clarke (1997) and Scott and Clarke (2020) are collections of some of the best of them. The *popcenter.org* website has many more. In Chapter 2, we saw several case studies that related to drink-driving, domestic burglary, and domestic violence. Of course, case studies can be complex, the evidence for effectiveness is seldom cast iron, the responsible ingredients in successful interventions with many components are difficult to discern, and the necessary conditions for success can be unclear. This puts crime prevention decision-makers who are keen to adopt an evidence-based approach in a quandary.

Let us take one example of a crime prevention case study to examine how case studies can fruitfully be drawn on by decision-makers. The example I'm going to use is the Kirkholt Burglary Prevention Project, already sketched out in Chapter 2 and referred to earlier in this chapter.

The findings of the Kirkholt project were published in two Home Office reports that were widely circulated to policymakers, practitioners, and academics (Forrester, Chatterton, & Pease, 1988; Forrester, Frenz, O'Connell, & Pease, 1990). They were part of a numbered series of *Crime Prevention Unit Papers* that had the imprimatur of a government department. The Home Office at that time was funding a 'Safer Cities' programme that was run by a research unit (see Tilley, 1993b). Safer Cities began by providing grants in 20 cities, staffed by specially employed Home Office appointees who were charged with managing a grant to support targeted crime prevention initiatives. These teams were encouraged to draw on the Kirkholt findings to address burglary problems in areas where levels were high in their cities. I was asked evaluate the projects that were put in place to see whether the success of Kirkholt was replicable. My findings were published in a subsequent Crime Prevention Unit Paper (Tilley, 1995, see also Tilley, 1996). They provide some evidence of what happens when case studies are drawn on.

The conditions for drawing on the Kirkholt Project within the Safer Cities Programme were promising. Those initiating projects had money and expertise. They were working in cities that had especially high rates of burglary at a time when national burglary rates overall were high by historic standards. What was revealed in the Safer Cities projects was the difficulty in knowing what was essential to Kirkholt. I wanted to treat them as replications to see whether the Kirkholt project's impressive successes were a fluke or were generalisable. Could we expect copies of Kirkholt to deliver similar benefits elsewhere?

As with most crime prevention projects, 'Kirkholt' had many components (including 'cocoon' home watch, removal of prepayment meters for gas and electricity, prompt security upgrades, a focus on those who had been victimised, and an initial survey and analysis of crime data better to understand the problem). The estate where it was delivered had distinct attributes (including housing types, layout, population, links to surrounding areas), and the implementation of the project had particular human and financial resources (including an experienced university team, a special grant from the Home Office, a dedicated and inspired project leader, substantial Manpower Services supplementary staff). What was essential was not clear. Both the areas themselves and what was done in them varied from project to project, albeit that all were supposedly based on Kirkholt. What would amount to 'fidelity' in replication was indeterminable. Selection from the Kirkholt project was unavoidable and decisions about what to select uncertain. Table 7.4 compares some of the attributes of the projects based on Kirkholt with those of the Kirkholt project itself (see Tilley, 1996 for more detail).

Table 7.4 Kirkholt and its 'replications.'

Kirkholt	Replication? 1	Replication? 2	Replication? 3
Well-funded demonstration project	Standard (much lower) funding	Standard (much lower) funding	Standard (much lower) funding
25% incidence rate for recorded burglary	Burglary rate quarter of Kirkholt's	Burglary rate third of Kirkholt's	Burglary rate fifth of Kirkholt's
Clear target area boundaries	No clear boundaries	Clear boundaries	Partial boundaries
Removal of utility cash prepayment meters	Few cash prepayment meters	Nothing on meters	Meters did not figure as a burglary issue
Extensive initial research	Different research	No research	Different research
Established effective police-led interagency partnership	Police and probation involvement. No specified lead	Safer-Cities-led interagency project	Police-led project-employing carpenter
Security upgrades for victims	Council tenant security upgrades	Security upgrades for all	Security upgrades for victims and those 'at risk'
Cocoon home watch round victims	Neighbourhood concern groups, not victim cocooning	No Neighbourhood/ Home Watch	No Neighbourhood /Home Watch
Domestic burglary focus	Domestic burglary focus	Domestic burglary focus	Domestic burglary focus

What Kirkholt and its intended lookalikes reveal is that some level of abstraction is necessary to go from the details of a specific intervention to distil its supposed crucial features. Replications can never be exact. Assumptions about what matters (and what doesn't) in any intervention are necessary. The efforts to replicate Kirkholt bring this to the surface. Decision-makers need to recognise the inevitability and complexity of abstraction from a given case study to work out what can be taken for achieving their objectives in their own conditions.

Much of what mattered most in Kirkholt has become clearer in the light of subsequent research and case studies that have drawn on it. First, the ubiquity of repeat victimisation patterns, discussed in Chapter 3, across places and crime types, has been revealed in many research studies. It is easy to forget the scepticism with which the initial findings on repeats in Kirkholt were greeted. I remember the shaking of heads in the Home Office at the time! However, the phenomenon of repeat victimisation and its use as a basis for targeting crime prevention interventions have become commonplace. Indeed, it lies, for example, behind the Killingbeck domestic violence prevention case study outlined in Chapter 2. Second, Kirkholt revealed the benefits of the problem-solving strategy, which lies at the heart of Chapter 6 and is now widely endorsed. Before deciding what to do to try to reduce burglary in Kirkholt, extensive data collection and analysis were undertaken to figure out the nature of the problem and what might most effectively be done to reduce it, the interventions were monitored, and the outcomes evaluated. Third, it exemplified the need for third parties to be involved in reducing opportunities for specific crimes in this case by removing prepayment meters, target hardening the most vulnerable dwellings, and surrounding burgled dwellings with cocoons to increase the risk to would-be return burglars. It may also have inadvertently helped reduce near repeat burglaries with its attention to neighbours of victims, who as we saw in Chapter 3 are at heighted risk as well as the burgled dwelling itself!

Given the impossibility of exact replication in crime prevention, a different term might better capture ways in which case studies can fruitfully be drawn on by decision-makers in dealing with their problems. I suggest 'emulation.' Emulation acknowledges that a project drawn on is being treated as exemplary and inspires efforts to effect similar achievements, but it does not imply that the project is simply being transposed to a new setting. Rather, selection and adaptation are needed to take account of different conditions. Some tailoring to idiosyncratic circumstances is provided for. Reported follow-up case studies can then help refine understanding of the causes behind Kirkholt's successes, and how its successes can be reproduced or improved. This is the story behind improvements in human flight following the Wright brothers and heart transplants following Christiaan Barnard.

Advice on accessing and using evidence

Popcenter.org provides a treasure trove of materials that those concerned with the prevention of crime can access easily and freely. Hundreds of problem-oriented projects can be found, the majority of which speak to case studies of efforts to reduce crimes of one sort or another. In addition, there is a range of background material on crime prevention, and especially situational crime prevention. Step-by-step guides to systematic problem-solving in diverse languages can be downloaded, on the basis of the original '55 small steps' written by Ron Clarke and John Eck (2003). There are links, too, to further sources of evidence and advice, including a useful 'library.' It is the obvious starting point for any crime prevention decision-maker concerned to draw on evidence.

Popcenter.org, thus, comprises a large warehouse, including bric-a-brac of varying quality as well as more substantial items. While the origins of *popcenter.org* lie in Goldstein's vision for *policing*, much of the material is relevant to others with crime prevention interests or responsibilities.

Problem-solving guides comprise the main original component of *popcenter.org*. These distil what is known in ways that are orientated to informing decisions about what to do in attempting to reduce specific crime problems. The first series comprise 'Problem Specific Guides.' At the time of writing, there were 74 of them. Examples include 'Robbery of Pharmacies,' 'Gasoline Drive-Offs,' 'Sexual Assault of Women by Strangers,' 'Theft of Scrap Metal,' 'Domestic Violence,' 'Drunk Driving,' and 'Assaults in and Around Bars,' as well as 'Shoplifting' which I drew on in Chapter 7. The guides are updated periodically to take advantage of new evidence.

These problem-specific guides have a common structure. They begin with a general description of the problem and what produces it, move on to what decision-makers need to do to understand the problem in their local situation, and then turn to how to select promising responses. An appendix summarises possible responses discussed in more detail earlier in the guide, under the following headings: Response (what could be done), How It Works (the underlying mechanism), Works Best If (the contextual conditions for the response to activate the change mechanism), and Considerations (mostly implementation conditions). Table 7.5 summarises the table for responses to pharmacy robbery (La Vigne & Wartell, 2015).

Evidence drawn on came from different countries, notably the United States, Canada, Australia, the Republic of Ireland and the United Kingdom. Sources included academic studies, government reports, industry body materials, news reports, trade magazine stories, and police service reports and presentations. Rather than rely only on reviews sifting out everything that failed to meet a particular standard for a particular methodology, here opportunist use was made of all sources and types of evidence which could help decide what to do to reduce the problems of pharmacy robbery.

Lest it be thought that focusing specifically on robbery in pharmacies, as against other business, involves too much specificity, a case study relating to the prevention of robberies in bookmakers (betting shops) in London highlights the importance of detail.

The Metropolitan Police Flying Squad (2011) project, as described in Chapter 2, implemented a problem-solving project aiming to reduce a specific robbery problem arising across London (causing financial losses as well as obvious distress to staff). Betting shops were frequent targets of armed robbery because they handled large quantities of cash, which was obviously attractive to criminals. The Flying Squad looked at the times when robberies tended to take place – at closing time when cash holdings were high,

Table 7.5 Responses to problems of pharmacy robbery.

Response	How it works	Works best if . . .	Considerations
Informing pharmacy employees about robbery trends	Heightens pharmacy staff vigilance and preparedness so as to minimise harm in the event of a robbery	. . . pharmacies provide routine training and updates to employees and communicate with police	Informing pharmacists alone will do little to prevent robberies, but, combined with other good security practices, it could aid them in protecting themselves and any customers present and seeking assistance quickly
Providing prevention guidance to pharmacy employees	Improves pharmacy staff compliance with robbery prevention policies and practices	. . . training is conducted on a routine basis and is reinforced by posters, checklists, and other literature prominently posted in employee break areas	Pharmacy staff turnover can be high, underscoring the importance of including prevention guidance as a part of new staff orientation processes
Managing risk factors	Reduces vulnerability of pharmacy to robbery	. . . pharmacy staff is educated about potential harms and what should be done specifically to reduce each risk	Risks vary for fraud, burglary, and robbery so there is a need to know each; risks also vary by pharmacy, depending on physical layout, staffing, etc.
Installing a panic alarm	Increases the probability of police apprehension	. . . the alarm is easily accessible, not obvious, and goes directly to police	Panic alarms will only deter robbers if they know generally that such alarms exist
Using a video surveillance system	Deters potential robbers who are aware of the system; increases the likelihood of identification and apprehension.	. . . the cameras as well as signs announcing the cameras are noticeable.	Pharmacy owners must be persuaded to install high-quality systems
Tracking the stolen drugs /offenders	Increase the likelihood of identification and apprehension; may be a deterrent for those who are generally aware they may be tracked	. . . all pharmacy staff are aware of and know how to use tracking methods, and police have the resources to respond quickly	Tracking devices are primarily investigative tools but may prevent robberies if offenders believe a pharmacy may be using these tools
Using deterrent signage	May deter individuals who calculate risks relatively carefully	. . . signs are placed in prominent locations both at the entrance of the pharmacy and near the pharmacy counter	In other crime prevention contexts, these forms of deterrence alone have not had much of an impact on criminal behaviour
Employing security measures			Measures will vary depending on store design (inside and out), staffing, and types of drugs that are dispensed

Measure	How it works	Condition	Potential problems
Increasing pharmacy lighting	Increases the risk of detection by police and identification by witnesses	...lighting is positioned so as to not cast shadows; lighting is combined with a wide array of security measures	Brighter lights alone are unlikely to prevent pharmacy robberies
Locking up drugs	Increases the difficulty in gaining access to desired drugs	...accessibility is limited and offenders believe that pharmacy staff cannot access drugs	Some potential for violent reactions by offenders upon learning that drugs are inaccessible; potentially higher costs for pharmacies and greater inconvenience for pharmacy staff in filling prescriptions
Installing physical barriers	Denies access to drugs; reduces the likelihood that pharmacy staff will be coerced into turning over drugs	...pharmacy staff know how to use barriers, and barriers are properly maintained	Higher costs for pharmacies and some reduction in 'personal touch' of customer service
Ensuring front windows are clear	Increases the likelihood that police or witnesses will detect a robbery in progress, which might be a deterrent	...there is clear line of sight from outside the store to the pharmacy counter	May increase costs to pharmacy if remodelling is required; some potential loss of advertising opportunities
Limiting the drugs available	Denies the desired drugs, at least in large quantities	...the fact that targeted drugs are restricted is prominently advertised through signage at the pharmacy entrance	Pharmacies may lose legitimate customers to pharmacies where these drugs are more readily available
Limiting the drug information available via telephone	Reduces the ability to determine whether robbery is worth the risk	...all pharmacy staff abide by not discussing drug availability with customers	Pharmacies may lose legitimate customers to pharmacies where it is easier for them to determine whether these drugs are available
Conducting focused surveillance and enforcement	Intended to increase the likelihood of apprehension	...a rash of robberies was concentrated at a few properties such that prospects of detection through surveillance were high, and there were few offenders in the community	
Increasing penalties for pharmacy robbery	Intended to deter through threats of harsh punishment	...enhanced penalties are widely publicised and/or known offenders are notified, and potential offenders believe they will be apprehended and punished	Many studies of the deterrence value of enhanced penalties suggest they do not prevent crime, mainly because offenders do not believe their risk of apprehension is high

staff numbers low, and punters few. They looked at what reduced risks to offenders at targeted premises – blacked out windows or windows covered in posters meaning that those outside couldn't see what was happening inside. The Flying Squad worked with bookmakers and bookmaker organisations to modify their operational practices and to change the layout and design of their premises in order to reduce their vulnerability. The aim was to change bookmaker robberies from being low risk/high reward to being high risk/low reward. This was the theory. The changes wrought applied the theory to the specifics of bookmakers. It was successful. But the circumstances for robberies of bookmakers differ from those of robberies of pharmacies.

Chapter 3 focused on targeting problems using evidence relating to crime concentrations, which is obviously relevant for decision-makers. This chapter has focused mainly on evidence about what to put in place to prevent crimes effectively and efficiently. Both types of evidence are needed by decision-makers.

For crime prevention decision-makers trying to make decisions relating to local problems, all the sources of evidence discussed earlier are useful. The problem-solving guides available at *popcenter.org* help match past interventions with present conditions. Even when no guide for the specific problem at issue is available, the reports show decision-makers the kinds of question they need to ask themselves in deciding what intervention(s) to use. Decision-makers can use well-documented case studies, but they need to work out whether and how they are relevant to their conditions. The controlled experiments that meet minimum Maryland Scale standards (and the warehouses of systematic reviews of them) can be drawn on for the past track record of intervention types that might be successful.

Discretion, evidence, and crime prevention decision-making

Those involved in crime prevention may or may not be given discretion to decide what to do. Their discretion may or may not be backed by evidence. Their non-discretion likewise may or may not be backed by evidence. Table 7.6 shows four possibilities.

Table 7.6 A typology of discretion and evidence in crime prevention decision-making.

	Backed by evidence	Not backed by evidence
Discretion not allowed	A	B
Discretion allowed	C	D

The least risky way of dealing with a presenting problem when there is no time or expertise to work out a bespoke one is A – to impose informed no or low discretion responses that largely disregard the specifics of cases. The results of RCTs and kindred study designs can be especially useful here, despite their shortcomings. The best response to a problem is C. Here, practitioners use discretion based on their informed understanding of the particulars of the situation and of relevant tested theory. The riskiest strategy is B – to require a response but one that is not backed by evidence, so that it may systematically fail or cause harm. There can be success in D – discretionary responses not backed by evidence, but it depends on creativity, common sense, and experience. Some decision-makers are more creative and have more experience and common sense than others. In the previous chapter on problem-solving, we saw examples where problems had been cracked by committed practitioners using their judgement and experience to work out what to do in the face of idiosyncratic situations. Written up as case studies, these inspired responses can be fed into the evidence-base for future emulation by others.

Table 7.6 is, of course, a simplification, presented here for heuristic purposes. Policies and practices can be better or worse backed by evidence. Moreover, crime prevention practitioners (and other decision-makers) can have more or less discretion. Nudge theorists draw attention to the use of 'defaults' to set standard (at best, evidence-backed) practice, which can be overturned in specific situations if there are good reasons for doing so (Thaler & Sunstein, 2008).

Car theft crime prevention provides a nice example of default-setting for drivers. One of the striking features of car security measures, referred to as an example in Chapter 2, is that their activation and deactivation largely no longer require action by the individual driver (see Farrell & Tilley, 2022). When we enter the car and drive it away, most of the security features are activated or deactivated automatically, as required. We can activate or deactivate them manually, but the default is that they are switched on and off automatically. This goes not only for electronic immobilisers but also for alarms, retraction of wing mirrors, and locking of doors. Other security devices are built into the car and do not need activation or deactivation, for example the distribution of components of the audio system within the vehicle rather than a removable device. Although the technology and its development may be complex and likewise the processes around decision-making to install them (see Laycock, 2004), once in place their operation requires little or no human agency. They are just there.

In the case of domestic violence, the Killingbeck experiment suggests that even where there will be many unique features to each incident and each case, sufficient commonality could be identified to inform non-discretionary escalating responses with successive incidents (A in Table 7.6). In these cases, decision-making is largely in the hands of those competent to specify non-discretionary interventions by those not sufficiently equipped to make them themselves. Sadly, discretion is often removed by powerful and confident decision-makers who do not know as much as those whose responses they are directing. This is catastrophic.

The creation of evidence

The problem-solving process of crime prevention described in Chapter 6 both uses evidence and creates it. It uses evidence in informing searches for patterns, in the identification of modifiable causes, and in selecting possible responses. It creates evidence in the discovery of new patterns, in the identification of local causal conditions, and in the assessment of achievements. At its best, it creates case studies that others can draw on and try to emulate, as indicated earlier in this chapter.

There is a huge technical literature on research methods in social science, criminology, and crime analysis. Data creation and collection are tricky. There are multiple bear traps into which the unwary can fall. Self-deception is also commonplace. One of the reasons for multiple blinding (recipients of treatment, deliverers of treatment, and analysis of data) in the best of randomised controlled trials is that biases very easily creep in. Placebo (experiencing positive effects unrelated to the activation of supposed active elements of the treatment for test) and nocebo (experiencing negative effects unrelated to the unintended activation of active elements of the treatment for test) responses are well-documented in research on medical interventions.

Here, I confine myself to a few general points on data and data sources that are drawn on in creating evidence for crime prevention, not so much for the specialist analyst who should be aware of them, as for the general reader and those who may create evidence more occasionally.

The first point to make is that all data are socially constructed. The notion that there are brute facts about crime that speak for themselves is mistaken.

The social creation of data is most obvious in interviews and surveys that involve interactions between the informant and the researcher. Questions are asked by the researcher (sometimes in questionnaires and sometimes face-to-face). The questions are interpreted by the respondent who configures his or her reply according to their understanding of what is being asked from them (and what they are prepared to say). There is always scope for alternative interpretations, and (consciously or otherwise) the respondent has to work out what is wanted. Take a simple question, 'Do you have children?'. The respondent may take it to include or not include stepchildren, adoptive children, children who have been taken into care, grown-up children who have flown the nest, adult as well as dependent children still in residence, children at university, dead children as well as those who are alive, resident grandchildren, foster children, and so on. The question may look simple, but the answer is unavoidably constructed in light of the respondent's perceptions of the interests and needs of the researcher. There is no brute, correct answer, and statistical summaries of responses are summaries of the data constructed through interviews. For some research questions, one answer to a number of children is needed, for others a different one! One reason for always explaining clearly the underlying reason behind questions used in an interview or a questionnaire is to try best to align respondent interpretations of questions with the interests of those asking them.

Crime surveys (also referred to as victimisation surveys) are widely used for collecting data on crime patterns. They are sometimes face-to-face and sometimes by phone and sometimes use questionnaires for the completion on paper or online. At best, they are very carefully designed to maximise the chances that the respondent understands what the question is about, for example in defining crimes that may not always be understood consistently or as intended: for instance in common parlance, burglaries are often referred to as robberies, albeit that a more precise understanding of both burglary and robbery is needed to elicit what the survey aims to uncover. There remain problems, however. There is quite an extensive literature on questions concerning emotional responses to crime, most notably fear, and their varying interpretations by respondents (see, e.g. Ditton, Bannister, Gilchrist, & Farrall, 1999; Farrall, Bannister, Ditton, & Gilchrist, 1997). Moreover, homing in on 'fear' may miss more significant emotional responses such as anger. There are known difficulties in recall when crime surveys ask about the experience of crimes, even if the crime type is understood as intended. Some respondents may include crimes that occurred outside the intended time period about which questions are asked (most often a year). Others may omit incidents either because they are forgotten or are taken to have occurred outside the intended time period.

Repeats pose special problems in crime surveys. For very frequent incidents, such as domestic violence in the case of individuals or shop theft among some retailers, estimating overall numbers can be very tricky, and different strategies have been adopted to try to deal with the issue (see, e.g. Farrell & Pease, 2007). For the estimation of the incidence of crime (the number of crimes of a given type over a given period in relation to the population at risk), including rare instances of very high numbers of crimes experienced by a small number of victims can have a dramatic effect on a sample survey and make trends hard to represent across repeat surveys. Contrariwise, disregarding the very high numbers of crimes suffered by some victims risks misleading users of crime surveys about the real experience of crime.

Crime surveys are expensive, and very large ones are needed to get any fix on relatively rare crimes, so coverage is always restricted. They generally fail to capture corporate crime victimisation. They are not useful for the analysis of crime problems in small areas: national surveys will have too few respondents. Local surveys are prohibitively expensive if done properly with a large enough sample. There is always some uncertainty over non-respondents. Their attributes may be compared to those of respondents, but this does not mean that crime experience is the same. Response rates for national crime surveys have been high, but levels are falling.

Self-report surveys are also conducted to collect data on offending behaviour. These can vary in ways akin to the variations in victimisation surveys and have similar limitations. Furthermore, there are greater risks to the truthfulness of responses. Self-report studies are hard to design but can be useful in demonstrating the normality of much criminal behaviour across the lifetime of individuals and in showing differences in the levels of criminal behaviour across age and gender.

Reports of results of individual interviews, focus groups, and participant and nonparticipant observational studies are obviously socially constructed. They depend on researcher interpretations of those interviewed or observed, on presentational contingencies at work for subjects of the research, and on recording practices. This does not of course invalidate the data assembled but means that they can easily be skewed or mislead, especially when collected by inexpert researchers with poorly designed research instruments and research practices.

In relation to crime, administrative data are routinely used. These relate to both victimisation and offending. Regarding patterns of crime event, the attraction of recorded crime is that it is relevant to small areas, and statistical records go back a long way (to 1898 in England and Wales!). Crime surveys were originally conducted to try to address the 'dark figure' of crime: crimes that had taken place but had been unrecorded either because they had not been reported or because, although reported, they were not recorded by the police. Reporting and recording depend on decisions by citizens and police workers. Confidence in the police and a belief that they can and will respond helpfully are likely to affect reporting decisions. Factors impacting recording decisions may include chances that the crime can be detected, the perceived credibility of the person reporting the crime, the category of crime into which the reported event can be slotted, and the costs and benefits of the one chosen.

Historical trends and comparisons across areas are undermined by variations and changes in crime reporting and recording practices, which themselves depend on a range of contingencies. For example the telephone made reporting crime easier as landlines, and then mobiles, became commonplace. For some offences, notably domestic violence and rape, an increase in the rates of reported incidents may reflect victims/survivors' increased confidence that they will be responded to properly rather than increases in numbers of offences. Contrariwise, a reduction in confidence in the police may reduce reporting if victims think nothing will be gained by it.

Crime-recording practices also affect the ease with which estimates of repeat patterns can be made. Inconsistences in location records have made estimating local rates tricky (Farrell & Pease, 1993). Some police services said they did not have a repeat problem based on their analysis of local records. On inspection, it has been found that they missed events due to recording inconsistencies. Moreover, failures to report and record crimes reduce the chances that repeat patterns will be found. Sometimes, failures to report successive incidents may follow from the perceived failure of the police to take action that is helpful to the victim.

Regarding victim attributes, the police can be coy about asking some questions, for example about age. In the first piece of crime prevention research I undertook, which related to domestic burglary, I asked the Police Inspector seconded to the project about the age and gender of the person reporting the crime. At that time, there were no computerised records. He told me that that would be easy to find out. It was recorded on the C4 form. A few days later, he came back to say that most of the women had been recorded as 'Over 21'!

Administrative data can also be drawn on in relation to offenders. But clear-up rates for many crimes are low and depend on police resources, police skills, the focus of police efforts, the skills of offenders, and available technologies. Detection is a social process, and charging depends on social processes, as do prosecutions and outcomes in court. Moreover, crime itself is a social event. There are direct or indirect relationships between offenders and victims. Offending is often a collective social process where some but not all may be apprehended. The numbers that we have about arrests; prosecutions or convictions; the trends in these; and about the attributes of those arrested, prosecuted, and convicted all reflect more or less complex social processes. The data are socially produced. What appear as neat brutal facts about offenders are socially constructed products of contingent social processes. They are drawn on as evidence to inform preventive strategies, but the raw material is socially created rather than simply reflecting an underlying reality.

Other administrative data sources that may be drawn on for evidence in crime prevention are also socially constructed and reflect social processes. Think, for example about police calls for service, calls to ambulances, hospital records, local authority records of antisocial behaviour, complaints data, fire service data, insurance claims data, and data held on crime by businesses. They all reflect decisions about and opportunities for reporting and recording over and above the events themselves. Box 7.3 briefly summarises influential discussions of the social construction of data used in the study of suicide rates.

Box 7.3 The social construction of data

The social construction of data was classically highlighted in a critical discussion of a study of suicide (criminalised in the UK until 1962) by one of sociology's founding fathers: Emile Durkheim, who published *Le Suicide* in 1897, with an English translation appearing in 1952 (Durkheim, 1952). Durkheim distinguished different types of suicide and compared rates to test his theory. In particular, he included a conjecture that Protestants commit suicide at a higher rate than Roman Catholics. Douglas (1967), Atkinson (1971), and Taylor (1982) highlight the decision-making processes involved in determining the cause of a death (accident, homicide, or suicide). What Durkheim took to be social facts about suicide rates turns out to be a function of processes of classification that may reflect social interests into which category is used, which will vary by the religious affiliation of the dead person and his or her nearest and dearest. For a recent book-length discussion of the social construction of data, see Becker (2017).

There are and can be no unequivocal data sources to furnish the raw material for analysis to create evidence for evidence-based crime prevention policy and practice. This does not mean that the data are of no value. It does not mean that it's okay to disregard them in favour of news reports or one's own agenda as we saw with the British Government's crime strategy. It does mean that we need to approach data critically and carefully to use the best available data and where possible to 'triangulate.' Triangulation involves assembling complementary data from independent sources to check whether they point to similar patterns and, where they do not do so, to figure out why and which is more dependable for decision-making.

It might be hoped that the foregoing points about the ways in which data for crime prevention are inexorably socially constructed, and about the need for this to be considered in their use to create evidence, are known and recognised by all established researchers, even though they are not always mentioned in academic papers. Their typical omission is likely because within the research community they are taken as read, and rehearsing them in each paper would be tedious and is unnecessary. However, they are needed for newcomers to research, as well as for those who may not be experts in social research but aim to draw on research findings in delivering evidence-informed crime prevention in their local areas.

Conclusion

I end this chapter with a few precepts for those attempting to collect or use evidence in crime prevention and to report their results to inform future decision-makers. Not all these precepts are derived from the preceding text but are included as guidance for those hoping to conduct studies and report findings that will have a positive impact.

- Use the best data sources that you can access, preferably more than one in relation to the phenomena of interest.
- When writing for user communities, note the social processes that lie behind the data used in reports of findings.
- Acknowledge the limitations of the data and why you think they are fit (or the best available) for crime prevention decision-making purposes.
- In analysing the data, use the simplest techniques which are consistent with clearly and accurately conveying the key findings, even if there are more sophisticated techniques for reporting findings in an academic journal or in an appendix to the report.
- Do not report more than is necessary to get the main findings for decision-makers across to them.
- Draw out possible implications for the crime prevention decision-maker.
- Be as brief as possible, with summaries of main points.
- In reporting findings from case studies, evaluations, and reviews, collect evidence that is as close to being EMMIE compliant as is practicable.
- Make critical use of evidence from relevant previous reports of crime patterns and experience of crime prevention activities.
- Spell out the key theory/ies of interventions (context, mechanism, outcome pattern conjectures). There will be lots of theories. Home in on the most plausible and most important for decision-making.
- In evaluations, look for data that speak to the expected processes and outcome patterns, which follow from the intervention theory. Try to anticipate possible unintended outcome patterns, as well as intended ones, and put in place provisions to capture them. Make sure you focus on possible negative as well as positive outcomes.
- If you are convinced that an RCT (or a research design akin to it) would be the best method of evaluating a crime prevention initiative, build theory in advance that will inform measurements focused on what may be important sub-group variations, albeit that there will rarely be enough cases for statistical analyses of them.
- Build on what has gone before, maximising the chances of cumulation in evidence-based crime prevention.
- Write in simple English, following the advice of John Eck in his book, *Writing with Sweet Clarity* (2022). For example use short words, short

sentences, an active voice, simple well-labelled tables and charts that are explained in the text.

- Be critical of all that you read/hear about – theories, data, methods, findings, inferences, applications, while recognising the ubiquity of fallibility and the need to come to decisions, be they about research, policy, or practice.
- Never lie. Try to avoid overstatement when you report. Be upfront about uncertainties.
- Finally, do read *Realistic Evaluation* (Pawson & Tilley, 1997) and follow-up texts (Pawson, 2006, 2013, Emmel, Greenhalgh, Manzano, Monaghan, & Dalkin, 2018, Farrell & Sidebottom, 2019) that will take you through the realist thinking that has informed much of this chapter!

Exercise: Assemble accessible information on patterns of knife crime and potential interventions to reduce it and prepare a short presentation of your findings for decision-makers to draw on.

References

Asthana, A. (2022). Rishi Sunak vows to increase prison capacity in crime crackdown bid. *ITV News*. Retrieved December 9, 2022, from www.itv.com/news/2022-11-18/rishi-sunak-vows-to-increase-prison-capacity-in-crime-crackdown-bid

Atkinson, A. (1971). Societal reactions to suicide: The role of coroners' definitions. In S. Cohen (Ed.), *Images of deviance* (pp. 165–191). Harmondsworth: Penguin.

Becker, H. (2017). *Evidence*. Chicago, IL: Chicago University Press.

Bowling, B., & Ross, J. (2006). A brief history of criminology. *Criminal Justice Matters*, 65, 12–13. doi:10.1080/09627250608553013

Brand, S., & Price, R. (2000). *The economic and social costs of crime*. Home Office Research Study 217. London: Home Office.

Broad, W., & Wade, N. (1983). *Betrayers of the truth: Fraud and Deceit in the halls of science*. New York: Simon and Schuster.

Campbell, D. T. (1957). Factors relevant to the validity of experiments in social settings. *Psychological Bulletin*, 54(4), 297–312. doi:10.1037/h0040950

The Campbell Collaboration. (2023). *Better evidence for a better world*. Retrieved July 16, 2023, from www.campbellcollaboration.org/better-evidence.html

Clarke, R. (1997). *Situational crime prevention: Successful case studies*. New York: Harrow and Heston.

Clarke, R., & Eck, J. (2003). *Become a problem solving crime analyst in 55 small steps*. London: Jill Dando Institute of Crime Science, University College London.

Cochrane, A. (1972). *Effectiveness and efficiency: Random reflections on health services*. The Nuffield Provincial Hospitals Trust.

The Cochrane Collaboration. (2023). *Cochrane library of systematic reviews*. Retrieved July 16, 2023, from www.cochranelibrary.com/cdsr/about-cdsr

College of Policing. (2023). *Crime reduction toolkit*. Retrieved December 14, 2022, from www.college.police.uk/research/crime-reduction-toolkit

Collins, H., & Evans, R. (2017). *Why democracies need science*. Cambridge: Polity Press.

Deaton, A., & Cartwright, N. (2018). Understanding and misunderstanding randomised controlled trials. *Social Science and Medicine, 210*, 2–21. doi:10.1016/j.socscimed.2017.12.005

Ditton, J., Bannister, J., Gilchrist, E., & Farrall, S. (1999). Afraid or angry? Recalibrating the 'fear' of crime. *International Review of Victimology, 6*, 83–99. doi:10.1177/026975809900600201

Douglas, J. (1967). *The social meanings of suicide*. Princeton, NJ: Princeton University Press.

Durkheim, E. (1952). *Suicide*. London: Routledge and Kegan Paul.

Eck, J. (2022). *Writing with sweet clarity*. London: Routledge.

Emmel, N., Greenhalgh, J., Manzano, A., Monaghan, M., & Dalkin, S. (2018). *Doing realist research*. London: SAGE.

Farrall, S., Bannister, J., Ditton, J., & Gilchrist, E. (1997). Questioning the measurement of the 'fear of crime': Findings from a major methodological study. *The British Journal of Criminology, 37*(4), 658–679. doi:10.1093/oxfordjournals.bjc.a014203

Farrell, G., & Sidebottom, A. (Eds.). (2019). *Realist evaluation for crime science*. London: Routledge.

Farrell, G., & Pease, K. (1993). *Once bitten, twice bitten: Repeat victimisation and its implications for crime prevention* (Crime Prevention Unit Paper 46). London: Home Office.

Farrell, G., & Pease, K. (2007). The sting in the tail of the British Crime Survey: Multiple victimisations. In M. Hough & M. Maxfield (Eds.), *Surveying crime in the 21st century: Crime prevention studies 22* (pp. 33–54). Monsey, NY: Criminal Justice Press.

Farrell, G., & Tilley, N. (2022). Elegant security: Concept, evidence and implications. *European Journal of Criminology, 19*(5), 932–953. doi:10.1177/1477370820932107

Forrester, D., Chatterton, M., & Pease, K. (1988). *The Kirkholt burglary prevention project, Rochdale* (Crime Prevention Unit Paper 13). London: Home Office.

Forrester, D., Frenz, S., O'Connell, M., & Pease, K. (1990). *The Kirkholt burglary prevention project: Phase II* (Crime Prevention Unit Paper 23). London: Home Office.

Gould, S. (1981). *The mismeasure of man*. New York: W. W. Norton & Company.

Health and Safety Executive. (2017). *Violence at work*. Health and Safety Executive.

Ipsos MORI. (2010). *Violence against Frontline NHS staff – Research for COI on behalf of the NHS Security Management Service*. London: Ipsos MORI.

Johnson, S., Tilley, N., & Bowers, K. (2015). Introducing EMMIE: An evidence rating scale for crime prevention policy and practice. *Journal of Experimental Criminology, 11*(3), 459–473. doi:10.1007/s11292-015-9238-7

La Vigne, N., & Wartell, J. (2015). *Robbery of pharmacies* (Problem-Specific Guides Series 73). Washington, DC: Community Oriented Policing Services U.S. Department of Justice.

Laycock, G. (2004). The UK car theft index: An example of government leverage. In M. Maxfield & R. Clarke (Eds.), *Understanding and preventing car theft: Crime prevention studies 17*. Monsey, NY: Criminal Justice Press.

Laycock, G. (2012). Happy birthday? *Policing: A Journal of Policy and Practice*, 6(2), 101–107. doi:10.1093/police/pas008

Laycock, G., & Tilley, N. (1995). *Policing and neighbourhood watch: Strategic issues* (Crime Prevention and Detection Series 60). London: Home Office.

Lewis, J. E., DeGusta, D., Meyer, M., Monge, J., Mann, A. E., & Holloway, R. L. (2011). The mismeasure of science: Stephen Jay Gould versus Samuel George Morton on skulls and bias. *PLoS Biology*, 9(6), e1001071. doi:10.1371/journal.pbio.1001071

Merton, R. (1973). *The sociology of science: Theoretical and empirical investigations.* Chicago, IL: University of Chicago Press.

Metropolitan Police Flying Squad. (2011). *Safe bet alliance.* London: Tilley Award Entry.

Pawson, R. (2006). *Evidence-based policy: A realist perspective.* London: SAGE.

Pawson, R. (2013). *The science of evaluation.* London: SAGE.

Pawson, R., & Tilley, N. (1997). *Realistic evaluation.* London: SAGE.

Perkins, C., Beecher, D., Aberg, D., Edwards, P., & Tilley, N. (2017). Personal security alarms for the prevention of assaults against healthcare staff. *Crime Science*, 6, 11. doi:10.1186/s40163-017-0073-1

Piza, E. L., Welsh, B. C., Farrington, D. P., & Thomas, A. L. (2019). CCTV surveillance for crime prevention: A 40-year systematic review with meta-analysis. *Criminology & Public Policy*, 18(1), 135–159. doi:10.1111/1745-9133.12419

Rew, M., & Ferns, T. (2005). A balanced approach to dealing with violence and aggression at work. *British Journal of Nursing*, 14(4), 227–232.

Scott, M., & Clarke, R. (2020). *Problem-oriented policing: Successful case studies.* London: Routledge.

Sherman, L. (1992). *Policing domestic violence.* New York: Free Press.

Sherman, L., Gottfredson, D., MacKenzie, D., Eck, J., Reuter, P., & Bushway, S. (1998). *Preventing crime: What works, what doesn't, what's promising* (Research in Brief National Institute of Justice). Washington, DC: US Department of Justice.

Sidebottom, A., & Tilley, N. (2020). Evaluation evidence for evidence-based policing. In N. Fielding, K. Bullock, & S. Holdaway (Eds.), *Critical reflections on evidence-based policing* (pp. 72–92). London: Routledge.

Sidebottom, A., Tompson, L., Thornton, A., Bullock, K., Tilley, N., Bowers, K., & Johnson, S. D. (2018). Gating Alleys to reduce crime: A meta-analysis and realist synthesis. *Justice Quarterly*, 35(1), 55–86. doi:10.1080/07418825.2017.1293135

Skivington, K., Matthews, L., Simpson, S., Craig, P., Baird, J., Blazeby, J., Boyd, K., Craig, N., French, D., McIntosh, E., Pettigrew, M., Rycroft-Malone, J., White, M., and Moore, L. (2021). A new framework for developing and evaluating complex interventions: Update of medical research council guidance. *BMJ*, 374, n2061. doi:10.1136/bmj.n2061

Spector, P., Zhou, Z., & Che, X. (2014). Nurse exposure to physical and nonphysical violence, bullying and sexual harassment: A quantitative review. *International Journal of Nursing Studies*, 51, 72–84. doi:10.1016/j.ijnurstu.2013.01.010

Taylor, S. (1982). *Durkheim and the study of suicide.* London: Macmillan.

Thaler, R., & Sunstein, C. (2008). *Nudge.* New Haven, CT: Yale University Press.

Tilley, N. (1981). The logic of laboratory life. *Sociology*, 15(1), 59–67. doi:10.1177/003803858101500108

Tilley, N. (1993a). Popper and prescriptive methodology. *Metaphilosophy*, 24(1 & 2), 155–166. doi:10.1111/j.1467–9973.1993.tb00454.x

Tilley, N. (1993b). Crime prevention and the safer cities story. *The Howard Journal*, 32(1), 40–57. doi:10.1111/j.1468–2311.1993.tb00758.x

Tilley, N. (1995). *Thinking about crime prevention performance indicators* (Crime Prevention and Detection Series 57). London: Home Office.

Tilley, N. (1996). Demonstration, exemplification, duplication and replication in evaluation research. *Evaluation*, 2(1), 35–50. doi:10.1177/135638909600200104

Tompson, L., Belur, J., Thornton, A., Bowers, K. J., Johnson, S. D., Sidebottom, A., Tilley, N., & Laycock, G. (2020). How strong is the evidence-base for crime reduction professionals? *Justice Evaluation Journal*, 4(1), 68–97. doi:10.1080/2475197 9.2020.1818275

UK Government. (2021). *Beating crime plan*. Retrieved December 12, 2022, from www.gov.uk/government/publications/beating-crime-plan

Weiss, C. H. (1999). The interface between evaluation and public policy. *Evaluation*, 5(4), 468–486. doi:10.1177/135638909900500408

Wells, J., & Bowers, L. (2002). How prevalent is violence towards nurses working in general hospitals in the UK? *Journal of Advanced Nursing*, 39(3), 230–240. doi:10.1046/j.1365-2648.2002.02269.x

8 Politics of crime prevention

Crime and crime control are inevitably and inescapably bound up with politics. The definition of what comes to be classed as a crime (or not a crime); the processes through which criminals are identified, tried, sentenced, and punished (or treated); the allocation of formal crime prevention responsibilities; the prioritisation of attention to one crime or another; the permissibility of (or requirement for) crime control measures; the funding for and the choice of public sector responses to crime; and even the funding for research that is designed to inform policy and practice, all involve political assumptions, political decisions, and political actions. Even crime prevention measures implemented by businesses and private citizens in their own interests in response to real or perceived crime threats, such as the shop theft prevention discussed in Chapter 6, are undertaken against a body of public policy, regulations, and a crime control framework set by governments. For example alarms and private security call for police and the criminal justice system; fire regulations constrain some uses of locks and window bars; gun control in many places restricts what self-protection measures can be used; etc.

We can look at the politics of crime prevention from several vantage points. First, we can look at them as detached observers, concerned as dispassionately as possible to draw lines between what is enacted as policy or practice and prevailing interests, powers, and ideologies. Second, we can look at them as committed critics concerned with righting wrongs, including crime-related ones, which are experienced disproportionately by certain sections of the population because of power structures or prevailing ideologies. Third, we can look at them as crime prevention policymakers and practitioners, trying to negotiate what can be put in place specifically to reduce or prevent crime and kindred harms, in a context of prevailing interests, power structures, and ideologies.

The focus of this chapter, in line with the rest of this book, is distinctly on politics as it relates to the delivery of effective, harm-reducing crime prevention. Effectiveness is not, however, a concern for some (otherwise quite interesting and insightful) perspectives on the politics of crime prevention.

DOI: 10.4324/9780429356155-8

Michael King (1991), for example, is candid about his indifference to issues of effectiveness, where he says,

> (We) should emphasise that we are not concerned . . . with the effectiveness of these schemes in reducing crime or the fear of crime, but in the ways in which the rhetoric and power structures associated with crime prevention promote or sustain specific political interests or policies.
>
> King (1991, p. 97)

I take the politics of effective crime prevention to relate to:

1. *Priorities in crime prevention endeavours.* More effective crime prevention will target crime concentrations: offences, offenders, and locations producing most crime harm. Chapter 3 discussed harms and crime concentrations.
2. *Responsibilities for crime prevention.* More effective crime prevention will make those who are competent to prevent crime responsible for doing so. Chapter 6 speaks to competence and responsibility in crime prevention and the mismatch that is sometimes found.
3. *Choices of crime prevention interventions.* More effective crime prevention will implement practicable measures that have demonstrated effectiveness or whose promise is informed by tested theory attuned to local conditions. Chapter 2 gives examples, and Chapters 4 and 7 discuss theories and evidence.

Because informed decisions on priorities, allocation of responsibilities, and selection of interventions require evidence, a separate section will discuss the politics of evidence construction.

The next section of the chapter proposes a generic framework for understanding the interplay of political forces that lie behind decisions over priorities, assignment of responsibilities, and choices over interventions. Chicago is then used as an example, drawing on a detailed case study of Chicago by Wesley Skogan. The chapter will then move on to separate discussions of the politics behind priorities, responsibilities, and interventions, before finally turning to research production and use.

Proposal for a generic framework

The aim of Figure 8.1 is to map the interacting groups that typically play a significant role in shaping crime prevention priorities, responsibilities, and interventions. The lines with either two-headed or single-headed arrows indicate directions of influence.

The specifics will vary from place to place and time to time.

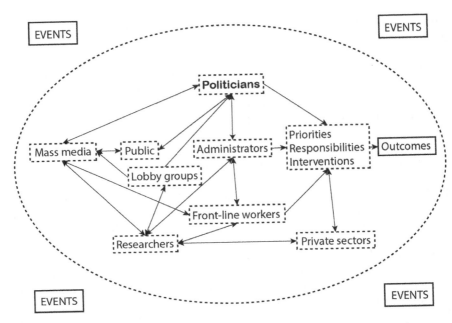

Figure 8.1 An analytic framework for the politics of effective crime prevention.

You will see that a dotted boundary surrounds the interactions portrayed, with 'EVENTS' around the boundary.[1] Inside the dotted oval are contextual conditions for all within and for their interrelationships. These can include, for example, culture, geography, class relations, demography, economic resources, technology, the legal system, political institutions, and prevailing crime patterns. The configuration of these shapes what is and what is not in practice up for decision-making.[2] 'EVENTS' refer to occurrences or developments that disrupt prevailing contexts. Examples include the COVID-19 pandemic or a war or a terrorist attack or a technological development, or a change in the law, or a high-profile policy/practice innovation elsewhere, or an unexpected spike or drop in crime.

The main actors within the model are also put in dotted boxes to capture their openness to other influences beyond those represented. Examples of other sources of influence include professional bodies setting standards for some occupational groups, families, neighbours, peer groups, vested interests, ideology, personal experience, resources, and expertise. Comprehensive accounts of specific crime prevention decisions would need to go into this.

What Figure 8.1 should make clear is that decisions about what comprise crimes and about prevention priorities, responsibilities, and interventions follow a complex interplay of disparate interacting influences, some of which will have little to do with effectiveness in reducing harms. The mass media can play a pivotal role in agenda-setting but are concerned with stories that are newsworthy and emotionally compelling rather than the relatively dull business of accurate reports of crime trends (unless they are upwards) or of successful efforts to prevent crimes and their harms. This is not to say that mass media have no positive roles to play – they can sometimes highlight neglected high-harm behaviours in need of prevention or criminalisation and harms engendered by the criminalisation of some behaviours.

Chicago: a case study

The best study I could find to exemplify political processes along the lines described in Figure 8.1 relates to the use of 'stop and frisk' as the police crime prevention strategy to reduce shootings and murders in Chicago (Skogan, 2023). This detailed, book-length, multi-method account focuses mainly on the 15 years from 2004. During this period, annual numbers of stops and frisk fluctuated between 380,000 (2011) and 718,000 (2014). Skogan has closely observed policing in Chicago over a much longer period (Skogan, 2006; Skogan & Hartnett, 1997). There is much devil in the study's detail. I strongly recommend it. Figure 8.2 puts Skogan's work on Chicago into the generic framework shown in Figure 8.1.

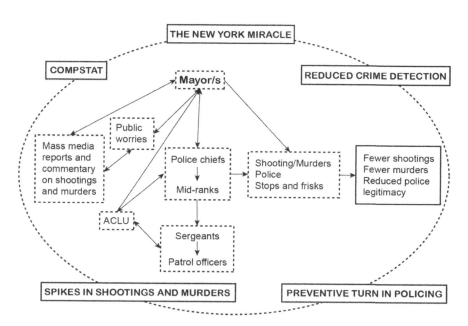

Figure 8.2 Chicago stop and frisk strategy.

News media attention to shootings and murders (especially in periods when newsworthy events were thin on the ground) prompted sustained policy attention to them, helping shape public opinion on crime and safety. This put pressure on the mayor (whose responsibilities included policing and crime control). The mayor in turn put pressure on the police to prioritise shootings and murders. Aggressive policing tactics (especially stop and frisk which in New York City allegedly produced a miraculous drop in crime) and a focus on hotspots (putting 'cops on dots') were influential developments in American policing. These made up a natural, credible, and popular strategy to try to reduce shootings and murders. To secure the delivery of the strategy, Compstat processes were used to check that stops and frisks were occurring in large numbers where shootings and murders were concentrated, mostly in African American areas of Chicago (a city which divides more clearly into African American, white, and Latino areas than most others). Intense pressure was applied from Chicago's Chief of Police down through the ranks to frontline officers. What was implemented were periods with very high rates of stops and frisks in African American neighbourhoods, a large proportion of which turned out to be of innocent people (stopped and frisked because the police looked for and found legitimate reasons to do so even though in the event nothing untoward was found). Many residents experienced multiple stops in some years, even though nothing was found to warrant further action.

Skogan notes two outcomes, one positive (harm-reducing) and one negative (harm-creating). The harm-reducing outcome was that the stop and frisk strategy did indeed save murders and shootings. Skogan undertook an exhaustive study, which drew on 15 years (180 months) of data on stops (the independent variable) and numbers of murders and of shootings (the dependent variables). He also collected data on some 20 variables that he built into his statistical model to take account of other factors that may have played a part. Skogan concludes that the best estimate of the numbers of murders prevented over the 180 months was 4 per month (range 2 to 6) and of shootings 24^3 per month (range 16 to 32). For every 1,000 stops (taking account of other factors), 0.141 murders and 0.868 shootings were prevented. Overall, over the 15-year period covered by the data included in the study, more than 700 murders were saved as were more than 4,300 shootings. This amounts to roughly an 8.5% solution to the problems of shootings and murders in Chicago.

The harm-increasing outcomes found by Skogan related to the loss of trust in the police, especially within African American communities where stops were concentrated. Community relations deteriorated. Police legitimacy fell. Innocent people were stopped and frisked, some repeatedly. Some were harmed by the police, especially when they reacted to procedural injustices. Evidence for this is provided, for example, through citizen surveys as well as patterns of police–citizen interactions and the injuries to some of those stopped.

The contradictory outcomes of the stop and frisk strategy make overall assessment tricky! The harms caused and created are qualitatively different. Judgements about trade-offs involve normative considerations. Wisely, Skogan does not try to provide an overall assessment using a common quantitative metric. Instead, he wonders about alternative strategies that would bring the harm-reducing benefits without the harm-producing costs of stop and frisk. The kind of focused deterrence noted in Chapter 2 and the kind of problem-solving (sometimes community involving) strategies described in Chapter 6 are possibilities.[4,5]

The next three sections will go through the production of priorities, responsibilities, and interventions, illustrated with examples.

Politics of crime effective prevention: priorities, responsibilities, and interventions

Priorities

Decision-making about what crimes matter for preventive purposes has often tended to reflect assumptions about, rather than evidence over, crime patterns and crime harms. Violence against women and children, corporate environmental damage and its human consequences, racial attacks, marital rape, and large-scale company frauds were, until relatively recently, either low on or absent from the crime prevention decision-making agenda, despite the harms they produce. Crime prevention had historically focused instead on street violence and volume property crimes and on those committing these types of crime. The crimes lower down or not on the agenda were largely those suffered by people with less power (women, children, black people, those living in less developed countries, and the general population) and committed by those with more power (men, adults, white folk, those living in rich countries, and owners of global corporations). The activities of those shown in Figure 8.1 are influenced by sets of background assumptions about what matters and what's up for debate at any point in time.

However, agendas change and may do so because of dramatic cases that elicit widespread public interest, the patient work of researchers who have endeavoured to highlight the neglect of crime harms, or the efforts of moral entrepreneurs and pressure groups. High-profile cases have marked turning points in preventive attention. In the UK, the abduction and murder of Sarah Everard by a serving police officer in March 2021 highlighted the vulnerability of women and girls to attacks in public places and kick-started greatly increased attention to them and to ways in which risks could be reduced. Likewise, the murder of Stephen Lawrence in a racial attack in April 1993 highlighted the extent and fatal consequences of racism. Both violence against women and girls and racist attacks were already serious problems to which researchers and interest groups had drawn attention, but the media spotlight furnished by the tragic events concentrated the minds of policy and practice decision-makers. In the United States, police violence against black people has become a focus of decision-makers' attention following the highly publicised killings of Tyre Nichols in Memphis in January 2023 and George Floyd in 2020, albeit that there had been many cases before either of these tragic and scandalous incidents, for example the killing of Rodney King in Los Angeles in 1991. In these cases, media attention to specific cases has helped prioritise the prevention of high-harm crimes.

News media seem, however, to be indifferent to (if not ignorant of) the sustained falls in crime experienced in most industrial societies beginning in the early-to-mid 1990s and maintained to the 2020s. Even serious news outlets appear to be uninterested in good crime-trend news.[6] Weatherburn (2011) describes mass media and politician misuse of crime statistics in Australia, and Gest (2001) describes the same in the United States. Strong evidence does not necessarily trump misleading and selective invocation of it.

National political decision-making on crime prevention priorities provides the context for local decisions on those same priorities. Funding, for example, is provided for attention to specific crimes. At the time of writing, crimes involving knives (which have been highly publicised) are being prioritised by the UK government, with special funds to encourage those in local areas to concentrate preventive efforts on knife crime. Likewise, attention to the prevention of violence against women and girls (following the Sarah Everard case) is being prioritised locally through a tranche of 'Safer Streets' funding in England and Wales.

Responsibilities

It can be in the interests of political decision-makers to assign responsibility for crime prevention to the police. Doing so accords with public expectations, often reinforced by media treatments of crime. It sits well with the notion that crime is prevented in proportion to the exercise of police powers. In the UK, government efforts in 2022–2023 to strengthen police powers to overrule rights to protest reflected neither police requests nor their wishes but rather governmental interests in allocating police responsibility for removing the inconveniences caused to the public from those protests. The police would then become accountable for removing those inconveniences (House of Lords, 2023). Importantly, this diverts blame from political decision-makers and towards the police.

However, as emphasised in earlier chapters, the police are not the only body with crime prevention competences. Politicians have sometimes assigned responsibilities to others with competence to prevent crime. For example in England and Wales, interdepartmental circulars were issued by the Home Office in 1984 (Home Office 8/84) and 1990 (Home Office 44/90) encouraging local organisations to collaborate with the police in developing and delivering crime prevention. Funding programmes, including Five Towns, Safer Cities, the Crime Reduction Programme, Safer Streets, and The Serious Violence Fund, have all encouraged partnership working involving those with competences to prevent crime, including the police but others besides. In 1998, the Crime and Disorder Act made the establishment of crime reduction partnerships mandatory. The Act also included a requirement for some specific action, including local authority consideration of crime consequences in deciding policy.

Home Office decisions about allocating responsibilities for crime prevention beyond the police and other parts of the criminal justice system have sometimes been informed by reputable and trusted in-house research, discussed in the section on the politics of research production and use later in the chapter. Spreading responsibility for prevention has had the advantage of drawing in those with the competence to prevent it and away from politicians who may lack competence.

For some bodies, the acceptance of responsibility is resisted. This is both because it can be onerous, but more particularly, responsibility is resisted where interests are threatened. For example Home Office research identified those makes and models of cars that were most at risk of theft (drawing on police recorded crime data). The manufacturers had been reluctant to build security measures into the cars. Publication of findings showing which makes and models were most at risk (and the ease with which they could be stolen) concentrated the minds of manufacturers who began to build in improved security along lines described in Chapter 6 (Houghton, 1992; Laycock, 2004). Here, manufacturers accepted responsibility to do something, rather than risk the imposition of statutory requirements.

The car security example highlights the challenges in assigning responsibility to competent bodies that do not suffer the costs of the crime they would be competent to prevent. There are many examples where a competent body might enjoy no direct benefits from the security measures they could put in place, but which would incur costs for them. One is thefts of and from cars in car parks, where a national security kite mark ('Park Mark') in the UK[7] has provided a carrot for car park proprietors to make their car parks more secure. The kite mark might attract more motorists because of the greater security offered for their vehicles.

Responsibility allocation at the national level is mirrored in the responsibility allocation at the local level, where again the challenge is to persuade those competent to act to take responsibility.

Interventions

News media seem largely uninterested in what is effective in crime prevention. They have likewise assumed that the way in which the police can best control crime is by using enforcement methods – detection, followed by prosecution, conviction, and punishment. Those on the right have tended to advocate stiffer sentences. They rail against being soft on criminals. Those on the left have stressed the need to address root causes and to assume that the root causes lie in social inequalities and inequities. The mass media have tended to focus on any evidence (strong or otherwise) of increases in crime or of failures to detect crimes, which pushes crime up the political agenda. They have been indifferent to robust evidence of what is effective in preventing crime.

Speaking at the Tory Party Annual Conference at the time of peak crime rates in England and Wales, the then Home Secretary Michael Howard, from the Conservative Party, used the slogan, 'Prison works.' He referred to 'a tidal wave of concern about crime' and stated that 'The silent majority has become the angry majority.' He claimed that '(T)he criminal justice system has been tilted too far in favour of the criminal and against the protection of the public.' He stressed deterrence, 'The time has come to put that right. I want to make sure that it is criminals that are frightened, not law-abiding members of the public.' Evidently, his speech was followed by a one-minute, 47-second ovation (Brown, 1993).

Tony Blair's slogan about being 'tough on crime and tough on the causes of crime' cleverly echoed the popular opinion being tapped by Michael Howard but added a reference to treatment which is more often embraced by those on the left (Blair, 1993). Being tough on the causes of crime referred to being tough on the root causes of criminality, whereas we now know that crime can often be prevented without attention to these supposed root causes and that traditional criminal justice responses to offenders often inflate rather than reduce their criminality. Being tough on crime meant detection and punishment of offenders. 'Being tough on criminals' and 'being tough on the causes of criminality' both fail to recognise the 'fundamental attribution error' discussed in Chapter 4. They thereby neglect the role of immediate conditions in producing deviant behaviour and the scope there is to alter those immediate conditions in the interest of crime prevention, the possibilities of which have been widely evidenced by researchers.

There appeared to be widespread public support for one situational measure in particular: Closed-Circuit Television (CCTV) in public places. The popularity of CCTV as a crime prevention measure was perhaps because it was deemed to contribute to the detection of offenders who could then be punished or because the increased prospect of detection would deter offenders. An amount of £38.5m was provided to local areas between 1994 and 1999 under the CCTV Challenge Competition – which funded 585 schemes nationwide; and a further £170 m was made available under the Crime Reduction Programme – funding a further 680 schemes (Home Office, 2011). Thus, over 1,200 local schemes in all were funded centrally. Political and public support for CCTV was high and was bipartisan. Although civil liberties groups opposed the invasion of privacy caused by CCTV, public resistance was muted in England and Wales (see Bennett & Gelsthorpe, 1996). The effectiveness of CCTV was unknown except through occasional anecdotes. There has since been quite a lot of research on the effectiveness of CCTV which finds it to have been effective in some specific conditions, for instance in car parks (see Welsh & Farrington, 2009 and Piza, Welsh, Farrington, and Thomas (2019) for overviews of findings). CCTV continues to be widely adopted with central government financial support, albeit without much attention to the conditions for its effectiveness (KANTAR, 2023).

Although the political context for crime prevention policymaking is not well-suited to the delivery of what is in practice known to be effective, this does not mean that governments have in practice stuck to headline policies and practices that simply echo what had been popular opinion, mass media rhetoric, or political party ideology. Both Conservative and Labour governments in the UK, for example, have included some support for the delivery of situational crime prevention on pragmatic rather than ideological grounds. Democracies, of course, rightly require decision-makers to attend to public opinion. Indeed, to neglect it would be politically suicidal, as would inattention to the prejudices of party activists. Requiring accuracy from the mass media in its treatment of crime would involve a form of censorship unacceptable in a free society. In practice, however, much decision-making is devolved to public servants and practitioners who enjoy wide discretion within the parameters set by politicians and who may also influence decisions made by those politicians.

Governments may choose not to apply crime prevention measures which they could implement, or try to implement, for reasons unrelated to evidence for their effectiveness. One example is alcohol taxation. There are strong empirical grounds for expecting that an increased levy on alcohol would produce a range of benefits, including a reduction in violent crime (Babor et al., 2010). The measure is not adopted presumably because of the powerful interests that would be threatened and the risk of electoral unpopularity. Likewise, in the United States, gun control measures remain very limited despite evidence that they could help reduce homicides, as well as a range of other firearms-related harms, for example suicides and accidental shootings. Again, gun control is not implemented due to a coalition between vested interests of the small arms industry and a powerful gun rights lobby (see Cook and Goss, 2014 for a balanced discussion of this).

Local decision-making about what to implement to try to prevent crime takes place in a context influenced but not determined by national steers and national funding. The various programmes funded by the Home Office incentivised the adoption of some measures, as noted before in the example of CCTV. Political and public support for CCTV has been high and bipartisan. Funding has been made available, and the adoption of this measure has become commonplace.[8] Where specific measures are known to bring down crime, they may occasionally be mandated. At an international level, a European Directive required that electronic immobilisers of a given minimum quality be fitted to all new cars (European Commission, 1995). Their effectiveness as a measure to prevent car theft has become well established (Brown, 2004; van Ours & Vollaard, 2013; Farrell, Tilley, Tseloni, & Mailley, 2011). Likewise, at a national level, the Netherlands has introduced regulations requiring minimum door and window security levels to houses, which have been followed by falls in domestic burglary (see Vollard & van Ours, 2011).

Politics of research production and use

I have been a participant observer of crime prevention research, and in this section, I draw on my experience as a secondee to the Home Office for around a decade (though never as a civil servant); as an advisor to a research group concerned with crime at a then Governmental Regional Office for a couple of years; as a researcher periodically conducting contracted research; and as a regular academic undertaking research funded by a research council as well as unfunded research. While these have given me a range of bird's eye views of some of the politics at work, they may also have created biases.

It is important to appreciate the politics of research production and application, because data and their analysis are crucial to the conduct of effective crime prevention: in selecting crime problems for preventive attention, in mobilising those with a capacity to prevent crime, and in decisions about what preventive measures to implement.

It would be disingenuous to say that 'facts' or 'data' are straightforward and speak for themselves. The previous chapter stressed the social construction of data. Data can be interpreted in different ways. There are gatekeepers who may or may not grant access to data sets. Data can be analysed in multiple ways. The old adage about 'lies, damned lies and statistics' speaks to real risk from opportunities for self-interested data production, provision, manipulation, and use.

Evidence analysis and use politics

While at the Home Office, I was generally kept away from policy people – that was for proper civil servants not hired research hacks! However, I recall one meeting where the policy official came with a request for any research that could support the Minister's policy to provide a warrant for it. I also remember crafting some guidance based on research where, at the behest of a minister, my careful reference to 'anecdotal' evidence was changed. The word 'anecdotal' was removed. I remember too preparing successive drafts of reports where any implications that policies had failed or were not based on evidence were softened in order not to make embarrassing waves for stakeholders. In this sense, text can be negotiated. Where researchers have an interest in their work's publication, we may be tempted to compromise on the text to avoid the risk that it will otherwise be quietly shelved. This is not to say that I saw pressure to tell lies, but I did see a subtle politics of research presentation.

More seriously, I recall a discussion with a junior researcher who had conducted a local Safer Cities evaluation. She found that the flagship project had had no discernible effect on the targeted crime. Her boss, who was responsible for fostering crime prevention partnerships, did not want this finding highlighted as it might discourage future participation. So, the text focused on the smooth implementation of the measure. The finding of failure was not omitted but included only in one of many footnotes.

As the government department with chief responsibility for crime prevention in England and Wales, the Home Office has both supported research that is related to crime prevention, and also funded several programmes focused on delivering crime prevention even though these do not always align well with popular conceptions of crime and of the most effective methods for controlling it. These programmes have required and have received agreement by relevant government ministers, and both research and crime prevention programmes have been funded by Conservative as well as Labour administrations.

The distinctiveness of the placement of research within the Home Office in England and Wales and its relationship with policymaking are highlighted by Laycock and Clarke (2001) in a comparison with the situation in the United States. Laycock and Clarke highlight the location of specialist researchers within the Home Office. Here, the focus of both internal and externally contracted research was decided in consultation with policymakers and was orientated to policy; the implications of findings for effective crime prevention policy and practice were made clear for policy and practice decision-makers; the theoretical orientation was informed by situational crime prevention; the output was published freely in readily accessible papers written with a non-technical readership in mind (though also often appearing in peer-reviewed learned journals); the findings had national reach due to relatively limited decentralisation; there were only 43 territorial police services to involve in research and in applications of findings; and research was led by specialist career civil servants rather than political appointees.

In contrast, in the United States, funding for research orientated to policy and practice was made available through the National Institute of Justice (NIJ). The NIJ had little in-house research capacity and hence oversaw rather than conducted research; bids for grants were open to externally formulated suggestions for the focus of research; output was not necessarily published in an accessible format; the main theoretical focus was informed by community policing with all its diffuse meanings; policy and practice implications were not necessarily made explicit; the federal system of government devolved much decision-making to states; there are many thousands of police agencies; and the director of the NIJ was a political appointee.

In making their comparison between the United States and United Kingdom, Laycock and Clarke show that the organisational context for research-informed decisions about what to implement in crime prevention can vary across democratic societies. They also show that political ideology, often fed by an ignorant mass media both reproducing and feeding into populist responses to crime, does not mean that better-grounded and evidence-based policymaking and practice are excluded. However, even in-house research may not be heard or be able to steer policy.

The price paid for research findings to have an impact on national policy and practice, as it has in the UK, may sometimes be that they need to be couched in terms that maximise their palatability to decision-makers, rather in the terms preferred by researchers. The politics for effective crime prevention may thus sometimes require uncomfortable compromises for researchers! That said, the location of research in the Home Office did not preclude research studies that cast doubt on taken-for-granted provisions for crime prevention. Home Office research was important in showing that neither the police nor offender treatments had reliably prevented crime (Brody, 1976; Hough & Clarke, 1984).[9] The Home Office Research Unit had also pioneered situational crime prevention as an alternative approach to crime prevention, which neither required nor was implemented by the police alone (Mayhew, Clarke, Sturman, & Hough, 1976; Clarke, 1980).

Data politics

Let us turn now to data, which is the lifeblood of effective, evidence-based crime prevention. There is politics involved in the creation and provision of the data that are analysed (see Maguire and McVie, 2012 for an overview focused on the UK). National victimisation surveys were developed to get a fix on crime levels and patterns, where numbers of crimes not reported and of reported but not recorded were unknown, referred to at the time as the 'dark figure of crime.' However, victimisation survey data are of no use when analysis turns to local problems and are of little use for relatively rare crimes even with large samples.[10]

Decisions to report and record crimes can be made for lots of reasons, including the perceived seriousness of the incident, the perceived chance that reporting it will lead to action, the requirement for a crime number when making an insurance claim, etc. Regarding recording crime, officers and their managers can and do exercise a great deal of discretion in deciding both whether to record an incident as a crime and if so which crime category to put it in. Moreover, the exercise of that discretion and influences over it change over time in ways that can be political.

Part of the unreliability of recorded crime data thus stems from their use for policy purposes, where counts and trends can affect resource allocation, incentivising inconsistent practices. The variability of crime-recording practices, however, means that caution is needed in interpreting trends over time, differences in rates across place, and concentrations of crime and crime harm, when it comes to trying to make informed decisions about which crimes to focus on in preventive efforts. Making such use of recorded crime data even more difficult, police responses to crime are liable to influence dispositions to report a crime: unsympathetic or unhelpful responses are clearly likely to reduce dispositions to report a crime, while sympathetic and helpful responses are liable to increase them (see Chapter 7 for more on the social construction of data).

Police officers can be candid about their role in recording reported incidents. While at the Home Office, I was once asked to develop a crime prevention performance indicator for the police. I presented some initial ideas to groups of police officers in various forces to canvass their opinions. They regaled me with the many ways in which they could fiddle and had fiddled the figures to fit with what was wanted by the police service in pursuit of their interests. One example was brought home to me with a story from a colleague. She had arrived home to find someone had attempted to break into her house. They had rung a neighbour's doorbell and been told to go away. They had then presumably rung her doorbell and, getting no answer, had smashed the glass in the door, but it had a deadlock so they couldn't get in. She called the police in line with what she took to be her civic duty, even though there was a vanishingly small chance that the crime would be detected. The call handler told her it was criminal damage. She argued her case. She knew it was an attempted burglary. At the time, police were being judged on their effectiveness in dealing with domestic burglary.

The decision to measure police service performance can affect the crime-recording practices. This in turn will compromise the integrity of local data for examining patterns and trends. Violence and sexual offences are notoriously slippery in terms of the categories available to capture them. Ironically, improved performance might be better achieved by higher rates of some recorded crimes, notably in the example of violence against women or racial attacks, where unsympathetic responses and reputations for them may produce reluctance to report. When the mass media report increases in crime as somehow a scandalous indictment of policing, they may be missing improvements in response to victims leading to higher rates of reporting.[11]

A National Crime Recording Standard (NCRS) was introduced in England and Wales to remedy police inconsistences in crime recording and was operative from 2002. Comparing the year before the introduction of NCRS and its first year of operation, Simmons, Legg, and Hosking (2003) estimated that the effect was to increase the overall number of recorded crimes by 10%, but this varied significantly by crime type: 23% for violence against the person, 9% for criminal damage, but only 3% for robbery and for burglary. For some years, the Audit Commission in the UK checked police adherence to NCRS, but its closure in 2015 (itself a political decision) ended the regular monitoring of crime-recording practices by that body. Because of uncertainties over recording practices and repeated findings that figures were unreliable in some places, recorded crime in England and Wales is not, at the time of writing, recognised by the Office for National Statistics as a National Statistic (except for homicide, which was restored in 2016 as meeting the required standard).

Conclusion

The politics of effectiveness in crime prevention revolve around decisions about which crime problems to address or to prioritise, about whom to try to involve in the delivery of crime prevention, and about which interventions to implement directly or to incentivise others to adopt.

Politics favours effective crime prevention to the extent to which a) it steers preventive endeavours towards the reduction of offences and offence patterns that are producing the greatest harms; b) it allocates responsibilities to those most competent to act in ways that will prevent crime; and c) it implements directly or prevails on others to implement interventions that promise to be effective in preventing crime harms, without producing serious negative side effects.

The politics of crime prevention are clearly complex. Political forces can sometimes generate decisions favouring effectiveness and equity, but they can also obstruct them. There is also space within the politics of crime prevention, as indicated in Figure 8.1, to exert influence in favour of effectiveness. Crime prevention researchers and partnerships between researchers and those at and close to the frontline of preventive activity, have, I think, much more to add in trying directly to inform key decision-makers. They could also work to improve public understanding of crime and crime prevention which would, in democratic societies, eventually contribute to better decisions.

Exercise: Take any decision regarding crime prevention priorities, responsibilities, or interventions and describe its politics, using the framework shown in Figure 8.1. If you think the decision was a poor one, explain why and what might have been done to improve it.

Notes

1 Inside the dotted oval are contextual conditions for all within and for their inter-relationships. These can include, for example, culture, geography, class relations, demography, economic resources, and technology.
2 See Lukes (1974) for an account of what is and is not up for decision-making.
3 This corrects the published number, following correspondence with the author.
4 It is not clear whether local research informed the stop and frisk strategy or whether it was adopted for other reasons, for example from the extensive commentary on what had happened in New York and on the trickle down of research of the kind referred to in Chapter 3 showing crime concentrations on small subsets of people and places. This explains why researchers feature in Figure 8.1 but not Figure 8.2. Skogan is a distinguished Chicago social scientist, with close knowledge of the city and of policing within it. He does not seem to have played any part in the formulation of the stop and frisk strategy. His account is that of an informed outsider, drawing on extensive independent research. However, it may well be that local research was, indeed, called on to feed into the development and delivery of stop and frisk in Chicago as the crime prevention strategy. Police data were certainly used, but who conducted the analyses and whether they enjoyed independence are not clear.
5 I should add that my brief account of Skogan's study does not do justice to his nuanced treatment of variations in rates of stop and search with different mayors, different chiefs of police, and changing rates of crime.
6 I once tried to interest the *Economist* in featuring crime drop patterns. They did not want to do so. Crime increases hit the headlines. Crime drops are boring. The headlines percolate through to public impressions of crime problems and crime trends. Political decision-makers perforce follow. Most strikingly we see this in the recent acknowledgement of strong evidence-based crime drops in England and Wales and their explicit, wilful disregard in policy! (UK Government, 2021).
7 Park Mark is police-owned in the UK: for details, see Safer Parking Scheme (2023).
8 I should add that CCTV has changed enormously over the period since it first began to be used as a crime prevention measure. In the early studies, the technology was crude by modern standards. The images tended to be grainy and monochrome. Moreover, it was new for offenders who may for a while have overestimated its technical capacities and not yet learned how to avoid it. What went by way of studies of effectiveness in the past may no longer hold in the present.
9 This echoed complementary findings in the United States for traditional police patrol (e.g. Kelling, Pate, & Brown, 1974) and offender treatment (e.g. Martinson, 1974, Lipton, Martinson, & Wilks, 1975).
10 Sample sizes obviously vary by country. Where large specialist surveys are undertaken, it can become possible to analyse patterns for less common crimes. Estévez-Soto has managed to analyse patterns of extortion against businesses in Mexico due to the large-scale commercial victimisation survey that has been run there (see Estévez-Soto, 2021, Estévez-Soto et al., 2021).
11 My suggestion for a performance indicator focused on reducing repeat victimisation. This attempted to sidestep some of the problems of recorded crime. However, unsympathetic police responses to victims might inadvertently be encouraged to reduce their inclination to report further incidents (Tilley, 1995)!

220 *Politics of crime prevention*

References

Babor, T., Caetano, R., Casswell, S., Edwards, G., Giesbrecht, N., Osterberg, E., . . . Sornpalsarn, B. (2010). *Alcohol: No ordinary commodity: Research and public policy* (2nd ed.). Oxford: Oxford University Press.
Bennett, T., & Gelsthorpe, L. (1996). Public attitudes towards CCTV in public places. *Studies on Crime and Crime Prevention*, 5(1), 72–90.
Blair, T. (1993). Why crime is a socialist issue. *New Statesman*, 29(2), 27–28.
Brody, S. (1976). *The effectiveness of sentencing – a review of the literature* (Home Office Research Study 35. London: HMSO.
Brown, C. (1993). *Howard seeks to placate 'angry majority': Home secretary tells party that balance in criminal justice system will be tilted towards public*. London: The Independent. Retrieved January 28, 2023, from www.independent.co.uk/news/uk/howard-seeks-to-placate-angry-majority-home-secretary-tells-party-that-balance-in-criminal-justice-system-will-be-tilted-towards-public-colin-brown-reports-1509088.html
Brown, R. (2004). The effectiveness of electronic immobilization: Changing patterns of temporary and permanent theft. In M. Maxfield & R. Clarke (Eds.), *Understanding and preventing car theft: Crime prevention studies 17* (pp. 101–119). New York: Criminal Justice Press.
Clarke, R. V. (1980). Situational crime prevention: Theory and practice. *British Journal of Criminology*, 20, 136–147. doi:10.1093/oxfordjournals.bjc.a047153
Cook, P., & Goss, K. (2014). *The gun debate*. New York: Oxford University Press.
Estévez-Soto, P. (2021). Determinants of extortion compliance: Empirical evidence from a victimization survey. *The British Journal of Criminology*, 61(5), 1187–1205. doi:10.1093/bjc/azab007
Estévez-Soto, P., Johnson, S., & Tilley, N. (2021). Are repeatedly extorted businesses different? A multilevel hurdle model of extortion victimization. *Journal of Quantitative Criminology*, 37, 1115–1157. doi:10.1007/s10940-020-09480-8
European Commission. (1995). *Directive 95/56/EC adapting to technical progress council directive 74/61/EEC relating to devices to prevent the unauthorized use of motor vehicles*. Retrieved July 16, 2023, from https://eur-lex.europa.eu/legal-content/EN/TXT/PDF/?uri=CELEX:31995L0056
Farrell, G., Tilley, N., Tseloni, A., & Mailley, J. (2011). The crime drop and the security hypothesis. *Journal of Research in Crime and Delinquency*, 48(2), 147–175. doi:10.1177/0022427810391539
Gest, T. (2001). *Crime and politics*. Oxford: Oxford University Press.
Home Office. (1984). *Crime prevention* (Home Office Circular 8/84). London: Home Office.
Home Office. (1990). *Crime prevention: The success of the partnership approach* (Home Office Circular 44/90). London: Home Office.
Home Office. (2011). *Cost of CCTV*. Retrieved January 27, 2023, from www.gov.uk/government/publications/cost-of-cctv
Hough, M., & Clarke, R. (1984). *Crime and police effectiveness* (Home Office Research Study 79). London: HMSO.
Houghton, G. (1992). *Car theft in England and Wales: The Home Office car theft index* (Crime Prevention Unit Paper 33). London: Home Office.

House of Lords. (2023). *Public order bill.* Retrieved February 1, 2023, from https://bills.parliament.uk/publications/49143/documents/2653

Kantar. (2023). *Evaluation of the safer streets fund round 1, year ending March 2021.* London: Home Office. Retrieved February 2, 2023, from www.gov.uk/government/publications/safer-streets-fund-evaluation-round-1-year-ending-march-2021/evaluation-of-the-safer-streets-fund-round-1-year-ending-march-2021

Kelling, G., Pate, T., & Brown, C. (1974). *The Kansas City preventive patrol experiment.* Washington, DC: Police Foundation.

King, M. (1991). The political construction of crime prevention: A contrast between the French and British Experience. In K. Stenson & D. Cowell (Eds.), *The politics of crime control* (pp. 87–108). London: SAGE.

Laycock, G. (2004). The UK car theft index: An example of government leverage. In M. Maxfield & R. Clarke (Eds.), *Understanding and preventing car theft: Crime prevention studies 17.* Monsey, NY: Criminal Justice Press.

Laycock, G., & Clarke, R. (2001). Crime prevention policy and government research: A comparison of the United States and United Kingdom. *International Journal of Comparative Sociology, 42*(1–2), 235–255. doi:10.1177/002071520104200110

Lipton, D. S., Martinson, R., & Wilks, J. (1975). *The effectiveness of correctional treatment: A survey of treatment evaluation studies.* New York: Praeger.

Lukes, S. (1974). *Power.* London: Macmillan.

Maguire, M., & McVie, S. (2012). Crime data and criminal statistics: A critical reflection. In A. Liebling, S. Maruna, & L. McAra (Eds.), *The Oxford handbook of criminology* (pp. 163–189). Oxford: Oxford University Press.

Martinson, R. (1974). What works? Questions and answers about prison reform. *Public Interest, 35*(2), 22–54.

Mayhew, P., Clarke, R., Sturman, A., & Hough, M. (1976). *Crime as opportunity* (Home Office Research Study 34). London: HMSO.

Piza, E. L., Welsh, B. C., Farrington, D. P., & Thomas, A. L. (2019). CCTV surveillance for crime prevention: A 40-year systematic review with meta-analysis. *Criminology & Public Policy, 18*(1), 135–159. doi:10.1111/1745-9133.12419

Safer Parking Scheme. (2023). *Park Mark®.* Retrieved February 1, 2023, from https://parkmark.co.uk/about-the-safer-parking-scheme

Simmons, J., Legg, C., & Hosking, R. (2003). *The national crime recording standard (NCRS): An analysis of the impact on recorded crime.* London: Home Office. Retrieved January 29, 2023, from http://image.guardian.co.uk/sys-files/Guardian/documents/2003/07/17/NCRS1.pdf

Skogan, W. (2006). *Police and community in Chicago.* New York: Oxford University Press.

Skogan, W. (2023). *Stop & Frisk and the politics of crime in Chicago.* New York: Oxford University Press.

Skogan, W., & Hartnett, S. (1997). *Community policing, Chicago style.* New York: Oxford University Press.

Tilley, N. (1995). *Thinking about crime prevention performance indicators* (Crime Prevention and Detection Series 57). London: Home Office.

UK Government. (2021). *Beating crime plan.* London: Home Office. Retrieved January 18, 2022, from www.gov.uk/government/publications/beating-crime-plan

van Ours, J. C., & Vollaard, B. (2013). *The engine immobilizer: A non-starter for car thieves* (CESifo Working Paper: Public Choice, No. 4092). Munich: Centre for Economic Studies and Institute, University of Munich.

Vollard, B., & van Ours, J. (2011). Does regulation of built-in security reduce crime? Evidence from a natural experiment. *The Economic Journal, 121*, 485–504. doi:10.1111/j.1468-0297.2011.02429.x

Weatherburn, D. (2011). *Uses and abuses of crime statistics* (Crime and Justice Bulletin, Contemporary Issues in Crime and Justice 153). Sydney: New South Wales Bureau of Crime Statistics and Research.

Welsh, B., & Farrington, D. (2009). Public area CCTV and crime prevention: An updated systematic review and meta-analysis. *Justice Quarterly, 26*(4), 716–745. doi:10.1080/07418820802506206

9   Better crime prevention

Things have got better in crime prevention. However, they can continue to get better still. There will need to be continuous adaptation to keep up with changes in crime trends together with technological, social, economic, and political developments. This chapter will include an overview of the improvements that we have witnessed over the last half century and an outline agenda for what's to be done to build improvement into policy and practice and in so doing maintain progress.

Improvements over the past half century

In 1970, Norval Morris and Gordon Hawkins published *The Honest Politician's Guide to Crime Control*. They drew heavily on the President's Crime Commission Report (US) of 1967. Morris and Hawkins highlighted the low levels of investment in research relating to crime prevention, the shortage of rigorous studies evaluating the effectiveness of crime prevention measures, the unpromising findings from the research that was available, and the dubiousness of the data provided by reported crime rates for tracing crime trends. Since 1970, there have been significant improvements, as witnessed in material covered in earlier chapters. These improvements include higher levels of funding for crime-prevention-related research and growth in the number of publications and reports speaking to crime levels and preventive activities. Many of these studies identified crime prevention effects from interventions such as those noted in Chapter 2, as well as the effectiveness of problem-solving initiatives in crime prevention as described in Chapter 6. Well-designed victimisation surveys have become widespread across jurisdictions and are conducted regularly to give a stronger fix on crime patterns, crime levels, and crime trends than police data for those crimes covered in the surveys. Moreover, surveys are now conducted that focus on crimes against businesses as well as against households and individuals. Victimisation surveys suggest that from the early-to-mid 1990s onwards, what had been major crime problems shrunk steadily across many jurisdictions up to the 2020s, notably vehicle theft and burglary.

In the concluding chapter of *The Honest Politician's Guide to Crime Control*, 'Research,' Morris and Hawkins made some specific suggestions.

DOI: 10.4324/9780429356155-9

They referred to 'possibilities' enumerated by the Commission's task force on science and technology. These included the following (Morris & Hawkins, 1970, p. 236), all of which have since been achieved:

1. 'Electronic computers for processing the enormous quantities of needed data
2. Police radio networks connecting officers and neighbouring departments
3. Inexpensive, light, two-way portable radios for every patrolman
4. Computers for processing fingerprints
5. Instruments for identifying criminals by voice, photograph, hair, blood, body chemistry, etc.
6. Devices for automatic and continued reporting of all police car locations
7. Helicopters for airborne police patrol
8. Inexpensive, reliable burglary and robbery alarms
9. Nonlethal weapons to subdue dangerous criminals without inflicting permanent harm
10. Perimeter surveillance devices for prisons
11. Automatic transcription devices for courtrooms.'

In an earlier chapter of their book, Morris and Hawkins advocated security measures to reduce auto theft and burglary. They referred to 'devices making ignition jumping impossible, locks on steering wheels, and alarms,' expecting these to 'reduce car stealing by 75 per cent at least . . . because UCR[1] data indicate that the majority (about 75%) of cars are taken for joyriding' (Morris & Hawkins, 1970, p. 102). Moreover, 'by making these devices compulsory throughout the automobile industry no manufacturer would suffer a competitive disadvantage' (ibid). In relation to burglary, which they referred to as, 'the most frequent kind of stealing' (p. 104), they said that, 'possibly the cheapest and most effective system might be a concealed push button alarm on the ordinary home telephone giving direct contact with the local police station' (pp. 103–104). Although, especially in the case of burglary, the details of what has turned out to be effective were incorrect, the focus on security measures was right and prescient in terms of later developments which have effectively driven these crimes down, not only in the United States but also in most industrialised societies.

Morris and Hawkins acknowledged the complexity of crime prevention. They advocated systems analysis as a method for dealing with the complexity. They said,

The essence of this technique is to construct a mathematical description or model of the system in light of which it is possible to conduct simulated experiments which may indicate how the real life system may be better organized and operated.

Morris and Hawkins, 1970, p. 240

The development and use of agency-based models for crime prevention deliver, perhaps in unexpected ways, on this suggestion (see Groff & Birks, 2008).

Unsurprisingly, writing in the 1970s, Morris and Hawkins were unable to anticipate some paradigm-shifting developments in ways to prevent crime. They largely (although as we have seen far from exclusively) focused on criminal justice system responses to criminality and on traditional means of trying to reduce criminality by intervening among offenders and those at heightened risk of becoming involved in crime. They did not anticipate situational crime prevention (other than target hardening) or the discovery of patterns of crime concentration (such as hotspots and repeat victimisation), both of which have since provided strong foundations for effective and well-targeted crime prevention.

Morris and Hawkins did not foresee the falls in crime that have occurred in many western countries since the early-to-mid 1990s. These can largely be accounted for by improvements in security which have reduced opportunities for what had been high-volume property crimes, notably vehicle theft and burglary, where the kinds of preventive measures they advocated have indeed become standard. Regarding car theft, reduced opportunities have had the happy side effect of cutting off a key route into adolescent crime careers, which include diverse offences (Tilley & Farrell, 2022).

Morris and Hawkins failed to consider the possibility of, and potential benefits from, building learning and attentiveness to local conditions into crime prevention decision-making. The practical incorporation of these has been facilitated through the emergence of local crime prevention partnerships as mentioned in earlier chapters. These partnerships often include experts, analysts, and independent researchers 'co-producing' informed crime prevention strategies alongside policymakers and practitioners (Crawford, 2017; Hodgkinson & Tilley, 2023).

Morris and Hawkins disparaged research focusing on the causes of crime in favour of applied research that is directly orientated to informing preventive interventions, but even among the most applied researchers, this is now seen as a mistake. Finding the causal mechanisms behind crime and victimisation to identify and target effective interventions is, as with health research, widely taken to be important (see Chapter 4). David Farrington echoes the point in relation to preventive work focused on family factors influencing offending, when he concludes,

> Ideally, intervention experiments targeting family factors should be included in longitudinal studies in order to establish causal effects more securely. A new generation of longitudinal studies should go beyond demonstrating that family factors predict offending and should seek to determine the key *causal mechanisms* involved. They should help greatly in designing family-based intervention programs to reduce crime.
>
> Farrington (2011, p. 148, emphasis added)

Not all the suggestions made by Morris and Hawkins to the honest politician have been acted on as they hoped, notably those regarding weapons control to reduce violent crime. Morris and Hawkins comment,

> It is unlikely that we could offer a program to diminish man's (sic) aggressions, his jealousies, greed and selfishness, which underlie violent crime . . . Our task is of lesser reach but of immediate promise in reducing the impact of those motive forces. It strikes not at the reform of man but rather at a modification of his environment which will reduce the suffering he inflicts on his brother.
>
> Morris and Hawkins (1970, p. 63)

Morris and Hawkins refer to the 8,870 gun-related murders in 1968 and the estimated 90 million firearms in circulation in the United States. They advocated increased gun control to reduce access to convenient and effective ways of killing people.[2] This has not happened. In 2018, there had been an estimated 390 million firearms in circulation in the United States. Using 2021 data from the Bureau of Justice statistics, which takes reports from most police services in the United States, Table 9.1 gives the number of homicides and the method used in committing the crime.

Table 9.1 shows that at least 11,628 of the homicides involved guns, around 80% of the total. Given that the figures don't quite cover all the United States and that some 'other weapons' may have included guns, the real number will be higher. It is certainly an increase in the number cited by Morris and Hawkins for 1968.

In England and Wales, there are periodic worries about homicides using guns or knives. There are strong gun control measures in the UK, and there are relatively few homicides involving guns, as shown in Table 9.2 (only 35 in 2020–2021, making up 6% of the total). Knives and other sharp implements are most used in homicides, with 235 in 2020–2021 (40% of the total). As Table 9.1 showed, after guns, knives were by far the most used weapon for homicide in the United States, accounting for just over 7% in 2021.

At the time of writing (February 2023), neither the United States nor the United Kingdom has put in place effective controls over the supply of the kinds of knives preferred for offensive purposes. Vested interests and political ideology still prevail, impacting what can be done in crime prevention, and this seems unlikely to end any time soon.

Maintaining improvement

There can never be complacency over what we know and what we should deliver by way of crime prevention. Researchers, policymakers, and practitioners have had to and will continue to have to respond to emergent conditions and emergent opportunities.

Table 9.1 U.S. homicides and methods used in 2021.

	Number	Percent
Handguns	6,012	41.0
Firearms, type not stated	4,740	32.3
Other guns	876	6.0
Knives	1,035	7.1
Other weapons (or weapons not stated)	1,059	7.2
Blunt objects	243	1.7
Personal weapons (hands/fists/feet/etc.)	461	3.1
Other	251	1.7
TOTAL	14,677	100

Source: Federal Bureau of Investigation (2021).

Table 9.2 England and Wales homicides and methods used in 2020–2021.

	Number	Percent
Sharp instrument	235	40.2
Hitting, kicking, etc. (without a weapon)	107	18.3
Other	52	8.9
Not known	52	8.9
Shooting	35	6.0
Blunt instrument	32	5.5
Strangulation, asphyxiation	27	4.6
Motor vehicle	20	3.4
Poison or drugs	16	2.7
Drowning	10	1.7
Burning	8	1.4
TOTAL	594	101.7

Source: Office of National Statistics (2023).

The crimescape for preventive attention has altered markedly since 1970. Changes in technology (e.g. the spread of the Internet and Internet services), routine activities (e.g. altered travel and leisure patterns), financial arrangements (e.g. decline in cash and spread of credit and debit cards), international relations (e.g. border controls), communications (e.g. the mobile phone), working patterns (e.g. growth in home working following COVID-19), methods of bringing up children (e.g. patterns of child surveillance and supervision), and global politics (e.g. the Russian invasion of Ukraine), for example, have all led to changes in crime patterns. Often, changed crime patterns are by-products of developments otherwise welcomed for the benefits they bring, such as the motor car, the computer, the portable radio, the Internet, social media, and the mobile phone. Changes in routine activities brought about as a by-product of the COVID-19 pandemic and regulations introduced in efforts to contain it, for a while, added some and subtracted or reduced other crime problems (Langton, Dixon, & Farrell, 2021; Nivette et al., 2021)

Sensibilities about the nature of crime harms have also altered with greater preventive attention paid, for example, to rape, child abuse, sexual exploitation, racial violence, and human trafficking. The importance of environmental crimes, of terrorist offences, and of corporate offending has become more apparent in view of looming climate change crises, political changes, and global interdependences. No one could have predicted these changes in 1970. Likewise, no one will be able to predict medium- to longer-term social and technological changes that will transform the crimescape, requiring new preventive strategies over the coming 50 years. There are thus good reasons for making crime prevention a continuously adaptive enterprise, rather than one that can reach any end state.

Scientific and technological developments have both changed crime opportunities. They have added some by introducing new targets and new techniques, both of which are exemplified in the mobile phone. They have also removed or reduced others, such as the disposable safety and electric razor as replacements for the aptly named cutthroat, and the change from cash to bank transfer as a way of paying wages.

Mutual adaptation by crime preventers and offenders builds in a need for continuous development of improved crime prevention techniques, as illustrated in the case of CCTV, tags to prevent shop thefts, locks, and safes (Churchill, 2016).

There is an inescapable complexity to crime prevention. There's a role for simplicity in science, where new and fundamental causal mechanisms are discovered. We rightly laud people such as Newton and Darwin, who discover them. However, in real-world conditions, complexity is at work. This is true for the physical and biological worlds (think short-term changes in local weather patterns and about processes of evolutionary adaptation), but even more so in the social world where there are multiple moving parts many of which interact creatively, intentionally, and adaptively. These processes mean that there will always be emergent properties to crime and to crime control.

For all these reasons, for the foreseeable future crime and crime prevention can never be expected to reach a steady state. There will continue to be changes. For most of those at the sharp end of crime prevention, continuous improvement and adaptation will be needed just to stand still. It may be that fundamental social changes, including reduced social exclusion, reform of fractured communities, replacement of poorly designed and criminogenic buildings and estates, reduced levels of patriarchy and misogyny, and an end to racism will, if they occur, have downward impacts on crime levels. However, a) they may not happen, b) they may not produce hoped-for crime prevention side effects, and c) they may create new crime problems as unintended side effects. Although all are in my view worth fighting for, depending on them for the prevention of crime-related harms would be a mistake.

Moreover, the social reforms listed in the previous paragraph would not touch many crime harms such as corporate offending against individuals and the environment. Some Marxists might welcome a revolution, which aims to deal with a whole range of crime and non-crime problems at a stroke by replacing capitalism with a transformed social order where crime would have no place because there would be no need for it. Maybe, but in the unlikely event of the revolution occurring, new crime opportunities and temptations could be expected requiring new preventive innovations. The literature on relative deprivation suggests that comparisons in practice tend to be made to those similarly placed rather than to those whose advantages are remote. Those similarly placed also generally live close to one another. Offenders don't travel far. This all suggests that even after a revolution, predatory crime against near neighbours would still take place and preventive action will be needed. That, or intrusive surveillance of the kind found in contemporary China, or the brutal repression in Afghanistan. There may be worse things than many types of crime. For many of us, likewise there are worse things than gun control including the huge suffering caused by firearms-related accidents, crimes, and suicides.

An engineering orientation is helpful in accommodating change and taming complexity in specific contexts (Tilley, 2016; Tilley & Laycock, 2016). Change, variation, and complexity are acknowledged, but goals are routinely achieved through an understanding of basic principles and their application in specific conditions. Safety margins are often built into engineering in order to minimise the chances that perturbations in the simplified worlds assumed are not catastrophic in their consequences. The designs of aeroplanes, bridges, boats, and buildings in this sense follow similar processes. Exemplars, past experience, and general scientific principles derived from tested theory are applied, paying attention to the specific idiosyncratic conditions for the particular project (see Petroski, 1996; Vincenti, 1990). The strength of the processes is shown in the low failure rates. The failures show the fallibility of what is done, often because some salient feature of the complex world for engineering activity has been overlooked. Lessons are learned from these failures, for example in aircraft accident investigations, to reduce the risk of future failures (Petroski, 1996, 2006). The history of hacking and the harms produced by it provides an excellent example of the ways in which the identification of system weaknesses and failures has required continuous adaptation both at the technical and human levels (Shapiro, 2023). Offenders actively search out system weaknesses that they exploit. As Holt and Bossler nicely put it, 'Hackers and malicious actors engage in problem-solving behaviors to find paths of least resistance to gain access to otherwise hardened targets' (Holt and Bossler, p. 179).

Problem-solving of the kind described in Chapter 6 is the approach to crime prevention that comes closest to an engineering orientation. The theory described in Chapter 4 and the case studies referred to throughout this book, but particularly in Chapters 2 and 6, comprise important raw materials for an engineering approach. Future developments in empirically tested theories of crime and criminality will comprise new resources that decision-makers in crime prevention can draw on in better anticipating, pre-empting, and reducing future crime and crime-related harm patterns.

What's to be done to build improvement into policy and practice?

The following is an improvement agenda, building on the material of the previous chapters.

1. Better understanding of crime and crime harms:

    a. *Better data*: well-kept administrative records, routinely made available in forms that facilitate quantitative analyses with clear qualifiers on coverage and quality, are essential. This needs to include details on offence, incident locations (virtual as well as physical), victims, known offenders, and modus operandi. Suppliers need to include, at minimum, the police, probation services, prosecutors, courts, hospitals, fire services, and local authorities, with built-in linkages to facilitate cross referencing in analyses. Regular victimisation surveys covering households, individuals, and other crime targets (e.g. businesses, transport providers, public sector organisations, and voluntary sector bodies) need to be conducted to complement administrative records.

    b. *Better theory and theory testing*: much theory simply hypothesises an association between variables or a pattern of succession between variables, and many tests simply measure these linkages. More nuanced theory is needed to identify causal mechanisms generating associations between (and succession of) variables and the conditions needed for these mechanisms to be activated, as described in Chapter 4. Tests of these theories need to focus on the detailed data signatures that would be expected through the conjectured activation of these mechanisms in specified contextual conditions.

c. *Better reporting of research*: much research is framed in ways that are inaccessible to potential user readerships. If it is to be drawn on by decision-makers, it needs to be presented in formats that make it as easily digestible as possible.

d. *Better translation of research findings for those working in policy and practice*: researchers are often reluctant to spell out what they take to be the implications of findings for decision-makers. Although implications may be debatable, a helpful starting point is the conclusions of researchers close to the data they are using. 'Pracademics' (practitioners who have also learned and honed research skills) have a useful role to play in crime-prevention-related research.

2. Better policy and practice application of what is known:

a. *Better problem-solving practice*: the problem-orientated approach to crime prevention focuses on crime problems that persist despite standard responses to them. This requires an understanding of those aspects of the context for that problem, which are relevant to the selection of interventions which can realistically be expected to trigger one or more preventive mechanisms. Practice routinely falls short of this ideal.

b. *Better routine practice*: large numbers of crime incidents requiring a response, but with limited time to deal with each of them, are dealt with by relatively inexperienced workers. These call for standardised (or default) responses that yield net best outcomes. Identifying these responses, monitoring their implementation, and checking that they continue to produce best outcomes across varying contexts comprise an important research, administration, and practice agenda. Refinement to improve nuanced standardised responses by contexts comprises an agenda for continuous improvement.

c. *Better co-production*: practitioner experience in dealing with crime incidents, criminals, and criminal groups yields informed ideas about crime patterns, crime and criminality causes, and criminal organisations and networks. Yet, this experiential understanding is fallible, based on selective experience and perception. It is also rarely articulated. High-quality researchers have a good understanding of what has been established from systematic study. Teacher–learner relationships between practitioners and researchers allow for the co-production of useful and useable tested theory to be drawn on in problem-solving and routine practice. Each 'side' can learn from and feed back to the others in a cycle of improved understanding and practice (see the contributions to Knutsson & Tompson, 2017).

d. *Better evaluation*: experimental studies of crime prevention interventions that are high on 'internal validity' provide strong evidence that something about an intervention produced the measured outcome in the particular place and at the particular time of the study. Generalisations beyond that are a matter of faith. Repeat studies try to replicate or emulate what was done but perforce are selective in what is delivered. Aggregation of findings has become technically highly sophisticated but remains conceptually weak (see Chapter 7). Typically, there are mixed findings across studies where contextual variation is high. Evaluations need to focus on diversity in outcome patterns across diversity in context and diversity in intervention target. They need to use multiple methods to test increasingly nuanced hypotheses focused on working out what works for whom in what contexts and how and likewise on what negative side effects are produced for whom in what contexts and how. Continuous improvement in intervention selection and targeting will ensue.

3. Better anticipation of emergent crime problems

a. *Better early-warning*: we have noted that the crimescape changes in ways that are intrinsically unpredictable, at least in the medium-to-long terms. This does not mean that it is entirely impossible to anticipate and hence prepare for more imminent changes in crime patterns. This is already routinely done in relation to seasonal events, such as 'mischief night' (Halloween) in some parts of Britain, and sporting events, such as football matches between traditional rivals. Beyond this, the advent of new technologies, new physical developments such as those for housing and business, and new regulatory regimes may give rise to predictable new crime opportunities. There is scope here for informed foresight to forestall 'crime harvests' that could otherwise be confidently expected (Pease 1997). This already happens to some extent in urban planning but could be extended to other new developments with predictable crime consequences. (See Tetlock and Gardner, 2019 showing what can be achieved in the improvement of short- to medium-term forecasting and on the difficulties in anticipating longer-term changes.)

b. *Better pre-emption*: it is one thing to be able to anticipate imminent emergent crime problems. It is another to work out what can be done to pre-empt them and to persuade those best placed to pre-empt them to do so. Past successes in retrospective developments of interventions and of mobilisation of those competent to take steps to avert the crime harvests are available as examples to draw on in attempts to pre-empt future ones.

c. *Better treatment of cyber*: It is already clear that cyber-dependent and cyber-enabled crime have marked a radical departure from traditional forms of crime and that future hardware and software developments will likely furnish new crime threats and opportunities (Holt & Bossler, 2016; Martin, 2019). Hacking began as a relatively innocent pastime, but weaknesses in systems have opened the way for a host of malign applications of viruses, worms, and their hybrid combinations (Shapiro, 2023). There is already an 'arms race' between those bent on using IT for criminal purposes and those trying to foreclose emerging criminal opportunities it provides. The advent of quantum computing poses a predictable threat to current encryption measures to secure data, access to which would provide the wherewithal to steal intellectual property, to bribe, and to extort. Evidently, encrypted data are being harvested pending the availability of the technology to decrypt them. ChatGPT is being used by students to produce essays that try to sidestep the technologies that spot potential plagiarism. Upcoming autonomous vehicles face the threat of hacks into their software, which will put users at risk. As noted in Chapter 3, numbers of crimes involving fraud (normally using computers) and computer misuse are matching the numbers of traditional crimes in England and Wales. Artificial Intelligence (AI) has been used to try to prevent crime. It may also pose dangers, including abuse by criminals and terrorists in pursuit of their objectives. It is highly likely that these and other emerging crime threats associated with IT developments, such as the burgeoning Internet of Things, will require adaptation of what we know so far about how to control crime and reduce crime harms, and who needs to be involved. It looks likely that innovations will be needed in both the technical and social worlds (Shapiro, 2023).

4. Better public understanding of crime

a. *Better mass media reporting of crime*: mass media treatment of crime patterns is weak and misleading, yet it is what has tended to shape public opinion, public debate, and public policy (see Chapter 8). The mass media have, however, also been important in highlighting neglected crime (and crime control) harms and helping to put them on the policy and practice agenda. Better agency engagement with mass media outlets (TV, radio, newspapers, and social media), aiming honestly and accurately to inform the public rather than to serve organisational PR ends, may create a better climate for policy decisions. Moreover, where media treatments of crime themselves can cause crime-related harms (e.g. fuelling racial attacks or riots), it is especially important that their reports are balanced and accurate.

b. *Better research engagement with mass media*: many researchers eschew engagement with mass media outlets for fear of misrepresentation. The bigger danger is that misleading impressions of crime problems, created by the understandable media focus on dramatic but relatively rare events, go unchallenged.

c. *Better repudiation of criminogenic, erroneous, and misleading reports of crime*: crime-related reporting, especially on social media, can quickly create crime multipliers by highlighting crime opportunities, focusing violence on targets of prejudice, and spreading intelligence on new ways of committing crimes. Correcting misapprehensions on social media can be bruising, especially when racists, homophobes, and misogynists threaten researchers. Countering criminogenic myths about crime and attempts to responsibilise media organisations are liable to become increasingly important with changes in types and uses of media outlet.

5. Better attention to ethics

    a. *Better evidenced ethical discussion*: ethics are obviously central to the law, law enforcement, and crime prevention. Utilitarian concerns with consequences mean that evidence relating to them is crucial. In crime prevention, this involves attending empirically to unintended negative consequences (including potential infraction of rights and affronts to aesthetic sensibilities) that are brought about and in what conditions, rather than a simple worry that they may sometimes be brought about. Moreover, where unintended harms are produced, measures to reduce or remove them may be possible. This again requires evidence to check whether such ameliorating measures are in practice having their intended effects (and again also whether they produce their own harmful side effects).

    b. *Better acknowledgement of trade-offs*: it may even be that trade-offs are sometimes called for between benefits, unintended harms, and infraction of cherished human rights. Informed decisions on this require the inclusion of evidence. Skogan's findings relating to stop and frisk in Chicago as a means of trying to reduce shootings and murders, as discussed in Chapter 8, provides a useful example (Skogan, 2023).

    c. *Better attention to ethics in devising and implementing interventions*: important issues of ethics may not be settled through evidence, but without evidence, discussions of them are impoverished. In crime prevention decision-masking, ethical issues inevitably arise in questions of prioritisation. They also arise in relation to potential threats to civil liberties, backfire effects, and aesthetic questions. These matters cannot be swept under the carpet nor can they be reduced to monetised comparisons of costs and benefits cranking out authoritative judgements. Ethical considerations in crime prevention decision-making require evidence but cannot be settled by evidence alone.

6. Better politics:

    a. *Better priorities*: The improvement agenda outlined already should lead to better crime prevention decision-making over priorities, responsibilities, and interventions, along lines discussed in Chapter 8.

b. *Better responsibilisation*: The importance of partnership in crime prevention has been emphasised over the past 40 years. Cybercrime is unlikely to be prevented effectively by police action alone. It is becoming the most widespread crime problem, causing massive harm. It will require action by many bodies. Governmental responsibilisation will be needed at both a national and international level (Williams & Levi, 2017).

A fitting conclusion to this chapter and this book was captured on a hoarding at the Oval (a cricket ground in London) in a test match between England and Australia in 2023, as I was putting the final touches to this book: 'BETTER NEVER ENDS'!

Exercise: Write a letter to a politician (of your choice) laying out a reasoned agenda for continuous improvement in crime prevention.

Notes

1 Uniform Crime Recording refers to an FBI programme to collect voluntarily provided standardised crime data from law enforcement agencies in the United States for use in statistical analysis. The data are available for analysis through the Bureau of Justice Statistics (BJS) website (https://bjs.ojp.gov/). The BJS website also includes many reports of U.S. crime patterns using both UCR and victimisation survey data.
2 Evidently this position cost Morris his nomination as head of the U.S. federal agency, the 'Law Enforcement Assistance Administration,' which was created followed the 1967 President's Commission on Law Enforcement and Administration, whose first aim was to prevent crime (Gest, 2001, p. 36).

References

Churchill, D. (2016). Security and visions of the criminal: Technology, professional criminality and social change in Victorian and Edwardian Britain. *British Journal of Criminology*, 56(5), 857–876. doi:10.1093/bjc/azv092
Crawford, A. (2017). Research co-production and knowledge mobilisation in policing. In J. Knutsson & L. Tompson (Eds.), *Advances in evidence-based policing* (pp. 195–213). London: Routledge.
Farrington, D. (2011). Families and crime. In J. Wilson & J. Petersilia (Eds.), *Crime and public policy* (pp. 130–157). Oxford: Oxford University Press.
Federal Bureau of Investigation. (2021). *Crime data explorer*. Retrieved February 5, 2023, from https://cde.ucr.cjis.gov/LATEST/webapp/#/pages/explorer/crime/shr
Gest, T. (2001). *Crime and politics*. New York: Oxford University Press.
Groff, L., & Birks, D. (2008). Simulating crime prevention strategies: A look at the possibilities. *Policing*, 2(2), 175–184. doi:10.1093/police/pan020
Hodgkinson, S., & Tilley, N. (2023). Independence and impact: A typology of researcher-user relationships for policing and crime prevention. *Policing and Society*, 33(3), 315–332. doi:10.1080/10439463.2022.2109631

Holt, T., & Bossler, A. (2016). *Cybercrime in progress: Theory and prevention of technology-enabled crime*. London: Routledge.

Knutsson, J., & Tompson, L. (Eds.). (2017). *Advances in evidence-based policing*. London: Routledge.

Langton, S., Dixon, A., & Farrell, G. (2021). Six months in: Pandemic crime trends in England and Wales. *Crime Science, 10*, 6. doi:10.1186/s40163–021-00142-z

Martin, P. (2019). *The rules of security: Staying safe in a risky world*. Oxford: Oxford University Press.

Morris, N., & Hawkins, G. (1970). *The honest politician's guide to crime control*. Chicago, IL: University of Chicago Press.

Nivette, A., Zahnow, R., Aguilar, R., Ahven, A., Amran, S., Ariel, B., . . . Eisner, M. (2021). A global analysis of the impact of COVID-19 stay-at-home restrictions on crime. *Nature Human Behaviour, 5*, 868–877. doi:10.1038/s41562-021-01139-z

Office of National Statistics. (2023). *Appendix tables: Homicide in England and Wales*. Retrieved February 6, 2023, from www.ons.gov.uk/peoplepopulationandcommunity/crimeandjustice/datasets/appendixtableshomicideinenglandandwales

Pease, K. (1997). Predicting the future: The roles of routine activity and rational choice theory. In G. Newman, R. Clarke, & S. Shoham (Eds.), *Rational choice and situational crime prevention: Theoretical foundations* (pp. 233–245). Aldershot: Dartmouth Press.

Petroski, H. (1996). *Invention through design*. Cambridge, MA: Harvard University Press.

Petroski, H. (2006). *Success through failure*. Princeton, NJ: Princeton University Press.

Shapiro, S. (2023). *Fancy bear goes phishing*. London: Allen Lane.

Skogan, W. (2023). *Stop and Frisk and the politics of crime in Chicago*. Oxford: Oxford University Press.

Tetlock, P., & Gardner, D. (2019). *Superforecasting: The art and science of prediction*. London: Random House Business.

Tilley, N. (2016). EMMIE and engineering: What works as evidence to improve decisions? *Evaluation, 22*(3), 304–322. doi:10.1177/13563890166565

Tilley, N., & Farrell, G. (2022). Security and international crime drops. In M. Gill (Ed.), *The handbook of security* (3rd ed., pp. 891–907). Cham: Palgrave.

Tilley, N., & Laycock, G. (2016). Engineering a safer society. *Public Safety Leadership: Research Focus, 4*(2), 1–6.

Vincenti, W. (1990). *What engineers know and how they know it*. Baltimore, MD: The Johns Hopkins University Press.

Williams, M., & Levi, M. (2017). Cybercrime prevention. In N. Tilley & A. Sidebottom (Eds.), *Handbook of crime prevention and community safety* (pp. 454–469). London: Routledge.

Index

For Product Safety Concerns and Information please contact our EU
representative GPSR@taylorandfrancis.com Taylor & Francis Verlag GmbH,
Kaufingerstraße 24, 80331 München, Germany

Printed and bound by CPI Group (UK) Ltd, Croydon, CR0 4YY
08/06/2025
01897009-0008